ISBN 978-0-282-07719-8
PIBN 10841926

1 MONTH OF
FREE
READING

at

www.ForgottenBooks.com

By purchasing this book you are eligible for one month membership to ForgottenBooks.com, giving you unlimited access to our entire collection of over 1,000,000 titles via our web site and mobile apps.

To claim your free month visit:

www.forgottenbooks.com/free841926

English
Français
Deutsche
Italiano
Español
Português

www.forgottenbooks.com

Mythology Photography **Fiction**
Fishing Christianity **Art** Cooking
Essays Buddhism Freemasonry
Medicine **Biology** Music **Ancient
Egypt** Evolution Carpentry Physics
Dance Geology **Mathematics** Fitness
Shakespeare **Folklore** Yoga Marketing
Confidence Immortality Biographies
Poetry **Psychology** Witchcraft
Electronics Chemistry History **Law**
Accounting **Philosophy** Anthropology
Alchemy Drama Quantum Mechanics
Atheism Sexual Health **Ancient History**
Entrepreneurship Languages Sport
Paleontology Needlework Islam
Metaphysics Investment Archaeology
Parenting Statistics Criminology
Motivational

THE

HISTORY AND LITERATURE

OF

THE CRUSADES.

FROM THE GERMAN

OF

H........ VON SYBEL.

EDITED BY

LADY DUFF GORDON.

LONDON:

CHAPMAN AND HALL, 193, PICCADILLY.

1861.

Crus 117.5

PREFACE.

HEINRICH V. SYBEL, whose Essay on the Crusades
is now introduced to the English reader, was born
at Düsseldorf, in the year 1817. His father, who
is still living, was well known as a strong advocate
for the Liberal party in the parliamentary history
of Prussia. From the Gymnasium at Düsseldorf,
v. Sybel was sent, at the age of seventeen, to the
University of Berlin, where he attended Leopold
Ranke's lectures, and shortly became one of the
Professor's most promising pupils. Under Ranke's
guidance, the original historians of the Crusades
were carefully examined. These studies influenced
v. Sybel's future career, and he determined thence-
forth to devote himself to historical research. His
first attempt as an author was an Essay, published
in 1837, ' De Jordanis Vitâ et Scriptis.' In 1841
he published his ' History of the First Crusade,'

a work which gives evidence of great industry and
critical skill. He subsequently printed, in various
Reviews, essays on the Second Crusade, on the
Kingdom of Jerusalem, and on the Legends of the
Crusades (1850); and in 1855, in Munich, he delivered four lectures on the Crusades. These works
have established the reputation of v. Sybel as the
best living authority on that remarkable portion of
history.

The first part of the work now submitted to the
public, is a translation of the lectures delivered at
Munich; the second part is taken from the preface
to his History of the First Crusade, published in
1841; and consists of an elaborate criticism on the
various original authorities in the eleventh and
twelfth centuries, and on the later historians of the
Crusades, down to the present time. There exists,
we believe, no such critical examination of the original authorities in any other language. The refer-
ences to them in Mills's History of the Crusades
are somewhat meagre; while Michaud, although
in his 'Bibliothèque des Croisades' he has given
ample extracts, has nowhere subjected the originals
to the rigorous and minute analysis they undergo
at the hands of the German Professor.

The first impulse to a critical examination of the original authorities of the First Crusade was given by Professor Ranke in his Historical Exercises ('Uebungen'). He began with the first books of William of Tyre, which he proved to be merely a repetition of earlier accounts by Albert of Aix, Raymond of Agiles, and from the 'Gesta Francorum.' He then examined Albert of Aix, whose work he considered to be derived chiefly from oral tradition. Professor Ranke's other avocations prevented his pursuing this subject any further; but sufficient was done to clear the way for other historical students ; and v. Sybel has carried out the method of his eminent teacher.

The narrative of the First Crusade, as given by Mills and other modern historians, v. Sybel regards as a mingled mass of truth and falsehood, of history and legend, founded chiefly on the account of William of Tyre. William of Tyre wrote in 1170, and with much that was valuable, he mixed tales borrowed from Albert of Aix (1130). The general character of the work is thought by the German Professor to be poetical and legendary.

To revert to v. Sybel's career. In 1839 he went to Bonn, and in 1842 he became Professor of

History at that University. In 1844, he and another Professor, of the name of Gildemeister, wrote a
pamphlet on the Holy Coat of Treves, and on holy
coats in general, which won for him the sympathy
of all opponents of ultramontane tendencies. The
Elector of Hesse hereupon offered him a profes-
sorship at Marburg. At that small University he
had ample leisure to devote to literary pursuits,
and in 1845 he published a work on the origin of
the German Monarchy ('Entstehung des deutschen
Königthums'). The book was subjected to some
adverse criticism at the time, but subsequent inquiry has done much to confirm the justice of
v. Sybel's views.

He then turned his attention to more modern
times, and went to Paris, where he ransacked the
public archives. The fruits of this journey were
two essays, one on Burke and the French Revolution, and another on Burke and Ireland; he subsequently wrote essays on the Duke of Wellington and
on Prince Eugene of Savoy.

The years 1848, 1849, and 1850, interfered with
his historical researches and pursuits. Like many
others, v. Sybel was carried away by dreams of German unity and by hopes of a great future for Prussia.

After the complete failure of these aspirations, v. Sybel returned to his Professor's chair, and to literature. He resumed his favourite subject of the French Revolution, and published the first volume in 1853.

In 1856, v. Sybel was invited to take the chair of Professor of History at the University of Munich, and was made a Member of the Bavarian Academy of Sciences. Spite of the opposition of the ultramontane party, who had not forgiven the part he took in the controversy on the Holy Coat of Treves, v. Sybel rose higher and higher in the estimation of the King of Bavaria. Besides occupying himself with the business of the Academy of Sciences, and with his lectures in the University, which were deservedly popular, v. Sybel found time to establish an historical school and an historical journal, the first volume of which appeared in 1859. Materials were placed by the King at his disposal for a history of Bavaria during the last century. He was also requested to superintend an edition of the Acts of the German Diets, and was named President of an Historical Commission which consisted of men like Pertz, Ranke, Droysen, and others. The first meeting took place in October, 1858, since which time

the Historical Commission have continued their labours with considerable success; v. Sybel's contribution being the history of the French Revolution,
three volumes of which have appeared.

Unfortunately v. Sybel's views of political matters,
which he was too honest too conceal, were so much
at variance with those of the King of Bavaria, that
he was compelled in 1861 to resign his professor-
ship at Munich, and he is now installed at Bonn
as Dahlmann's successor.

CONTENTS.

PART II.—LITERATURE OF THE CRUSADES.

CHAPTER I.

CHAPTER II.

CHAPTER III.

CHAPTER IV.

PART I.

HISTORY OF THE CRUSADES.

HISTORY OF THE CRUSADES.

CHAPTER I.

THE subject of these pages, that series of great wars which we designate as the Crusades, is one of the greatest revolutions that has ever taken place in the history of the human race. They have been repeatedly described in various instructive and celebrated works, and without doubt there are few who have not heard of those armed pilgrimages to the Holy Land; of the fame of Peter the Hermit and Godfrey of Bouillon, of the feats of Richard the Lion-hearted, or of the sufferings of St. Louis. Nevertheless the interest and importance of such events is, from its very nature, inexhaustible. During their progress a universal change takes place in the condition of the nations involved in them; and every new commentator must find fresh subject for interest and instruction according

B

to his own requirements and inclinations. This may also be said of the wars of the Persians, of the migration of the northern hordes, or, after them, of the Reformation and the French Revolution. Each of these events, like the Crusades, marks a new epoch in the state of Europe; and it shall be my task to place these last plainly before you under this aspect, although, with such an extensive sub-ject, this narrative can at best only assume the pro-portions of a slight sketch.

We cannot understand the importance of the Crusades if we look upon them as a mere sequel and extension of the pilgrimages to Jerusalem. Such a complete change in the history of the world does not arise out of such insignificant causes. The Crusades must be regarded as one great por-tion of the struggle between the two great religions of the world, Christianity and Mahomedanism; a struggle which began in the seventh century, on the confines of Arabia and Syria, and embraced in quick succession all the countries round the Medi-terranean, and after thousands of years and changes has disturbed our own century, as it did that of Gregory VII. The history of the human race re-cords no contest more violent or more protracted than this. There is none which filled a greater arena; none which roused the passions or the capabilities of the people to a greater degree. When the prophet Mahomet began his career at Mecca, Arabia was hardly known to the rest of the world. Fifty years after his death his followers were already ruling the land from the Indus in the East, the Caucasus in the North, to the coasts of the Atlantic in the West. The world never before saw a quicker or more complete invasion. Mahomet had succeeded in setting the ardent imaginations of his countrymen on fire with the idea of a holy war. In short, vigorous sentences, he preached to them the greatness and power of one Almighty God. He did not reason or explain, but he carried men away with him. He painted the rewards of Paradise and the tortures of the damned in glowing colours; and his whole religion was contained in these words: Obedience to God and to His Prophet. His teaching was the announcement of a new rule, without dogmatic mystery, and without any philosophical foundation. Man could alone be just in that he learned God's will from the Prophet, and then fulfilled the Prophet's ordinances. God does not deliver, but he rules; and religion is not to become one with him, but to obey him implicitly. Thus, his mission from the first was not one of instruction, but of subjugation; unbelievers were rebels, who were to be smitten with the edge of the sword, and forced to conform to his doctrines, or to pay tribute. War necessarily arose out of the first principles of his religion ; and no sooner was he acknowledged in Mecca than he sent threatening admonitions to the Persian King and the Byzantine Emperor. The scorn with which they answered the unknown fanatic, was met by the most furious attacks; neither Roman·nor Persian troops were able to withstand the masses of brave men, which, with the rapidity of· lightning, inexhaustible, and with exulting contempt of death, spread in torrents over the country. They had no other thought than fanaticism for the Caliph, no other delight than war against the infidel, no other hope than entrance into Paradise. They were men with but few wants, brave in battle, and insensible to fatigue, easily put in motion, and equally untiring ; inaccessible both to luxury and to civilization. They dwell, says one of their poets, beneath the shadow of their lances, and cook their food upon the ashes of the conquered towns.

In the year 715 these hordes had overrun all Western Asia, the whole northern coast of Africa, and Spain, even beyond the Pyrenees.

Muza, the ambitious conqueror of Spain, conceived the plan, which, though vast, was not too extensive for men accustomed to subdue the world ; —by two great simultaneous attacks to render the whole of Christendom subservient to the Prophet. For this purpose an army was to advance from Asia Minor towards Constantinople, and another to march across the Pyrenees upon the empire of the Franks; then from east and west to unite their triumphant forces in Rome, the centre of Christianity. Luckily for Europe, Muza at this time fell into disgrace with the Caliph, and his great project was only carried into effect piecemeal, and consequently without success. He began by attacking Constantinople, and blockaded that town for three years by sea and land. The Emperor Leo III. defended himself with great courage, destroyed the Mahomedan fleet with the newly invented Greek fire, and at last, in 718, forced their army to retire. Ten years then elapsed before the empire of the Franks was attacked in the west. In Muza's time this attack might have been successful, because the Franks were then torn by internal discord. Since then, however, Charles Martel, one of the bravest warriors of any time, had taken his place at the head of the Frankish empire; he beat the Arabian and African hordes in six hotly contested battles at Poitiers. The people of the East, says one of the Spanish historians, the German race, men deep-chested, quick-eyed, and iron-handed, have crushed the Arabs. After this double failure the great onslaught of Islam was checked. Christendom had suffered much; it had lost its birthplace, Palestine, and its earliest Churches in Asia Minor and Africa; but it had saved its existence, and soon after Charles Martel's death it found a representative of its unity and power in his grandson Charlemagne, who, as Emperor of Western Christendom, extorted some acknowledgment even from the Caliph himself. The struggle between the two religions now remained in abeyance for some centuries, except some insignificant feuds on the frontiers of Spain, in the Italian Isles, and on the coast of Asia Minor, as symptoms of the smouldering embers of discord.

From this moment the inward development of the two worlds were totally opposed. In the Mussulman country the religious element had thrown all others into the shade; religious warfare was the sole occupation of the inhabitants, and supremacy of the Caliph was the sole basis of political life. After the ninth century, this distinctive peculiarity was broken down on all sides. Earthly enjoyments, secular culture, and national independence asserted their power; the arts and sciences flourished extensively; the dominion of the Caliph was broken, and limited to spiritual supremacy; on every side temporal institutions sprang up under and around him; political, intellectual, and manufacturing interests

displaced the enthusiasm for the war of faith.
Islam as a conquering religion lost its terrors, and
its warlike power fell into gradual decay. This
change from fanaticism to culture, was in reality
the greatest gain to the Mahomedans; and to this
period belongs nearly everything effected by Islam
for the real or lasting interests of humanity, for intellectual progress and the refinement of manners.

In the West, things took a different course. While
the Mahomedans attained political life and intellectual progress at the expense of religious vigour
and unity, the European nations, from the ninth to
the eleventh century, confined themselves more and
more exclusively within the narrow ecclesiastical
paths. This tendency is visible even in Charlemagne. The worldly, political, and national elements
are brilliantly represented in his reign : the imperial
dignity was restored and endowed with unprecedented power; and the Pope of Rome was subservient to him like any other bishop of his dominions.
Science of every description was fostered, ancient
Roman writers imitated, old German heroic legends
collected. But with all this Charlemagne looked
upon his imperial mission as more particularly a religious one. On the first Diet after his coronation,
he orders, that now the imperial dignity is restored,
all men are to entertain the true belief in the Trinity,

and to lead a godly life in Christ. Wherever he discovered, within the limits of the Empire, defects in church government, remains of heathenism, or schismatic tendencies, he opposed them with the whole weight of the power of the State. He had no foreign war more at heart than that against the barbarians, that is to say, the heathens, the Saracens in Spain, the pagan Germans, Danes, and Slaves. Where he conquered he converted; and although the spreading of Christianity was useful in consolidating the temporal power of the State, yet the first feeling was that the Emperor was lord of the world, and the defender of true belief on earth.

The clergy and all ranks of the people held the same ideas. We are accustomed now to look upon religion as a purely personal and intimate feeling, the closest, and at the same time freest intercourse of each individual soul with God, a conviction of the heart, which is only of value in so far as it is of inward and spontaneous growth. In those ancient times men strove, it is true, to attain this frame of mind; but they were convinced that the only true path to it was by the outward observances of the Church. These therefore were enforced by penal laws, and force of arms; religion was looked upon above all as the direct command of God; and whoever did not profess the true faith, was persecuted as a rebel against the majesty of the Lord.

Soon after the death of Charlemagne, the Empire fell to pieces, the organization of the State was dissolved, and anarchy spread over the whole of Charlemagne's former dominions, Germany, France, and Italy. It is true that Germany raised herself from this second period of disorder, to unity and power, under the great Imperial House of Saxony, under Henry I., and Otho the Great. For a moment the glory of the Carlovingians seemed renewed; half Europe recognized the power of the Emperor of Germany, and under his vigorous protection, German song and the study of antique art put forth rich blossom. But this edifice was fated to last no longer than that raised by the Carlovingians. No sooner had Otho the Great closed his eventful career, than one country after another tore itself away from the Imperial supremacy, France and Burgundy, Italy and Poland, the Wends and the Danes. Meanwhile none of these succeeded in establishing for themselves any lasting government; the monarchies sank into a state of complete impotence; unruly petty tyrants trampled all social order underfoot, and all attempts after scientific instruction and artistic pleasures, were as effectually crushed by this state of general insecurity, as the external well-being and material life of the people. This was a dark and stormy period for Europe, merciless, arbitrary,

and violent. In Germany a few powerful sovereigns
maintained a commanding position for a time : such
were Conrad II. and Henry III., men of iron will,
like their followers. But with them the imaginative
impulse, the bright hope, and the mental activity,
which distinguished the days of Otho the Great,
were wanting. It is a sign of the prevailing feeling
of misery and hopelessness, that when the first
thousand years of our era were drawing to a close,
the people in every country in Europe looked with
certainty for the destruction of the world. Some
squandered their wealth in riotous living, others
bestowed it for the good of their souls on churches
and convents : weeping masses lay day and night
around the altars ; some looked forward with dread,
but most with secret hope, towards the burning of
the earth and the falling in of heaven. Their actual
condition was so miserable, that the idea of destruc
tion was relief, spite of all its terrors.

In this hopeless and depressed condition of the
world, men's thoughts turned, as is always the case
in any great tribulation, towards Heaven, for God's
salvation and refreshment. All other interests had
become worthless ; no possession and no existence
was safe from rude force ; nowhere was to be found,
after the splendid line of the Othos had passed away,
a character or a great idea capable of exciting the

imagination of a noble heart. There was nothing
for the deadened race of mankind to hold to, save
religion: and, at last, a state of feeling arose, full
of the bitterest hatred against this earthly world;
and, burning with desire for the joys of Heaven,
men fled from their families, occupations, and
neighbours; they tore themselves from all worldly
ties: the son abandoned his parents, the husband
his wife; the vassal left his feudal lord, and the
prince his people. Monasteries were more filled
than ever; new orders were instituted, the rules
and practices rose to the highest degree of asceticism and penance. Monastic seclusion soon ceased
to satisfy the growing desire to fly from the world
and those who dwelt in it. Men sought the depths
of the forest, the loneliness' of mountains, or the
untrodden wilderness, in order to mortify the flesh
in solitude, and turn their thoughts, with undisturbed zeal, on immediate intercourse with God,
his angels, or his saints. They awoke, with con-
vulsive terror, to the consciousness of their sins;
they spent night after night in breathless pleadings
for enlightenment and grace; their fancy drove them
in perpetual change, through images of infernal
torture, and divine beatitude, till at length a moment
of exhaustion and ecstasy succeeded,—refreshing and
dazzling visions gave to the struggling heart a cer-

tainty of union with God. In order to understand
the character and deeds of that time, we must not
for a moment lose sight of this mystical excitement,
full of contempt of this world; we must not forget
that it was the only thing that touched the imagination of that century, and that it was then a common and everyday occurrence. More particularly in
France, Spain, and Italy, the three countries which
spoke the Roman tongue, this feeling was spread
through all classes, and pervaded every order. Every
happiness, every earthly enjoyment, was deemed
dangerous. The body was looked upon as the dead
weight which hindered the soul in its flight to heaven. Men turned with contempt from science and
art. "Upon such toys," wrote the celebrated English Bishop Lanfranc, "upon such toys we have
wasted our youth, but now we have cast them from
us." The duties of a patriot, a subject, and a citizen,
lost their value and power, under the ruling passion
of that age, because they belonged to this mortal
and corrupted world. Men no longer had any perception of that plain human feeling which sees God's
service in useful labour, and which feels the support
of God's presence in the monotony of everyday life.
Such feeling was not enough for those overheated
imaginations. They wanted to see the Divinity with
mortal eyes, and to grasp the mystery with the bodily

senses. Owing to the condition of public feeling, pilgrims and palmers became more numerous than ever before. There was, indeed, hardly any other intercourse between nations; commerce hardly existed, and no one thought of travelling for pleasure, as the smallest journey was attended with difficulties and dangers of every kind. But many thousands of people went every year to the famous Abbeys of Clugny or Monte Casino, to the graves of the Apostles, to Rome, or to St. Jago di Compostella; and, above all, crossed the sea to Palestine, to the land which Christ trod, and to the rock which is said to have been his grave. High and low took part with equal zeal. Within the space of thirty years, we find in Jerusalem two Counts of Flanders, one Count of Toulouse, one Duke of Normandy, and a number of German bishops, all filled with the same belief, that they stood on the threshold of Heaven, and all equally horror-struck that unbelieving Mussulmans were desecrating this holy place. When religious enthusiasm had impregnated mankind to such a degree, anger against the unbeliever arose of its own accord, and war against the false religion appeared to be the most holy and praiseworthy action. Wherever the war against Islam had lasted, it now gained fresh vigour and life from the quantities of volunteers who flocked to victory, or death and Paradise,

under the banner of the Cross.   Burgundians, Provençals, and Normans, helped the Spanish king to
besiege the Caliph of Cordova, and to take Toledo.
The Normans from Naples settled themselves in
Sicily; and the fleets of Pisa and Genoa, decked
with Papal flags, stormed the harbour of Palermo.
Thus the Christian faith became in time the badge
of a great system of national defensive and offensive
alliance, which was animated by a sacred fire, and
eager for deadly warfare against all unbelievers.   If
from the seventh to the ninth centuries, Islam had
harassed the Christian nations by its vigorous ag-
gressions, now, in the eleventh, came the day of
reckoning, in a no less violent attack, on the part of
Christendom, upon the whole Mahomedan world.

Every great war must have a commander-in-chief
to direct, and a ruler to command it.   In the days
of Charlemagne and Otho, Christendom possessed
such a leader in the person of the Emperor.   Now
that was at an end, for the Imperial power was barely
tolerated by the German and Italian nobility, and
not recognized at all by the rest of Europe.   To fill
up this void, and give to the Latin world a new head,
the same ecclesiastical spirit which had roused the
war against Islam was now at work. Temporal sovereigns did not appear capable of leading mankind
to salvation : they were worldly and sinful, like the

rest. There existed on earth but one institution in
which the Spirit of God constantly and actively manifested itself; this was the Church with its servants,
and its head, the Pope. They, and they alone, were
called upon to govern the earth. Now that the Emperor had become incapable of representing the Christian world, the Pope was quite ready to grasp the
temporal as well as the spiritual power, and in the
character of chief military commander of Europe to
begin the crusade against Mahomedan Asia. Pope
Gregory VII. was the first Pope who assumed this
position in the face of Europe in its full force and
extent.

Gregory was without doubt one of the most remarkable men of any age. Never, as far as we
know, has religious enthusiasm been united with
such far-sighted policy, or spiritual fanaticism with
such pronounced talents for government. Hildebrand, as he was originally named, was the son
of a poor carpenter in a small Tuscan town. He
received his first instruction in Rome, but soon
fled in disgust from the lawless profligacy of that
town to the retirement of the convent. There, like
hundreds of others, he had prayed, watched, and
scourged himself, and had experienced ecstatic de-
lights, tearful penitence and humiliation, had shared
the belief that only by thus renouncing the world

could Heaven be gained. An unexpected occurrenca however soon gave a different impulse to his life. The Church was in the same state of disorganization as the temporal power; the Emperor Henry III., bent upon enforcing order and discipline, did not hesitate to intervene even in Rome, deposed three contending Popes, and appointed their successor himself. The young monk, who was personally attached to one of the three dethroned Popes, accompanied him into exile in Germany, equally indignant at the corruption of the Church on the one hand, and the attempts to cure it by the profane intervention of Imperial power on the other. He had brought the idea with him from his monastery that all the powers of this world were as nothing compared to the glory of the Church. That a layman, even though the Emperor himself, and with the most praiseworthy intentions, should dare to dictate to the Church, filled Hildebrand with holy indignation; and this it was that suddenly aroused his eminently practical nature from the unproductive contemplation of monastic life. Not to flee from the world, but to redeem it by absolute submission to the purified Church, became henceforth the task of his existence. In the year 1048 news came to Germany of the death of the new Pope, and the Emperor instantly named the Bishop of Toul as the future head of the Church.

He—Leo IX.—whose honest and unassuming piety was at first alarmed by the difficulties of his new calling, turned to Hildebrand for help, and requested him to come to Rome as his adviser. The answer was a resolute refusal. He could serve no Pope who held his office by virtue of an Imperial decree. His personal character and appearance were even then so commanding that the Pope trembled before the simple monk. Leo promised to go a barefooted pilgrim to Rome, and there to submit to the canonical election. Hildebrand, mollified by this, became henceforth the soul of the Papal government, till he ascended the throne of the Vatican himself in the year 1073.

Scarcely had he grasped the reins of ecclesiastical government when this carpenter's son developed such a universal genius for ruling as has only since been displayed in the two greatest self-made men of modern history—Cromwell and Bonaparte. He had the knowledge, the ability, and the will, to do everything. He became a reformer of the Church, a statesman, and a conqueror, a demagogue and a diplomatist, all with equal vigour and masterly skill. While his conviction rested unshaken on a steadfast belief in God's directing power, he knew that God compassed his ends by means of human agencies, and was unceasing in his endeavours to employ

c

every earthly means for the consolidation of his spiritual power. In the height of his enthusiasm he went further than any man had dared to dream of doing before him. "All princes," he wrote, " shall kiss the Pope's foot; he alone shall wear the imperial insignia ; he alone is answerable towards God for the sins of kings." "When Christ," he again wrote, "said to Peter, 'Feed my sheep,' he did not except kings ; what king has ever performed miracles like so many popes and lowly monks'?" He accordingly demanded, on no other title than this religious one, the oath of allegiance from the King of England, declared Spain to be the property of St. Peter, summoned the Kings of Poland and the Russian Czars to appear before his tribunal, declared the Emperor Henry IV. of Germany deposed, and made his antagonist Rudolph promise homage and allegiance to him. For these schemes, which embraced the whole of Europe, he strengthened himself by retirement and daily sincere and anxious prayer. "I behold myself," he wrote to the Abbot of Clugny, " so sunk in sin that prayer from my lips is of no avail. My life, indeed, is blameless, but my actions are of this world; therefore do I entreat you beseech the devout to pray for me." A longing after the contemplative quiet of the cloister dwelt in the mind of the proud prince of the Church amid the

struggle for supremacy in the world : it was the root
of his nature and the source of his power. Fortified anew by devotion, he again rushed into the
thick of the fight, in order to enforce by worldly
weapons that obedience which he had already demanded from kings as his due. He gained adherents in all countries, and bound them by solemn
oaths and military organization to follow his guidance. In Germany Duke Guelf, of Bavaria, con-
sented to hold his dominions on feudal tenure from
the Pope. In France a knightly army was assembled
for his service by the great Counts of Burgundy
and Toulouse and the renowned Abbot of Clugny.
In Italy he relied on his alliances with the Norman
Duke of Naples and the Countess Matilda of Tus-
cany, while zealous fanatics excited the populace of
the Lombard cities in his behalf. In a word, Gregory did not for an instant rest satisfied with establishing a universal supremacy over crowned heads,
but without hesitation took their subjects into his
own allegiance ; he was on the high-road to the destruction of all the existing governments of the
world, in order that he might embody them in his
great spiritual dominion. This was but the commencement of strife, attack, and turmoil; and, as
was to be expected, opposition to such an unheard-
of system arose in every quarter; but the plan of

the edifice was drawn by a mighty hand, and the
temporal supremacy of the Popes was announced
as a new spiritual and warlike impersonation of
Christianity.

This power at once turned its attention to foreign
affairs. Gregory had counted, not only upon the
obedience of the Latin nations, but also upon bringing back the Greek schism to its allegiance; and
then, upon leading both combined to a decisive attack upon Islam. A motive was furnished by a
warlike movement which broke out in the bosom of
Islam itself. At two points its dominions had been
invaded by unruly hordes of half-savage tribes, who,
like the Arabs in Mahomet's time, had no wish but
perpetual warfare, no culture beyond fierce religious
zeal. Among the Kabyles of the desert in Northern
Africa arose the empire of the Morabites, who, after
subjugating in rapid campaigns, the whole district
between the Syrtes, the Sahara, and the ocean, burst
upon the Christians of Spain in a furious invasion.
Simultaneously, the wild tribes of the Seljukes, from
the steppes of Bulgaria, poured in upon Asia, laid
waste the possessions of the Caliph of Bagdad, and
advanced on Asia Minor, and the dominions of the
Greek Emperor, whom they, in a few campaigns,
drove across the Hellespont, in disgraceful flight.
It seemed as if the times of Muza had returned,

and Rome was again to be threatened both from the
East and from the West. But Gregory VII. felt
himself more secure than Charles Martel, and resolved to anticipate the attack. In France he plead-
ed, with great effect, to obtain assistance for the
Spaniards; in Rome he got together, in 1074, an
army of 50,000 men, faithful followers of St. Peter,
whom he intended to lead in person to the relief of
Constantinople, and the destruction of the Turks.
He called upon the German Emperor, Henry IV.,
with whom he was still at peace, to help him in this
undertaking, and at the same time expressed his
intention of first bringing back the Greeks and Armenians to the unity of the Church of Rome; after
which he should lead the triumphant army to the
Holy Sepulchre at Jerusalem. It affords a fresh
evidence, that with all his enthusiasm, the turn of
his mind was eminently practical and calculating,
that he should look upon the Holy Sepulchre only
as the final ornament of victory, whilst the task he
saw before him was the gradual extension of conquest, and the establishment of a solid foundation in
Constantinople, whence the expulsion of the Turks
from Asia Minor and Armenia, and his own tri-
umphal entry into Jerusalem, would follow as a
matter of course. It was the first, and for many subsequent centuries the last time that so vast and so

methodical a plan of attack upon Asia had been conceived in Christian Europe.

Gregory VII. was not, however, destined to reap these laurels. Like Napoleon, seven hundred years later, he was to begin his career with dreams of oriental supremacy, and then, through life, to devote all his energies to the subjugation of the West. Within a few months, the dispute with Henry IV. broke out, in which the Pope was victor, and saw the successor of Charlemagne vanquished and trembling at his feet, while all Europe was convulsed with civil war. Gregory did not live to see the end; he was forced to fly from Rome before the renewed power of the Emperor, and died during his flight, under the protection of the Normans of Naples. Meanwhile, the Turks in Asia made alarming progress; they took Mecca and Jerusalem. The pilgrims complained bitterly of the excesses committed by the brutal soldiery at the tomb of the Saviour. The Greek Emperor Alexius sent the most pressing entreaties for help to the Pope, saying, that if he did not wish to see Christianity perish in the East, he must render him assistance. Urban II., an acute and subtle man, now sat on Gregory's throne; not to be compared with his predecessor in energy and large mould of mind, but penetrated with the same religious views, filled with ambition, and, although more pliant, his superior adroitness in the management of details rendered him, on the whole, more successful than Gregory. He thought it a religious triumph to stir up the son of Henry IV. to rebellion against his father, and thus to deal a terrible blow to the Imperial power; he had prevailed upon himself to forego for a time his pretensions to political supremacy in England and Spain, and thus to obtain the ecclesiastical obedience of those monarchs. By these means his influence, in the year 1094, was more generally recognized and honoured than Gregory's had ever been. When, in the summer of that year, a Greek embassy was sent to him, he decided on using his mighty influence against the East, and calling upon the Latin nations to make war upon Islam.

We see here a great difference between the two men. Urban did not think of taking the command and leading the attack in person. But that was not the chief distinction : in like manner as he had given up that immediate temporal supremacy, which Gregory had insisted upon in all lands, he left out of his warlike plans those great ideas of military method and politico-ecclesiastical conquest upon which Gregory had impressed the stamp of his character. Urban viewed the task by the light of that mystical piety, which, disregarding all earthly considerations, and setting aside all earthly ambition, strives to follow the straight path to the heavenly Paradise. After making a preliminary announcement of his intentions in a Council at Piacenza, he crossed the Alps late in the autumn to the south of France, and held a great Council at Clermont on French affairs; at the end of this, he called upon the people of Europe to aid him, not in delivering Eastern Christendom, but the Holy Sepulchre. According to worldly ideas, such an attempt on Jerusalem was quite illusory without a firm footing in Constantinople or Egypt; it could not have the slightest prospect of lasting success unless a fatal blow could thence be aimed at the whole edifice of the Turkish Sultanate. But Urban's hearers were not disposed to listen to the wisdom of this world. In drunken religious zeal, they revelled in the idea of rescuing the tomb of the Saviour from the defilement of the heathen; they looked upon Christ enthroned in heaven as their leader, and hoped to see the gates of the heavenly Jerusalem thrown open at the same time as those of the earthly. Fifty thousand warriors had volunteered to carry out Gregory's reasonable plan; at Urban's enthusiastic appeal more than three hundred thousand men fastened the Cross upon their shoulders. In a few months the cry, "God wills it," had flown from Clermont over half Europe,—throughout France and England, Italy and Scandinavia; with one passionate outburst the people sought to free themselves from the pressure of earthly wretchedness. They said, God had never permitted a time like the present, filled with blasphemy, disunion, and immorality; civil war was raging, truth and honesty had ceased to exist, famine and earthquakes had threatened destruction. In the depth of this misery the Lord had sent salvation. The time was fulfilled, of which it is written, " Whoso will go with me, let him take up his cross and follow me." Since the creation of the world, and the mystery of the crucifixion, writes a chronicler, nothing had been seen like this Crusade, which was a work of God, not of man. On the 4th of April, 1095, says another, fire fell from heaven like small stars, far and wide over all lands, since which time France and Italy had gone armed to the Holy Sepulchre without any temporal commander, led only by the spirit of the Lord. In a moment all evil had been banished from the Christian world, since Christ had once more vouchsafed his saving presence as their leader and Lord of Hosts. Earthquakes had ceased; a year of unexampled plenty followed the scarcity; peace and union returned among believers. Filled with these hopes, the western nations entered upon the First Crusade.

CHAPTER II.

WHEN Pope Urban II. announced the Crusade at Clermont in November, 1095, he secured to himself the leading position in the enterprise, by naming the Bishop Adhemar of Puy as his Legate and representative with the army, and by officially announcing to the Greek Emperor Alexius the forthcoming help against the Turks. Preparations on a large scale were making in most kingdoms of Europe. In Lorraine, Duke Godfrey of Bouillon, a religious and brave but not very wise man, was collecting a numerous army. In France, the brother of King Philip, Count Hugo of Vermandois, and the warlike Count Robert of Flanders, were enlisting men; the unruly and rash Duke Robert of Normandy mortgaged his whole territory in order to raise a splendid troop of French and English knights; besides these, Count Stephen of Blois, possessor of as many castles as there are days in the year, a

stately, proud, but morally weak man; and lastly,
as leader of all the Provençals and Gascons, Count
Raymond of Toulouse, more versed in war and
richer, but also more obstinate and violent than all
the rest. Italy, Pisa, and Genoa equipped their
fleets, all the Norman knights of Naples ranged
themselves under Bohemund of Tarentum, a lean,
pale, ambitious prince, who was for ever silently
forming comprehensive but constantly changing
schemes, always at work and yet always patient,
until the moment arrived for sure and victorious action; he was perhaps the only man in that army
who had nothing of the devout pilgrim spirit, and
only thought how he might on the way entrap his
old enemy the Greek Emperor, and at all events
found a splendid kingdom for himself in the East.
Everywhere the greatest activity prevailed: princes
assembled their vassals, knights their retainers; no
compulsion was used towards these dependents, but
very few of them stayed behind. The most perfect
. personal freedom prevailed during the whole Crusade in this unprecedented army. Each knight
served at his own pleasure, first under one prince
and then under another, as higher pay or greater
fame attracted them. Nothing but the common
impulse towards Jerusalem kept the whole mass
at all together. Christ was looked upon as com-

mander-in-chief, and therefore of course, according
to the then existing views, his representative would
have been the Papal Legate : but as he was without any military capacity, a war committee of the
most renowned leaders and bannerets, ten, twenty,
thirty, just as it happened, took the command ;
sometimes named a head of the whole army, whose
power lasted as long as his commission, or as he
could enforce obedience. We shall see that singular good luck was needed, in order to secure the
most moderate success in the midst of such anarchy.

Nearly a year had passed since the Council of
Clermont in 1095, before these knightly troops were
armed and collected. Many prepared never to return ; nearly all looked forward with beating hearts
to an unknown and distant land, brilliant with all
the glory of miracles and the splendour of fairy
tales. Such a state of mind, we, in our fast and
far-travelling days, can hardly understand ; it was
much as if a large army were now to embark in
balloons, in order to conquer an island between the
earth and the moon, which was also expected to
contain the heavenly Paradise. The lower classes
were frantic with excitement. The peasants and
artisans, who took no part in war, and were not
admitted into the regular armies, were those upon
whom the sufferings of that period fell hardest, and

they pressed with the wildest zeal to join in the Holy Crusade. In various countries, the Crusade was preached to them through peculiar organs. On the Rhine, a certain turbulent and ill-famed Count Emicho got together a troop several thousand strong, with whom he began the war for Christ's sake, by a bloody massacre and plundering of the Jews. In the north of France a native of Amiens, Peter the Hermit, travelled about dressed as a pilgrim, with sunburnt face and beard reaching to his middle, riding upon an ass, and told the gaping people how he had been in Jerusalem, where the heathen desecrated the Holy Sepulchre with all manner of filthiness, and how there one night Christ appeared to him in all his glory, and gently addressed him, saying, " Sweet friend, tell my beloved Christian Church, that the time is come in which to help me; I have longed for her, I shall rejoice in her, and Paradise is open to her." His hearers beat their breasts, forsook their hovels, and followed the hermit with their wives and children; their number grew to sixty thousand. In this case delay was impossible, and the wild fantastic train poured though Germany in the summer of 1096, down the Danube and through Hungary into the Greek kingdom. In Constantinople the Emperor Alexius welcomed with alarm the tumultuous

guests, who proclaimed their leader as the true
apostle of Christ, and the author of the whole Crusade; and who resorted to plunder to supply their
wants, not even sparing the churches. He did all
he could to hasten their transit to the shores of
Asia, where, regardless of his warnings, they rushed
with blind zeal into the midst of the enemy's land,
and in the course of a few weeks were nearly all cut
to pieces by the Emir of Nicæa. With the small
number of survivors, Peter returned to Constantinople and awaited the coming of the main body.
A heterogeneous mass of camp-followers had joined
the army; and as the princes and knights took no
notice of them, they formed into a separate body,
numbering about ten thousand beggars and ma-
rauders, who followed unarmed in the wake of the
army, and though they often increased the difficulty
of maintaining it, they sometimes did good service
as spies, servants, and baggage porters.   Peter the
Hermit became their spiritual leader and saint;
they moreover elected a military commander, whom
they called Tafur, the Turkish for King of the Beggars; and laid down certain rules: for instance, no
one was to be tolerated among them who possessed
any money; he must either quit their honourable
community, or hand over his property to the King
of the Beggars for the common fund.   The princes

and knights did not venture into their camp except in large bodies and well armed; the Turks said of the Tafurs, that they liked nothing so well to eat as the roasted flesh of their enemies.

In the autumn of 1096 the first princely troops arrived at Constantinople; others followed in rapid succession, till the spring of 1097, some by water, some by land. The northern French mostly came through Italy and Epirus, the Provençals through Dalmatia, and the Lorrainers through Hungary. The Emperor Alexius was not without misgivings when he saw them arrive. He knew the hatred of the Latins towards the Greeks, particularly Bohemund's strong hostility towards himself. But their scattered order somewhat reassured him, and indeed inspired him with an idea of making use of them to forward the interests of his own empire. He informed them that Syria and Asia Minor were provinces of the Roman Empire, and only alienated from it for the time by the superior might of the Turks, and that he therefore expected that when they were driven out the pilgrims would acknowledge him as their legitimate Sovereign, and swear fealty to him: under these conditions he would furnish them with provisions, and assist them with troops. Count Hugo, who landed first, made no difficulty; but Duke Godfrey replied, that "his only master was the Lord Jesus Christ, and him only would he serve." Hereupon he was attacked and beaten by the Emperor's troops, and obliged to take the oath, to save the rest of his army. Bohemund, the one whom the Emperor most dreaded, submitted at once; he saw that most of the pilgrims had no mind to fight near Constantinople, which would have delayed their departure for the Holy Sepulchre; so he resolved, when once arrived in Asia, to disregard his oaths, and to act according to circumstances. His example determined the rest, except the stubborn and hot-headed Raymond of Toulouse, who would sooner die than acknowledge any other lord than Christ. He conceived a bitter and lasting hatred against Bohemund on this occasion; and when Alexius, who by no means trusted the crafty Norman, in spite of his oaths, perceived this, he tried to secure the friendship of the Count, by overwhelming him with presents, and marks of honour, and letting him off the oaths. One of the chief officers of his Court, Tatikios, accompanied the army as the Emperor's representative in the States that were to be conquered.

After many months had passed in these transactions, the troops at last landed on the long-desired Asiatic soil; and the war against the enemies of Christ began with an attack on the Emir of

Nicæa. It was fortunate for the pilgrims that the power of the Seljukes was greatly broken and decayed. Several pretenders were quarrelling for the Sultan's throne, and the emirs, or governors of provinces, had made themselves quite independent, and were waging war with each other. Several Armenian princes belonging to the subject Christian population had risen in arms in Taurus, and on the banks of the Euphrates and in Mesopotamia. On the south the Caliph of Egypt had just commenced a general war against the Seljukes, and was advancing towards Palestine by the isthmus of Suez. Thus the Crusaders found every barrier levelled before them. When they arrived in Asia, the Emir of Nicæa was fighting against the Prince of Melitene, the Emir of Aleppo besieging his neighbours of Damascus and Emessa, and the Emirs of Sebaste and Mosul were engaged in war with the Armenian leaders; all feeling of unity and even of religious zeal among the Turks was entirely crushed by these manifold feuds. On the other hand, the Armenians were awaiting the arrival of the Crusaders with impatience. Some Frankish knights, sent on before the army, were cordially welcomed by them, and even the Caliph of Egypt, although seeking to seize Jerusalem for himself, received a deputation from the pilgrims,

D

who offered him their alliance against the common
enemy, the Seljukes. A year before, an alliance
with one Mahomedan against another would have
been regarded with horror by the pilgrims; but in
the face of reality, even fierce zealots could take a
practical course.

Nicæa, abandoned to its fate by the other emirs,
fell before the Crusaders in July, 1097. The con-
querors then marched, amid fatigue and hardship,
diagonally across Asia Minor. They had confided
to Count Stephen of Blois the direction of their operations, or rather, the presidency of the council of war,
and he chose, on arriving at the foot of the Taurus,
to follow the road along the north of the range as far
as the Euphrates, and then, after a considerable circuit, to cross the mountains and advance into Syria;
the object of this deviation was probably to render as
much help to the Armenians as possible. Numerous
small garrisons were left behind in the hill forts;
Cilicia was called to arms by a division under Bohemund's adventurous cousin Tancred, and Count
Baldwin, Godfrey's brother; and shortly afterwards
Baldwin was sent with a fresh detachment across
the Euphrates into Mesopotamia, where he showed
so much vigour and discretion in his dealings with
the Armenians, that in the course of a few months
they proclaimed him their sovereign in their capi-

tal city of Edessa. The main army meanwhile marched down the course of the Orontes upon the most important and best fortified of all the Syrian towns, Antioch, where years of fighting, triumphs, and disasters of all kinds awaited the Christian forces.

In Antioch ruled an aged emir, related to the Sultan's family, by name Bagi Sijan, who had always distinguished himself by rude energy and valour: he was now determined to resist to the last gasp. The Christians poured over the rich and fruitful country. More than a hundred of their knights established themselves in the castles and fortresses of the surrounding land, unmindful of the wants of the army, or the progress of the siege. The great princes were meanwhile encamped before the several gates of the town, without power to blockade the entrance, much less to make an assault upon its strong and lofty walls. Bagi Sijan's horse scoured the adjoining country in incessant sorties, destroyed scattered bodies of Christian troops, and cut off the supplies of the principal camp. Day after day passed; winter came with endless floods of rain; want, hunger and sickness began to thin the Christian forces to a fearful degree. Of the 300,000 fighting men, only half were at their posts; the horses were all dead, save a few hundreds; the commander-in-chief, Stephen of Blois, fell sick, and had himself carried away from the camp to the nearest seaport town of Alexandretta. The others still persevered. By degrees they erected small entrenchments and forts before the gates, stopped the passage of the bridge over which the Turks had been able to cross the river, and repulsed some of the emirs who tried to succour the garrison. In the spring, matters mended; the sickness ceased, many scattered parties returned, and a Genoese fleet brought abundant supplies, and gave the command of the Mediterranean. On the other hand, internal discord began to show itself. Bohemund had cast his eye on Antioch, and therefore persecuted the Greek Tatikios with all kinds of threats and insults, till he drove him from the camp; he then declared, that if the princes would promise him the hereditary possession of this important town, he would deliver it into their hands. He had ample ground for this assurance. It is true that there were fiercer warriors among the pilgrims than the Prince of Tarentium. Count Robert of Flanders was held to be the best lance in the army, and no sword was more dreaded than that of Duke Godfrey, whose powerful arm had, in one of the recent skirmishes, cut a fully armed Turk in two, so that the head and breast fell to the earth, while the lower half of the body was borne back by the horse into the town. Nevertheless, the Turks unquestionably looked upon Prince Bohemund as the head of the army, and the centre of all its movements; and accordingly Firuz az Zerrad, a grandee of Antioch, moved by personal hatred to Bagi Sijan, made propositions to him to the effect that he would receive baptism, and betray the town into his hands. When Bohemund made known this offer to the council of war, the princes hesitated: Count Raymond of Toulouse, bitterly envious of his more cunning comrade, strongly protested against it, on the score of the oath by which they had all acknowledged the claim of the Emperor Alexius, and thereupon the others declared it impossible to agree to Bohemund's request. He shrugged his shoulders and withdrew from the siege to bide his time. Before long a general lassitude seemed to prevail in the Christian camps, and threatening news arrived from the East. The Sultan having mastered his rival, had commanded the Emir Kerbuga of Mosul, to gather together all the force of his dominions, and to sweep the ribald crew of unbelievers from the face of the earth. He collected above half a million of men, who, fortunately for the Crusaders, spent several weeks in fruitless skirmishes against Baldwin before Edessa. At last their leader saw where the decisive blow ought to be struck, and led his

enormous army towards Antioch. The anxiety
then became great among the Christians, for the
worst might be anticipated, if they were shut in
between the yet unconquered town and the overwhelming force which was advancing to its relief.
In this strait the princes applied to Bohemund, but
he, cool and unmoved, reiterated his former demand.
Already Kerbuga's light horse had reached the first
outposts of the Frankish position, danger was imminent, when Raymond retracted his opposition,
and the town was promised to Bohemund. During
the night he, accompanied by sixty knights, scaled
one of the towers of the town wall guarded by
Firuz; and through the nearest gate, which he
instantly opened to them, the army poured into
the town, and overpowered the Turkish garrison,
amid a frightful struggle and bloodshed. The old
emir fled, but was killed in the mountains by a
troop of Christian peasants; his son however succeeded in throwing himself with a few followers
into the citadel, where he repulsed Bohemund's hasty
attacks.

This occurred on the 6th of June, 1098; on the
9th, Kerbuga's forces appeared in endless array; so
near had Bohemund's absorbing ambition allowed
destruction to approach. The Christians were still
in great danger; after the assault, they had plun-

dered, revelled, and wasted the small stores they
had found, and a blockade of a few days must
inevitably produce a famine. The enemy, too, within the walls, entrenched in the citadel, which stood
on the south side of the town and commanded
it, had at once opened communication with Kerbuga. In that quarter of the city, the struggle was
carried on day and night, almost without ceasing.
Elsewhere Kerbuga contented himself with a strict
blockade, and used his numerical superiority to
keep throwing fresh troops into the citadel, whence
their attacks constantly increased in violence.
Weariness and despair now seized upon the Christians; their sufferings from hunger were frightful;
men were seen gnawing roots of trees, and shoes,
and fighting for dead rats and cats. Some sank
down in the heat of battle unwounded, but tired
to death, heedless of the strife going on above their
heads. Thousands gave up all hope and concealed
themselves in the houses, which neither promises
nor threats could induce them to leave. In this
misery the council appointed Bohemund commander-in-chief with unlimited power. He saved them
again this time, by ordering the town to be fired,
so as to drive the soldiers into the streets. Up-
wards of two thousand houses were reduced to
ashes. This produced a complete revulsion of feel-

ing, which, from a state of deep depression, at once
rosé to fanatical enthusiasm.   The strong religious
feeling which for awhile had subsided beneath the
influence of strange and foreign impressions, re-
vived with renewed energy.   Led by a vision, a
Provençal discovered in a church the lance with
which Christ was pierced on the cross; pilgrims
daily appeared before the council of princes, to announce fresh apparitions of the Virgin and other
saints, who exhorted the army to sally forth and
fight.   Bohemund himself had no other project;
help was not to be hoped for, and if they were not
to starve, they must conquer.   In the enemy's camp
dissension and insubordination prevailed; considerable bodies of men, offended by Kerbuga, had dispersed, and when, on the 28th of July, the Franks
sallied forth from the town, they succeeded after a
short struggle in scattering the disconnected and
unwieldy masses in all directions.   This settled
the whole war; a boundless dread of the Christian
arms spread throughout the East; if the pilgrims
had then advanced, they might have taken possession of Palestine without the least fear of opposition.

  But a new difficulty now arose among the princes
themselves.   Raymond of Toulouse, who occupied a
few towers in Antioch, reverted to his former refusal
to deliver them up to Bohemund.   The other princes

did not wish to offend either of these two mighty
chiefs by a hostile decision, and a bitter quarrel,
which soon spread among the troops, and often led
to bloody strife between the Provençals and the
Normans, paralyzed all their movements. At last,
in January 1099, when the dispute between Bohemund and Tancred was repeated, on occasion of the
taking of the neighbouring town Maara, the pilgrims would endure it no longer. A wild outburst
ensued; the pilgrims exclaimed that they would go
on to Jerusalem; the princes might quarrel about
the things of this world, but Christ would guide
his own people. The old fanatical spirit broke
through all the political and military considerations
by which it had been restrained for some time. Spite
of all Raymond's anger, he was forced to evacuate
Antioch, and to follow in the wake of his excited
fellow-countrymen. Then the army, in fact without
head or leader, rushed wildly on towards its original destination. Jerusalem had meanwhile fallen
into the hands of the Egyptians, whose inclinations
were originally friendly; but to the excited feelings
of the Christian forces, the Egyptian infidels appeared as hateful and worthy of death as any
Seljukes. The town was surrounded and taken
by storm on the 15th of July. The Christian fury
against the infidels vented itself in a sanguinary

struggle, and in some places the besiegers waded
knee-deep in blood; they then, with tears of rapture, and in a state of ecstatic piety, threw themselves down to pray at the Holy Sepulchre, surrounded with heaps of the slain.

After eight days passed in the intoxication of victory, the princes met to take counsel as to the best
means of keeping possession of their conquest. The
most important question was evidently the choice of
a ruler. The men of the highest eminence were by
this time no longer with the army. The Count of
Blois had fled homewards from Alexandretta on
Kerbuga's approach. Bohemund had remained in
Antioch, and the Papal Legate had died soon after
the victory over Kerbuga. The princes offered the
crown of the new kingdom to Count Raymond;
he, however, declared that he was unworthy to wear
an earthly crown in so holy a place. According
to some accounts, they then turned to the Duke of
Normandy, but received the same answer. It is
certain that at last they applied to Duke Godfrey,
who, although he, like Raymond, refused the title
of King, accepted the command and power in the
course of the following month. He succeeded in
beating an Egyptian army near Ascalon, and thus
secured the southern frontier of the kingdom. After
that however it became impossible to restrain the

masses of pilgrims who, after the fulfilment of their vow, longed to return home. Godfrey and Tancred were left at Jerusalem with about two hundred knights and two thousand effective men-at-arms. Count Raymond attempted, with still fewer followers, to found for himself a kingdom in Tripoli; the numbers at the disposal of Bohemund in Antioch, and of Baldwin in Edessa, were rather more considerable. To the duration and fate of these small territories we will afterwards turn our attention. I will now offer a few remarks upon the effect which these events produced both on those who took part in them and upon the European public, an effect which manifested itself in manifold, and in some cases very remarkable recitals and descriptions.

First, the princes themselves, in letters to the Pope, to their relations and friends, gave their eager and curious countrymen accounts of the great events of the war. Nine such letters have been preserved, some of them instructive and full of detail. There were also several men with the army who kept an accurate and continuous record of the occurrences as they succeeded each other—a Norman knight, a Provençal priest, a chaplain of Count Baldwin of Bouillon; and as they belonged to various countries and detachments the reports of each supply the omissions of the rest, and thus form a tolerably complete whole.   What they had written they sent by the first opportunity to Europe, where these journals were expected with the greatest eagerness, and, on their arrival, received with avidity, and extensively read and copied.   There were neither newspapers nor telegraphs, and in order to spread the much-desired news as fast as possible, the expedient was hit upon that the priests should read the newly-arrived reports, on Sundays, from the pulpit, and forward them one to another, from place to place, for this purpose.   These tales were, indeed, much shorter than the eagerly listening crowd wished; they were also drier, from their very accuracy, than minds thirsting for the marvellous had expected.   But the same taste had spread among the Crusaders, as well as in Europe, and was working with creative energy for the satisfaction of that kind of curiosity.   There has never yet been a large army without its bards and poets, faithful men-at-arms, grenadiers, or hussars, who, while sitting round the watchfire at night, invent songs in praise of their General, of their sweetheart at home, or of their fallen comrades, which pass from mouth to mouth, gaining new verses at every repetition.   The eleventh century was, indeed, as we have seen, an eminently unpoetical period, with its gloomy contempt for the world, and its fanatical enthusiasm; during that time hardly one piece of real poetry was produced on European soil. The Crusade, however, in which that fanaticism vented itself, at once produced an agitation favourable to liberty and progress. While it lasted, men's minds, it is true, were still affected by fierce religious enthusiasm, but, at the same time, their senses were impressed and captivated by the spectacle of an entirely new world. Thousands who till then had never caught a glimpse of anything beyond the narrow circle of their own parish, now beheld the splendid colouring of southern nature, the magnificence of the Greek imperial palaces, and the strange customs of the Mahomedan world, whose culture, even in its decay, was so far superior to that of the Europeans, as to inspire them with respect. The excitement produced by such impressions, was augmented by the danger which was imminent at every moment. Death was ever before their eyes, and every faculty of body and mind had to be exerted to preserve life, and at last to reach the glorious goal. Their intoxicated eyes still beheld visions of the saints and armies of heaven, but they no longer appeared in the lonely cloistered cell, or during nightly penance and flagellation. They were now seen in the thick of the battlefield, with shining weapons, and mounted on white steeds, dashing into

the midst of the Turkish army, and opening the
way for the heroes of the army, the darlings of the
troops, through the swords of the infidel masses.
Thus, religious sentiment was still the basis of this
movement; but it took a new turn, from monkish
devotion to chivalrous enthusiasm, from ascetic renunciation of the world to knightly valour. A new
sort of heroism was thus called into existence, and
with the heroes, heroic poetry arose. It showed
itself during the war among all ranks of the army.
Each nation celebrated its warriors, and, after every
great battle, sang the deeds of the victorious leader,
the goodly blows dealt by the foremost knights, and
the heavenly joys which rewarded the fallen heroes.
In the fragments of these songs which still remain,
we see the natural disposition to attribute the deed
which decided the common victory, to the hero or
prince of each particular race, and to claim for him
a prominent and leading position. Thus, the French
extolled Count Hugo, the brother of their king, as
the Duke of Dukes and the greatest leader of the
army. The men of Lorraine tell us that even in
Asia Minor, Duke Godfrey was the head of all the
princes; that the attack on Antioch remained so long
unsuccessful because of his illness; and that he and
his friend Robert of Flanders, had, on that memo-
rable night, been the first to set the ladders against

the walls of Antioch, and to enter the town. Even the mob of King Tafur had their songs in praise of the Hermit, who, in consequence of his vision in Jerusalem, had induced the Pope to preach the Crusade, and had then set all Europe in motion.

Altogether, we see with amazement how far, perhaps even on the very day after the event, the imagination of these poets and their hearers led them astray from the truth. The Council of Clermont was held in November; here we find it transposed into May, when the fields are green, and thrushes and blackbirds are singing: for Nature must needs rejoice and adorn herself in honour of such an event. This poetical license is continued through the whole course of the Crusades: side by side with the real events runs a fantastic story, glittering and multiform; a legendary creation, growing out of actual present history. We see how religious and warlike enthusiasm excites the love of adventure, and stimulates the power of invention, but also how untrustworthy are the observations and reports made under its influence.

I cannot deny myself the pleasure of giving a few extracts from these poems, which have come down to us in a later but slightly altered form. They are written in French rhymes. The translation has been abridged, and only aspires to render the general tone and colour.

THE TAKING OF THE CROSS AT CLERMONT.

At Clermont in Auvergne were met great hosts from near
 and far,
From France, and from all Christendom, unto the Lord his
 war;
Was none so young but thitherward must fare, and none so
 old.
Came prince and peer and paladin, came knights and ba-
 rons bold,
Each with his stout retainers, pennon and pennoncel;
The abbot brought his crosier, the cowled monk left his cell.
The King rode with his following, armed at point from head
 to heel,—
Stout Hugh the Lord of Maine, and Count Raymond of St.
 Gilles,
Stephen the stalwart Duke of Blois, and Bishop Adhemàr,
Than whom was none more valiant of all those men of war;
Came Godfrey of Bouloigne, with his two brothers fair,
Baldwin the sturdy striker, Eustace the debonair;
Robert the Count of Flanders, Robert the Monk also:
To tell the tale of all that came, were weary work, I trow.

When that their steeds were stabled and fairly foddered all,
That night at board and beaker they feasted them in hall,
And fair disport and solace they held till morning-tide.
When that the Pope in all his might, he borne him forth to
 ride,
The King and all his paladins gave him attendance due,
With the merry bells a-pealing, the minster doors unto;

And when the Pope had read the Mass, the multitude of folk
Out at the doors, all in hot haste, crushing and crowding,
    broke.
There were so many thousands there gathered, as men sayn,
Nor house nor hall, nor minster wall, e'er built, might them
    contain.
It was a fair May morning, the birds sang roundelay,
The trees were white with blossom, buds sprang on every
    spray ;
All golden lay the meadows in the sunlight's gladsome sheen,
As they sat them down by companies upon the springing
    green ;
To left and right as far as sight could stretch they hid the sod;
The Pope he stood alone, and preached the pilgrimage of God.
From son to sire like holy fire God's spirit spread his word ;
Was not one eye of thousands dry, was not one heart un-
    stirred.

When now the Pope had ended, the King rose in his place,—
" In God's name, Holy Father, hearken my words with grace.
Well dost thou say ; but I am grey, and lacking youthful heat ;
A frail man and a feeble, for such pilgrimage unmeet.
'Twere well, in lieu of _me_, that my brother Hugo ride ;
Of all my peers and paladins is none hath him outvied;
To him I render all my might."—The which when Hugo
    heard,
His heart within his bosom with rapture swelled and stirred.
A joy past joy it seemed to him in such good grace to stand,
To ride with ban and arrière-ban, unto his Lord's own land.
Quoth he, " Gramercy, Brother," and kissed him foot and
    hand.

E

Then to the Pope he louted low, the cross on him to take,
And knights and barons after him like act and vow did make;
Both lords of France and England, and lords of Norman
    line,
They prayed and pressed to take the cross, the holy pil-
    grim's sign;
So great the throng were many swooned, and died there as
    they lay.
Two hundred thousand took the cross at Clermont on that
    day.
Then loudly wailed the noble dames, and maidens wept for woe:
" Out and alas for us that here henceforth alone must go
In widowhood and orphanage! woe worth this princes' day,
That strikes, as with a single blow, our joyaunce all away!
'Tis sad in tower, 'tis dark in bower, all empty, cold, and lone;
Silent all sound of singing, disport and solace flown."
And many a gentle dame, I wis, her youthful lord bespake,—
" Fair husband, that with choice of heart me for your love
    did take,
Winning my favour with all vows that gain a lady's ear,
For God and Mary mother, when forth o'er sea you steer,
And look upon the city, where our Lord hung on the tree,
Keep thy true wife unforgotten, and give a thought to me."
There were gentle eyes a-weeping, and tears on tears they
    flowed,
And many a wedded woman there took the cross of God;
But the maidens sadly wended their weary way again,
Back to their fathers' castles, with their lonely weight of pain.

THE LEAGUER OF ANTIOCH.

Now lithe and listen, lordings, while the Christians' hap I
　　tell,
That, as they lay in leaguer, from hunger them befell.
In evil case the army stood, their stores of food were spent:
Peter the holy Hermit, he sat before his tent:
Then came to him the King Tafùr, and with him fifty score
Of men-at-arms, not one of them but hunger gnawed him sore.
"Thou holy Hermit, counsel us, and help us at our need;
Help, for God's grace, these starving men with wherewithal
　　to feed."
But Peter answered, "Out, ye drones, a helpless pack that cry,
While all unburied round about the slaughtered Paynim lie.
A dainty dish is Paynim flesh, with salt and roasting due."
"Now, by my fay," quoth King Tafùr, "the Hermit sayeth
　　true."
Then fared he forth the Hermit's tent, and sent his menye
　　out,
More than ten thousand, where in heaps the Paynim lay
　　about.
They hewed the corpses limb from limb, and disemboweled
　　clean,
And there was sodden meat and roast, to blunt their hunger
　　keen :
Right savoury fare it seemed them there; they smacked
　　their lips and spake,—
"Farewell to fasts : a daintier meal than this who asks to
　　make ?

'Tis sweeter far than porker's flesh, or bacon seethed in
    grease.
Let's make good cheer, and feast us here, till life and hunger
    cease."

While King and host, on boiled and roast, were making
    merry cheer,
The savoury reek of Paynim flesh 'gan rise into the air,
Till to the walls of Antioch the winds that smell did blow;
Then rose within an angry din, and all were wild for woe.
On house and hall and 'battled wall the swarming Paynim
    hung,
While all around the sharper sound was heard of woman's
    tongue.
Up to his topmost solar was y-clomb King Garsiön,
With Isaës his nephew, and Sansadon his son.
Quoth Garsion to his children,—" Now, by the great Mahoun,
These devils eat our brethren : look, in the plain adown."

Tafùr the king looked up from meat; he saw the Paynim
    stand,
Men, wives, and maids, on every wall that might a view com-
    mand ;
No ruth the sight awakened, but thriftily he bade
That they should see the corpses picked from where the
    heaps were laid ;
Bade roast whatso was fresh, and whatso rotted bade them
    throw
Into the stream that by the walls of Antioch did flow.
" We'll give the fish," quoth he, " the smack of Paynim flesh
    to know."

It happed that for a chevauchie did with Count Robert join

Count Tancred, and Count Bohemund, and Godfrey of Bouloigne;

All closed in steel from head to heel they chanced to pass
that way,

And knightly greeted they the King, and laughingly 'gan
say,—

" How fares it with the King Tafùr ?" " In sooth," the King
replied,

" If I said ' ill,' fair sirs, meseems, so speaking, I had lied.

Had we to skink a cup of drink, for food we've here our fill."

" Now, by my fay," quoth Godfrey, " Here's drink, an if you
will ;"

And straight bade bring a pitcher, filled with his own red
wine.

Then drank Tafùr, and well I wot, ne'er seemed him drink
so fine.

Then from his solar where he stood, loud called King Garsiön

To Bohemund, unto whose ear the wind brought every tone

Of that fierce sound,—" Now, by Mahound, malapert knaves
ye bin,

To do dead bodies such foul wrong is insolence and sin."

But Bohemund made answer,—" Fair Lord, what here ye see

Is none of our commanding, nor wight thereof have we :

'Tis King Tafùr's devising, his and his devil's crew ;

An evil rout are they, God wot.   The brutish taste we rue

That boar or deer holds sorrier cheer than flesh of Paynim
slain.

Yet ask not us to chide them, but unto Heaven complain."

THE GATHERING OF THE PAYNIM.

Not far from Samarkànd an open meadow lay,
Girt with dark stems of cypress, laurel, and olive grey,
And round the place a fragrant hedge of balsam thicket
    went;
Upon that mead the Sultan bade pitch his royal tent.
The tent-poles were of elmen-tree, with silver wrought full
    rare;
The tent-stuff was all diapered, like to a chess-board fair,
Half of the white and cramoisy, half of the gold and green,
And in the chequers, ouches and stones that glittered sheen:
Twelve thousand men beneath its shade had lain at ease, I
    ween.
And 'mid the household stuff that filled the fair pavilion
    round,
Was set on high, in beaten gold, an image of Mahound.
Between four magic-loadstones, all free in air it hung,
And hitherward and thitherward, as the wind listed, swung.

Then fourteen lords came lowly forth, each lord a king's
    own son,
And featly at the Sultan's high board have service done,
And after to the idol their sacrifice they made,
And, grovelling upon the ground, their gifts before it laid,
And censered it with incense, and prayed, and still the sound
That ended all their litanies was "Hear us, great Mahound."

While all were still on kneeling knees, in sudden fury broke
Prince Sansadon before the rout, and loud and wrathful
    spoke,—

" Up, weakling wittols that ye are, blind fools that here are
    laid,

Not knowing this Mahound of yours is powerless all to aid.

'Tis through that lewd false faith of his, and trusting in his
    name,

That I have lost my people and all mine own fair fame."

Then high uprist, he clenched his fist, and smote the idol
    down,

And trampled it beneath his feet: whereat there rose a
    stoun,

A wild uproar and hellish rout of that mad paynimrie ;

The knives they rained about his head, the shafts flew fast
    and free ;

" Accursëd !" cried the Sultan, "who taught thee mock
    our creed ?

Who art thou ?   What thy lineage ?   A rope were thy fit
    meed."

Prince Sansadon declared his name, and sadly 'gan to tell

The evil that on Antioch by Christian leaguer fell ;

Told of the Christian archers that waste no shaft in air,

The Christian knights, all sheathed in steel, that steel-
    sharp lances bear,

" Each one of whom," quoth he, " if down upon our hosts
    he bore,

Would spit of our light horsemen three files, I ween, or
    four."

Then scornful waxed the Sultan,— "Now, stout Knight
    mote thou be !

Who'd learn faint-heart and cowardice may go to school
    to thee "

Then up and spake grim Corbaran,—" Nay, Lord, as I opine,
He hath too much y-drunken : his head is hot with wine."
"Now nay, thou Persian Admiral," Prince Sansadon replied,
" Light words, soon said, but by my head I swear thy jape
    goes wide.
Tis not faint-heart, nor cowardice, nor wine that speaks
    in me.
King Garsion bade me ride to you as fast as fast may be.
For your good aid he prays you : he is right sore bested.
Behold, I bring this token, to seal what I have said."
And with the word, out of the pouch that like a post he
    wore .
Girt round about his waist, his sire's grey beard he bore.
But when the Sultan saw it, right sorry waxed his cheer.
" Now of a truth, when Garsiön did brook his chin to shear,
Things stand, I wot, in evil case ; his need it is not small.
To counsel how we best may bring him succour, one and all."

Long all was hush : both prince and peer sat silently and
    still,
As stricken to their inmost souls to hear King Garsion's ill.
Then random counsel counselled they ; some this advised,
    some that ;
At last out spake King Kangas, on Rubia's throne that sat.
" Now, by Mahound, great Sultan, this seemeth best to me :
Send through thy land, on every hand, swift posts as swift
    may be,
And to Coronda summon all your lords, with their array,
And, before all, the Caliph that in Bagdad holdeth sway.
Comes he, our Pope, salvation and strength come at his side,
And mightiest following of all with him will eastward ride."

"So be it," cried the Sultan, "a wise word hast thou said;
Four hundred posts with letters shall ere to-night be sped."

A moon had waxed, a moon had waned, and one in crescent
    stood,
When all ways to Coronda flowed arm'd warriors like a flood
Of horse and foot; by night and day the mighty muster goes,
With swords and staves and spears and glaives, with maces
    and with bows.
From Bagdad rode the Caliph, that all the country round
Had raised in arms by promise of the blessing of Mahound.
Came the swart and sinewy Arabs, that make their godless
    scorn
Of Christ his resurrection; and, the foul Fiend's brother
    born,
Leu, fiery-red, and gnashing his teeth as he were wode,
Behind whose heels of Turkish spears four hundred thou-
    sand rode;
Came from the furthest East a folk of strange and eldritch
    kind,
In whom, save teeth and eye-balls, no white speck mote you
    find.
And in the vanward of this rout, high set you might behold,
Upon a dromedary tall, Corbaran's mother old.
Grey was her hair, her eyes were blear, but still her wits were
    strong;
Strange things she knew from sun and moon, that to black
    art belong;
Could read the courses of the stars, and in those lights on
    high,
Foresaw at will the secrets of mortal destiny.

Their hosts up in the rearward the Kings of Mecca brought,
Bearing their image of Mahound, of hollow gold y-wrought;
Wherein through spell of gramarye an evil spirit sate,
And the Paynim danced before it, for worship and for state.
I trow it was a sight to see, that image of Mahound
Moving to din of shawms and drums, with harp and viol's
　　sound.

So to its journey's end in state the golden idol came,
Where with his host the Caliph sate to greet Mahound his
　　name.
Whereat the lying spirit that in this idol sate,
Blew himself up for pride before the Caliph and his state:—
" List what I say, and weigh my words and rightly under-
　　stand :
The Christiäns have never right unto the Paynim's land,
For that they worship God on high; this land I give to ye;
Heaven 'longeth to the Christian's God—the land be-
　　longs to me."
Then merry were the Paynim, and loud they cried, I wot,—
" Right well Mahound hath spoken;—a fool that trusts him
　　not."

Then, as chief captain of the host, the Sultan chose a man,
The Admiral of Olifern, the valiant Corbaran.
By beat of drum the heathen rout he marshalled there and
　　then,
In two-and-thirty squadrons, each of threescore thousand
　　men.
His foot was in the stirrup, his grasp was at the mane,
When his old mother, Calabra, his armëd hand hath ta'en

'Twas twice ten years since in the stars, by her black art she read,

TheChristians should be victors, the Paynims should be sped.

"Fair Sir," quoth she, "now wilt thou ride in good sooth to the field ?"

"Yea, and in sooth, good mother, and unseemly 'twere to yield,

While still in Antioch's leaguer the Christians flout our bands ;

I trow 'twere pity of his life, that in my danger stands."

"Son, take good counsel : homeward to Olifern repair.

These Christian knights are terrible ; their stars show bright and fair."

"What prate is this, good mother ? Say, is the story true,

That Bohemund and Tancred are their goddikins, the two ?

That for their early breakfast, whene'er they crave to eat,

Two thousand beeves will scarce suffice this doughty twain for meat.

So runs the tale." Then said the witch, "Son, leave this flouting tone ;

No gods these Christians worship, save Christ the Lord alone.

Never a man of all this host shall Christian might defy.

Of all the heads I count, not one but it shall lowly lie."

Heavy of heart that chieftain waxed, but featly hid his pain :

"Now let her yelp : so old she is, she grows a child again,

'Twere a good deed to cut her throat." Then into selle he sprang,

And forward marched the Paynim host to the trumpet's shattering clang.

When the Crusade was ended, and the mass of pilgrims came pouring back to the places of their birth, they imparted these more picturesque descriptions to their fellow-countrymen. We can imagine in how lofty a strain they would relate these tales; how imperceptibly the materials would grow beneath their hands; how conjecture would become certainty, and feeling take the form of undoubted fact. What awakened the interest of their hearers the most was undoubtedly the choice of a King of Jerusalem. During the expedition there had been songs in praise of Count Hugo's and Duke Robert's deeds, as well as of Duke Godfrey's; but the attention of Europe was now almost exclusively fixed upon the ruler of Palestine and the protector of the Holy Sepulchre. All the world wished to know his birth and parentage, to hear of his deeds and virtues; his fame became decidedly and exclusively prominent, and cast the real or fictitious greatness of the others completely into the shade. He was made into a descendant of the fabulous Knight of the Swan; it was reported that he had ever been the protector of innocence and the defender of the weak; that he once sinfully fought against Pope Gregory in the service of the Emperor, since when he had lain in heavy sickness till the time of the Crusades; then, by God's command, and as a sure

sign of his heavenly calling, the fever had left the
hero. Twenty years after his death, a priest of Aix-
la-Chapelle, named Albert, collected all the songs,
and verbal communications in praise of the Duke,
and incorporated them in a prose recital, which
is extremely graphic and lively. Partly from this
source, and partly from later poetical versions of the
original songs, subsequent writers have drawn all
their knowledge of Peter the Hermit as originator,
and of Godfrey of Bouillon as commander of the
Crusade; here Torquato Tasso found the so-called
historical subject of his great poem; but, as we now
know, he did but employ his master hand in polish-
ing and completing the great poem of a former century.

I have ventured to divert the attention of my
readers from the contemplation of facts to the much-
decried domain of scientific investigation and criticism. We often hear complaints that investigation
is dry and criticism destructive. I must admit that
in this instance Godfrey and Peter the Hermit have
been shorn of their false glory; and yet, if I mis-
take not, the picture of those remarkable times
loses nothing of its freshness or completeness. A
critical examination of the original sources* shows
us that certain events never really took place, and

* See Part II.

existed only in the creative fancy of contemporaries; but we know, and have here fresh proof, that
history does not consist solely of battles and sieges;
the achievements of the mind and the productions
of fancy are among its most important features;
and with regard to the Crusades, I have no hesitation in looking upon the composition of those
songs as an event almost greater than the taking of
Jerusalem. The territorial possession was lost in
a few years, and indeed it was untenable from the
first; but in those legends we see the first stir of a
vigorous new life, the first pulsation of renewed
mental activity after a century of oppressive and
gloomy fanaticism. This direction once taken, was
never again lost by Europe, but gradually carried
along the whole hemisphere in its course.

CHAPTER III.

THE Frankish States founded in Syria by the First Crusade had no easy task. With an army consisting at the most of seven thousand horse and five thousand foot, they could not hope for succour from their distant native countries; scattered among a scarcely conquered hostile population, and surrounded by powerful and naturally implacable foes. At first the great battles of Antioch and Ascalon produced great moral effect. Internal dissensions among the Turkish potentates, helped the Christians through the first period of danger, and then, attracted by the reports of the Crusade, the European countries sent perpetual reinforcements, which arrived sometimes in small and sometimes in large bodies, by water and by land, some intending to settle there entirely, but most for a limited period. From all this, however, Duke Godfrey derived little advantage; he was so powerless that, in even Jeru-

salem itself, he was obliged to acknowledge himself
the vassal of an ambitious prelate, Dagobert, who
had been chosen Patriarch of the Holy City; and
he died as early as 1100, after a short and unevent-
ful reign. He was succeeded by his brother Baldwin of Edessa, a vigorous and able ruler, who
overthrew the supremacy of the Patriarch by arbitrary force, and established the royal authority on
all points. Within ten years he took all the seaport towns from Tripoli to Jaffa, and thereby secured what was most important, freedom of communication with the Western world; the last years
of his life were employed in defending the southern
boundary of his kingdom towards Egypt by a succession of fortresses, which he planted partly round
Ascalon, still held by the Egyptians, partly in the
wilderness, on the spurs of the Arabian desert.
His successor, Baldwin II., who reigned from 1118
till 1130, carried on this warlike movement with
even greater energy and a more far-sighted policy.
The rule of the Caliphs of Egypt was then in a
feeble and decaying condition; moreover the desert,
and the naval predominance of the Christians, rendered any serious attack impossible. The probable,
indeed the only danger to the Franks was from
the East; in case any leader of eminence should
arise among the vigorous and warlike Seljukes, re-

concile or control the dissentient emirs, and then break into the country with a united force. Baldwin II., who, like his predecessor, had once been Count of Edessa, had a vivid conception of this danger, and accordingly wished to direct the military force at his disposal in Jerusalem and Antioch to that quarter; and there if not wholly to destroy the Sultanate, at least to secure a safe and defensible frontier. According to this plan, they must have taken Damascus, Aleppo, and all the places between Antioch and Edessa : then a sufficient defence would have been formed by the Taurus mountains on the north, the Euphrates on the north-east, and the Syrian desert on the south-east, as the boundaries of a compact kingdom. Baldwin followed up this idea by unceasing warfare and incredible exertion. Once, when taken prisoner by a bold adventurer, he lay for years a prisoner among the Turks. After his release, this misfortune only served to spur his activity into redoubled vigour. During his life the supremacy of the Cross was maintained in those countries. Haleb and Damascus were not conquered indeed, but they paid tribute, and the Mussulman merchants trembled as they passed along the roads between the Euphrates and Tigris, in fear lest the lances of the Frankish knights should appear on the horizon. If all the Christians had

F

shared the ideas of their King, his plan would in all
probability have been carried out, and perhaps a
lasting foundation of European power and civilization would have been laid in those lands.

But Baldwin stood alone among his comrades in
his political and military views.   They were never
wanting in ardour, courage, or religious zeal.   No
sooner did an enemy appear, than they received
the sacrament with fervent tears, and rushed with
enthusiastic contempt of death into the fight, where
the overwhelming weight of the Frankish armour
always told with effect.   Their abilities, however,
extended no further; convinced that they were protected by God himself, they attended little to earthly
considerations.   Instead of supporting the King in
his conquests in the north, the barons and burghers
of Jerusalem lamented his leaving the vicinity of
the Holy Sepulchre so often, and even neglecting it
for such distant undertakings; besides dragging
about that invaluable relic the Holy Cross, on those
accursed campaigns.   Thus hindered and thwarted
on all sides, Baldwin was unable to accomplish his
great design.   The heroes who drew their swords
and shook their lances so gallantly in Christ's honour, were quite incapable of understanding the
political motives and consequences of their undertaking.   It may even be said that they would not

understand them. Every earthly consideration seemed
to them a presumptuous interference with God's
ordinances, an impious intermingling of earth with
heaven. They thus ruined their kingdom by the
same one-sided religious zeal which had given them
the energy to conquer it. Instead of striving to
frame their society according to religious principles,
and then allowing politics to obey political rules,
and war military ones, they started upon the supposition that the very existence of their dominion
was a wonder of God's own working, and they were
convinced that for every fresh danger which threatened it, God had a new miracle in store. They
were soon to discover that such a notion was as
destructive to religion and morality, as to political
and warlike success.

It has been remarked, in all times, that the exclusive piety which holds itself superior to human
reason, is just that which panders most to earthly
vices. Amidst the most ardent enthusiasm for the
Church, all the most earthly passions soon asserted
their sway. The princes of Edessa and Antioch
quarrelled among themselves quite as fiercely as the
emirs of Aleppo and Damascus. Ere long, even a
knight like Tancred sought Turkish help against his
Christian adversaries, though, according to the fundamental ideas of the Crusade, any alliance with a

Turk was an abomination, and their blood the only
pleasant offering to the Lord. It was, however, in-
evitable that the bitterness of religious hatred should
gradually subside.   Each day brought forth social
and commercial relations with the infidels, as well as
war.   The Franks saw with amazement that people
who in Europe were held to be worse than wild
beasts, half-demons, half-brutes, could be lived with,
dealt with, nay, even that much might be learnt
from them. The idea dawned for the first time upon
the Franks, that human nature could exist under
other conditions than those of their own Church, ,
that God's light might be reflected in a thousand
different ways.   Such an idea is now welcome and
consolatory to our religious feelings, but then it was
entirely subversive of all 1eceived opinions.   It was
the same in all other transactions. Spite of all the devotion to the Holy Sepulchre, the Crusaders plunged
deeper and deeper into the earthly joys of Oriental
life. Baldwin's successor, King Fulco, was old and
somewhat infirm; he forgot the orders he had just
given, mistook his best friends, and had no memory
but for the commands of his imperious wife Melisende, which he executed with tremulous exactness.
Under this prince, the warlike impulse of the Baldwins completely died away. The Christians devoted
their whole attention to personal luxury and splen-

dour. The numerous clergy led the way by their example. Barons and prelates vied with each other in the race for political influence, rich benefices and livings, wealth, and pleasure. There was no kingdom in Europe in which the beauty and power of women played so conspicuous a part, as in the community at the Holy Sepulchre. Much as Fulco feared his queen, he was so jealous of her that he brought the handsome and proud Count Hugo of Joppa, whom he thought she distinguished, in danger of his life, by a criminal suit. Thereupon Hugo fled to the Egyptians, and commenced a devastating war against the kingdom; this was assuaged with much difficulty, and Hugo was recalled to Jerusalem, as it proved, to his misfortune, for an assassin attacked him in the high-road, and wounded him severely, which induced him to fly anew, to Europe. We find the same scenes repeated in the north. Count Joscelin of Edessa, a dwarfish, misshapen man, with a black beard, sparkling eyes, and gigantic bodily strength, left his capital in order to live joyously with numerous mistresses in shady country palaces, on this side of the Euphrates. In Antioch, Eliza, the widow of Bohemund II., withheld the inheritance from her daughter Constance. Count Raymond of Poitou, a handsome and brilliant knight, cast an eye on the rich heiress, but soon perceived, that though favoured by her, he could not gain possession of the throne against the will of her resolute and clever mother. Upon this, he changed his tactics, and appeared as the mother's passionate adorer, obtained a favourable answer, and led her in brilliant array to the altar, but no further. When there, he suddenly turned to the daughter, married her, and then, before the very eyes of the astounded and bewildered mother, proclaimed his and his consort's accession to the throne. Amid such occurrences, it was no wonder that the war against the Turks did not progress. The desire for further conquest was extinct, and the Christians only prayed to heaven that things might but remain as they were.

Such stability is not, however, the portion of human affairs. While the Franks rested and enjoyed life, trusting in God's help, a man arose among the Turks, who was destined to be the author of their destruction. Shortly before the Crusade, the brother of the Seljuke Sultan had caused one of his most able emirs to be executed, and had thought himself merciful and gracious because he spared his young son, Emaleddin Zenki. Deprived of fortune or favour, this boy worked his way up, from a common horse-soldier, by the strength of his arm and his intelligence. Amid the disorders of civil war, and more particularly since the invasion by the Franks, his sharp sword, his undaunted courage, and his keen and accurate judgment, had quickly become famous in the Syrian countries. He rose rapidly, from step to step, and all the Seljukes praised Allah when Zenki obtained the emirate of Mosul, with the distinct commission to wage an exterminating war against the Franks. The adversities of his youth had made him stern and harsh; he was more indignant at the indolent anarchy of his countrymen, than at the hostility of the Christians, and, while, from the beginning of his government, he left them not a moment's rest, perpetually attacked them unawares, and soon gained from them the dreaded title of the "bloody prince," he was entirely without mercy, or even justice, towards a Seljuke who was lax in the prosecution of the holy war, or, still worse, was suspected of friendship for a Christian. Military unity and energy were thus once more established under the Prophet's flag, and soon made themselves felt in bloody attacks, now upon the kingdom of Jerusalem, now upon the northern principalities. In a short time the Turkish possessions, from the Tigris to Lebanon, were under one rule, and in 1145 one of the most important Christian cities, Edessa, was taken by storm. Zenki died directly after, and Count Joscelin, roused from his life of indolence, hastened to free the town from the Turkish garrison. Scarcely had he set foot in it, when Nureddin, Zenki's son, approached with a large army, and, after sharp fighting, took Edessa for the second time, and nearly destroyed it. From that time, the whole of Mesopotamia remained in the hands of the Turks. The Christians discovered that there was no help for this state of things, and that Antioch must now serve as the northern frontier town instead, and, as far as they were concerned, profound peace prevailed in the land. Occasionally they exhorted Europe to send them a few reinforcements, at their earliest convenience.

There, the Holy Land had for a long time occupied but a small share of public attention. The reason lay in the general intellectual movement which had suddenly sprung up among the nations of Europe at the beginning of the twelfth century. The ascetic piety which despises the things of this world, and which had culminated in Gregory VII. and the Crusades, called forth a general reaction by its violence. In France, one of the acutest and boldest thinkers of any time, Abelard, dared to demonstrate the fallibility of the dogmas of the Church, and to vindicate the independence of philosophical speculation, with an energy which gathered around him thousands of enthusiastic disciples. The sunny air of Provence began to resound with the ardent poetry of the Troubadours, free in tone, glowing in colour, full of the joys of this world, and the passions of love and war. From Italy news spread on every side, that the great code of the Emperor Justinian had been discovered; it was read and taught in Bologna with untiring zeal, to a concourse of eager listeners; and a picture was unfolded before the eyes of a wondering generation, of a bygone period, in which a united government was really all-powerful, and the heads of the Church were only its first servants and officers. The effect of this was powerfully felt in Germany as in Rome. The abbots in Germany complained that even their own monks could not be got away from their legal studies to attend to the services of the Church. Arnold of Brescia addressed the Roman citizens with electrifying eloquence, and called up before them the image of the old *Populus Romanus*, inciting them to open rebellion against the temporal power of a Church, which was, he said, a scandal to religion and morals, and ought to be made to disburse its treasures for the public good.

The Papal power had however been too firmly established since the time of Gregory VII., to succumb to this first movement. Too many important interests were bound up with it, and every antagonist was met by a host of enthusiastic admi-

rers or energetic partisans, and, as usual, an unsuccessful rebellion only served to strengthen the power
and ambition of the government.   About 1140 it
was principally the Abbot Bernard of Clairvaux,
who in France and Upper Italy kept the people to
their allegiance towards the Pope and the Church.
He was sufficiently well grounded in philosophy
not to shun the conflict with Abelard; he brought
back the great Order to which he belonged to strict
rules and hard study; he won over the Lombards
and Provençals, who for a time had upheld a schis-
matical pope, by his impassioned and persuasive
eloquence.   The weak and sickly man gained the
ear of the whole population of the West.   Without
ambition, and free from passion, by nature contemplative and quiet, Bernard obtained a European
influence, solely by his fervent devotion to the leading ideas of the time.   His letters, in which much
pains was evidently bestowed on the elegance of
the style, and the impressiveness and sentiment of
the imagery, were current in all the land, breathing
a still dominant and irresistible spirit.   He himself would be nothing more than a plain and humble monk; any call to leave the walls of his beloved
Clairvaux for a higher place he obstinately refused
to obey; but kings listened to his sermons, and
Pope Eugene thought absolute reverence for the
Abbot his greatest virtue.

Under these circumstances, Europe was obviously
not in a favourable state for another great undertaking for the relief of Jerusalem, and warfare
against the Turks. The political condition was
no less unfavourable. The general confusion into
which Gregory VII. had thrown all the European
nations, and which, like an earthquake following a
volcanic outbreak, had found vent in the First Crusade, was at an end.

Political power had everywhere gained strength,
the European States showed signs of new life, and
great national interests were fermenting. Germany
was under the rule of the first king of the race of the
Hohen-Stauffen, Conrad III. Always an opponent
of the Popes, he was constantly at war with their
allies, particularly the mighty sovereign house of
Guelf. The latter, when conquered in Germany,
called foreign comrades to their aid,—the turbulent
Hungarians from the east, the ambitious Norman
King of Naples, Roger II., from the south. Conrad,
on the other hand, entered into an alliance with the
Emperor Manuel of Constantinople, who, like himself, had suffered endless vexations from the Normans and the Hungarians. Roger hereupon determined instantly to fall upon the Greek provinces
with redoubled vigour, and earnestly begged King
Louis to support him either with a fleet against

Manuel, or by land against the German king. In a word, Europe was split into two great alliances, on one side the German king with most of his princes and the Greek Emperor; on the other, the Guelfs, Louis of France, the Hungarians, and Roger of Naples. In this state of things, no one thought of a Crusade, least of all the Syrian Franks, who wished indeed for the arrival of a few detached bodies of troops, but not for the presence of a whole army, in their land.

It happened, however, that King Louis VII., on the occasion of an insurrection in the town of Vitry, in Champagne, stormed the place, cut down a number of the inhabitants, and, amongst other buildings, burnt the churches also. His excitable temper made him ungovernable in rage, and crushed by remorse after the first outburst was over; he was accessible to but one idea at a time, and incapable of taking any comprehensive views. No sooner was the battle ended than he repented, with horror and bitterness of spirit, his offence against the churches, feared for the salvation of his soul, and vowed a Crusade as the expiation for his crime. Bernard, to whom he applied for assistance, tried to dissuade him, saying that it was better to fight against the sinful inclinations of his own heart, than against the Turks. When, however, the King obtained from

the Pope an order that Bernard should preach in
behalf of the Crusade, he, with humble obedience,
exerted all his talent in aid of the purpose which
he disapproved, and with such success that in
France an army of seventy thousand knights joined
the King.   King Roger joined the undertaking with
great eagerness, in the full hope of involving the
French monarch in a quarrel with the Greeks by the
way, and of thus being enabled to carry out Bohemund's old plans against Constantinople.   In the
meantime, Bernard had gone to Germany, but at first
found very little sympathy from either king or people.
This was natural enough.   An uncommonly strong
resolution was needed in order to leave all domestic
cares and quarrels, from purely religious motives, and
to march straight away to the East, there to make
an alliance with those who had been enemies hitherto, and thus indirectly to break off with Emperor
Manuel, who had been a faithful ally.   But Bernard
did not despair.   One Sunday, when Conrad was
hearing him preach, he suddenly addressed from
the pulpit such warning, promising, and threatening
words to the King, that he was overcome, and in a
soft fit of repentant piety, put on the cross.   The
number of knights who accompanied him was, however, small, and the chief part of the German Crusaders consisted of rabble, of the stamp of the

Tafurs. The Pope, who, like Urban in 1095, put himself at the head of the whole undertaking, was little pleased with this reinforcement, and blamed the King for putting on the cross without asking leave from Rome; to which the King could only reply that the Holy Spirit bloweth where it listeth, and allows no time for tedious solicitations.

Both armies marched down the Danube, to Constantinople, in the summer of 1147. At the same moment King Roger, with his fleet, attacked not the Turks, but the Greek seaport towns of the Morea. Manuel thereupon, convinced that the large armies were designed for the destruction of his empire in the first place, with the greatest exertions, got together troops from all his provinces, and entered into a half-alliance with the Turks of Asia Minor. The mischief and ill-feeling was increased by the lawless conduct of the German hordes; the Greek troops attacked them more than once; whereupon numerous voices were raised in Louis's headquarters, to demand open war against the faithless Greeks. The kings were fully agreed not to permit this, but on arriving in Constantinople they completely fell out, for while Louis made no secret of his warm friendship for Roger, Conrad promised the Emperor of Constantinople to attack the Normans as soon as the Crusade should be ended. This was a bad beginning for a united campaign in the East, and moreover, at every step eastward, new difficulties arose. The German army, broken up into several detachments, and led without ability or prudence, was attacked in Asia Minor by the Emir of Iconium, and cut to pieces, all but a few hundred men. The French, though better appointed, also suffered severe losses in that country, but contrived, nevertheless, to reach Antioch with a very considerable force, and from thence might have carried the project which the second Baldwin had conceived in vain, namely, the defence of the north-eastern frontier, upon which, especially since Zenki had made his appearance, the life or death of the Christian States depended. But in vain did Prince Raymond of Antioch try to prevail upon King Louis to take this view, and to attack without delay the most formidable of all their adversaries, Noureddin. Louis would not hear or do anything till he had seen Jerusalem, and prayed at the Holy Sepulchre. The brilliant prince had better success with Louis's wife, Eleanora, the Golden-footed Queen, as the Greeks called her, whose favour he won by such open homage, that Louis flew into a violent passion, and ordered an instantaneous departure from Antioch. In Jerusalem he was welcomed by Queen Melisende (now regent, during her son's minority, after Fulco's death), with praise and

gratitude, because he had not taken part in the distant wars of the Prince of Antioch, but had reserved
his forces for the defence of the holy city of Jerusalem.
It was now resolved to lead the army against Damascus, the only Turkish town whose emir had always refused to submit to either Zenki or Noureddin. Nevertheless Noureddin instantly collected all his available
forces, to succour the besieged town against the common enemy. It appeared as though, if Damascus
should not fall before his arrival, a great collision must
inevitably take place. Events however took a curious
turn. On the one hand, Melisende had heard that
if the town were taken, Louis intended to give it,
not to her, but to a French Count; on the other,
the Emir could not doubt that if Noureddin should
relieve the town, his supremacy could no longer be
resisted. Both Queen and Emir were equally dissa-
tisfied with either prospect. To these small rulers, the
hostility between East and West, Islam and Christianity, had become indifferent; they wished for nothing but the continuance of their own comfortable
local rule, without the interference of the great oppressive potentates. Accordingly, a secret compact
was made between Jerusalem and Damascus, in
consequence of which the Syrian barons, by trea-
cherous manœuvres, forced King Louis to raise the
siege, and the Emir then hastened to send the

joyful news to Noureddin, that he need give himself
no further trouble.   The German king, long since
tired of his powerless position, returned home in the
autumn of 1148, and Louis, after much pressing,
stayed a few months longer, and reached Europe
in the following spring.   The whole expedition,
undertaken in a ferment of piety, just as a man
might dedicate a taper, or found a chapel; undertaken without reference to the great political relations, or the true interests of the respective States,
had been wrecked, without honour and without
result, by the most wretched personal passions, and
the most narrow and selfish policy.   We see in the
First Crusade the strength, in the Second the weakness of mediæval religious feeling.   It was only
fitted for rapid, violent, and instant action; lasting
combination, fruitful action, or enduring results, it
was unable to produce.   It evaporated in heated
enthusiasm, and narrow contempt of the world; it
rushed madly on, with eyes turned to heaven, in
expectation of some wondrous miracle, and fell
crashing to the ground, its feet entangled in some
miserable creeping weed.

Speedy, irresistible, overwhelming retribution
overtook the Syrian Franks for their folly.   King
Louis had hardly set sail, when Noureddin arose
more terrible than his father had ever been.   He

G

first attacked Antioch, and misfortune rudely overtook Prince Raymond after all his social triumphs.
He was killed in battle, half his army destroyed, and
his territories traversed in all directions by the victors.   No less heavily did Noureddin visit the rest
of the dukedom of Edessa on this side the Euphrates.   Count Joscelin was taken prisoner, and
the country finally subjugated by the Turks.   The
power which Zenki had founded rose higher and
higher against the weak bulwarks of the Christian
States. Noureddin grasped it with a firm and steady
hand, embracing the whole of the East in a comprehensive glance, allied now with Cairo, now with Iconium, and even on friendly terms with the Greek
Emperor Manuel.   He had inherited the bravery,
earnestness, and religious zeal of his father, and he
was especially distinguished by an unwearied spirit
of order and regularity, which showed itself in his private dealings as strict conscientiousness, and in his
political conduct as methodical forethought.   His
serious and thoughtful nature could only be roused
by the strongest religious motives.   Against the
meanest of his subjects he appeared before the judge,
like any other citizen, and never departed a hair's-
breadth from the precepts of the law, or was un-
faithful for a single moment to the principles he had
once recognized as true.   His Court had the same

serious tone; there was little outward splendour, but the Sovereign never relaxed from his silent and dignified carriage. All who were about his person acquired a subdued and careful demeanour, and his relations and great courtiers dared not be guilty of any wantonness or insolence, for their master was as inexorable to offenders as he was just to merit. All the harshest part of his resolute nature was felt by the Christians and their friends. He burdened his Christian subjects with intolerable taxes, the produce of which was devoted to the holy war. He excited the fanaticism of Islam against them by every means in his power. In all the neighbouring Turkish States he possessed friends and adherents in the most pious priests, the holiest dervishes, and the penitent fakirs, through whose influence the mass of the people were roused to such enthusiasm, that not one of the neighbouring Princes would have dared to disregard Noureddin's call to arms. The Sultan did not forgive the Emir of Damascus his treaty with Jerusalem. "Damascus," he said, "is useless to the cause of Islam, and the Christians will take it if I do not anticipate them." Every kind of warfare, every means of victory were justified, in his eyes, by this argument. He sowed dissension between the Emir and his officers by one agent, and by another between the

people of Damascus and their ruler, whose principal
vizier, a Kurdish chieftain, Eyoob, was also in intimate correspondence with his brother Shirkuh, Noureddin's chief officer.   The prey was thus completely
surrounded, and in the year 1154 Noureddin took
the town and its dependencies without a blow. Thus
the whole eastern frontier of Jerusalem was laid bare
to his victorious arms.

Meanwhile the Christians did their utmost to render success easy to him. It never occurred to King
Baldwin III. to secure Damascus against him, either
by taking possession of it himself, or by sending
assistance to the Emir.   Instead of this he turned
the politics of his country into a channel which
quickly led to the catastrophe.   He directed his
arms not against the strong and really dangerous
enemy, but against the weakest and most impotent
of his neighbours, against Egypt.   He took Ascalon
in 1153, and in 1156 he made destructive inroads
as far as the Nile. The consequence was that Egypt,
until now exceedingly jealous of Noureddin, was
compelled to call on him for aid, and Baldwin's
scattered forces were several times almost cut to
pieces by the Sultan.   Nevertheless, in 1164, Baldwin's brother Amalric, who succeeded him, obstinately pursued the same disastrous course.   He
was a fat, solemn, stammering man, with a great

taste for the study of history and geography, for
legal and theological researches, and a strong pro-
pensity for sensual indulgence, which he knew how
to excuse with dry humour; but above all, he was
eager in the pursuit of gold or treasure. In order
to extort money, he began a new war with Egypt
immediately upon coming to the throne. He obtained considerable sums, but at the same time inspired such a feeling of desperation, that one party
in Egypt unconditionally embraced Noureddin's
cause; and his vizier, Shirkuh, led a troop of
cavalry across the desert into the country, on whose
appearance Amalric retreated, utterly disheartened,
into Palestine. Fortune once more offered him
means of escape. Shirkuh behaved with the greatest insolence as the conqueror and ruler of Egypt,
and the Caliph, a stupid and apathetic man, was a
puppet in his hands. But the Caliph's vizier Shawer,
enraged at the Kurdish chief, suddenly changed
sides, and now appealed to King Amalric for relief.
Shirkuh was unable to resist with his handful of
light cavalry, and hastened to Noureddin at Damascus to beg for reinforcements, describe the thoroughly
disorganized and rotten condition of Egypt, and
plan a systematic conquest of that country. Noureddin hesitated. These designs were too remote
and uncertain for his cautious mind; he thought

the volatile, cunning, and foolhardy Shirkuh deficient in the necessary foresight and trustworthiness, and at last, in 1166, only confided to him
a small division, which was repulsed by Amalric
on its arrival in Egypt.   The country became,
in fact, a Frankish province, Cairo was garrisoned
by Christians, and a considerable yearly tribute
was paid to Jerusalem.   It was an unexpected, and,
properly used, would have been an immense gain
to the Christian cause.   But once more everything
was ruined by Amalric's narrow selfishness.   He
thought he could wring more spoil from Egypt,
scoffed at the notion of its resistance, and in 1168
demanded, under the threat of a devastating war,
a tribute of two million pieces of gold.   This
was too much for the Vizier to bear; his deepest
feelings of indignation were roused; "Let Shirkuh destroy us," he cried, "we shall at least not
have submitted to unbelievers."   In spite of the
recent disagreements, he once more implored Noureddin's help.   The Sultan saw that he had no
choice left.   This time Shirkuh hastened across
the desert with eight thousand horsemen, defeated
all the preparations of the Franks by his rapid
movements, and while Amalric still thought him
on Asiatic ground he was before Cairo, welcomed
by the acclamations of its inhabitants.   Hereupon

Amalric quitted the country for ever, and Shirkuh took care that it should not again be lost to the Turkish rule. A fortnight after the retreat of the Franks, his young nephew, Saladin, ordered the Vizier Shawer to be arrested and executed, and the feeble Caliph gave the vacant office, and with it the government of the country, to the Turkish con- queror. When, a few weeks after, Shirkuh died, Saladin, with Noureddin's sanction, succeeded him.

He was then in the first fresh bloom of youth, and had given but few proofs of political or mili- tary talent. He had been living in the gardens of Damascus; dividing his time between scientific studies and social pleasures, and had followed his uncle to Egypt with the greatest reluctance. " I was as miserable," he said later, " as though I had been led to death." He did not, as we see, seek fortune, but she sought him. Once in action, however, he showed himself energetic and ardent; his mind developed itself largely and vigorously, each suc- cessive difficulty and danger called forth, out of his joyous and pleasure-loving nature, the highest faculties of dominion and conquest. He had no- thing of Noureddin's somewhat pedantic manners; he loved to be surrounded by happy faces, and to lay aside his external dignity in personal inter- course, sure of being able at any moment to resume

the character of an absolute commander. He was
not so stern a judge as Noureddin towards others
or towards himself; he often acted with great indulgence, and sometimes also with harsh and arbitrary caprice, but was afterwards ready to acknowledge his injustice, and to make ample amends.
He was altogether more amiable, frank, and natural
than Noureddin; his was one of those splendid
natures, which, in the plenitude of genius, half unconsciously grasp the dominion over a people, but
know no other rule or limit than their own personal power and inspiration. They in every sense
overstep the bounds of everyday life, they break
through all rules, and not unfrequently neglect the
commonest duties; they feel their own strength,
and are possessed with the desire to give full
scope to their faculties. The young commander,
who a year before had angrily lamented that the
command of the Sultan had driven him to endure
fatigue and hardship, now held a vast kingdom in
his firm and supple grasp; he had no feelings save
those of a born ruler, and all who gainsaid him
felt the whole force of his resentment. Several
insurrections in Egypt were put down with such
promptitude and so much bloodshed, that the people in fear and trembling gave up all thoughts of
rebellion; and when, in the year 1171, the faint-

hearted Caliph made a feeble attempt at independence, the news suddenly spread through the land that he had ceased to live; and the race of the Fatimites was extinct after a reign of two hundred years. To none was the rise of Saladin more dangerous than to the Franks in Palestine, who were now surrounded, and threatened on all sides by a united, unmerciful, and ever restless power. Noureddin on the east and Saladin on the west, had only to advance with their masses of troops, and the Frankish States must have been crushed at once by the mere force of numbers. But an unforeseen complication of affairs on the side of the enemy delayed the catastrophe for a few years; it happened that one of the great Turkish rulers had for the present moment a personal interest in maintaining the existence of the Christians.

Saladin had come into Egypt as Noureddin's subaltern, and ruled there with the title of the Sultan's viceroy. In reality, he governed quite independently, owing to the great distance between Damascus and Cairo, and the necessity of quick and decisive measures in Egypt. It was however certain that his absolute sovereignty would cease directly the two countries should be united by the conquest of Palestine; and for this reason Saladin delayed under every conceivable pretext whenever

Noureddin sent him orders to begin the holy war.
Noureddin endured this for two years, and then
sent for his nephew Saifeddin from Mosul to Damascus, entrusted to him the government of Syria,
and prepared to march in person at the head of a
mighty army, in order to call the ambitious upstart
to account. Saladin in the meantime conquered
Nubia and part of Arabia, in order to take refuge
there on the appearance of his angry chief. At
this important crisis a higher power interposed in
favour of the younger potentate. In the year
1174 Sultan Noureddin and King Amalric died
within a short time of each other, both leaving
sons under age, who became the centres of anarchy
and party feud. Thus Saladin, yet in the flower of
life, beheld a boundless field open before him, and
the future destiny of the East within his grasp.
His first step was to declare to the ambitious emirs
and pretenders to power in Noureddin's dominions
that he should resent every injury to young Ismael
as one offered to himself, and that he looked upon
the son of his benefactor as his natural ward. But
when Ismael came forward with unexpected vigour,
and humbled all his relations and officers beneath decisive and rapid strokes, Saladin suddenly changed
his policy, appeared with an army in Syria, conquered Damascus, and as an open proclamation of

his own supremacy, assumed the title of Sultan. Several years were passed in confusion and fighting, during which the Christians were blind enough to take Saladin's part. In 1181 Ismael died, Saladin strained every nerve, and in the course of three campaigns, reduced all the Syrian emirs, those of Mesopotamia, and at last of Mosul itself to acknowledge his supremacy. In the year 1184, he was sole ruler from the sources of the Nile as far as the river Tigris, and now he began the last decisive attack upon the Christians, whom, spite of the general largeness of his mind, he hated with relentless hate, worthy of Zenki or Noureddin.

. In the Frankish States the near approach of dissolution was foretold by inward decline, by division and anarchy, by miserable cowardice, and insolent rashness. The young King Baldwin IV. lay incurably ill with leprosy; they sought, as his future heir, a husband for his sister Sibylla, and Baldwin hastily pronounced in favour of Count Guy de Lusignan, a Gascon bully, without wealth or power, and what was worse, without understanding or character, so that his elevation provoked a storm of indignation throughout the kingdom. Two great parties were instantly formed. At the head of one stood nominally Baldwin and Guy, but really Reginald of Chatillon, a desperado athirst for war and plunder, and physically and morally ungovernable; a man who under other circumstances might have been a common pirate, or possibly a great conqueror; he fully perceived the desperate state of affairs, and exhorted the Christians—as at the worst they could but lose their lives—to fight without delay or cessation. The opposing barons ranged themselves against him under the former regent, Count Raymond of Tripoli, a clever but vacillating and weak man, who, halting between honesty and ambition, aspired to the crown, half from selfish, half from patriotic motives, and warmly advocated a peaceful and yielding policy towards Saladin, as the only chance of safety. Amid these hopeless disputes, Saladin's mighty onslaught burst upon them, from Egypt, from Damascus, and from the sea, simultaneous, and well combined, with armies each more numerous than the whole Christian force. Once more disturbances on the Tigris, in which the Sultan was involved, gave the Franks a moment's breathing-time; Raymond of Tripoli used it to remove the incapable Guy, and proclaim Sibylla's son heir to the throne; but when King Baldwin sank under his disease, and the royal boy died unexpectedly, Sibylla, in spite of all objections, recalled her husband, and placed the crown upon his head. The Count of Tripoli, beside himself with rage,

forgot every consideration of duty, and applied to
Saladin for help. Guy and Sibylla thought themselves fortunate to obtain by heavy sacrifices an
armistice from the mighty Sultan, who showed himself merciful from contempt. But they were not
strong enough to compel Count Reginald to keep the
peace; from the fortresses of the Arabian desert he
sallied forth and attacked the peaceful caravans on
their passage, and thereupon Saladin declared the
measure to be full. The Count of Tripoli, in his anger against Guy, allowed the immense army which
Saladin brought from Damascus to pass through his
dominions, and on the 1st May, 1187, Saladin gained
his first victory over the advanced Christian troops
posted on the river Kishon, and led his overwhelming army upon Jerusalem. Before this terrible danger
party hatred at last was silent; the Christians collected all their forces, and even the Count of Tripoli
repenting the fearful consequences of his breach of
faith, joined his former adversaries. But even so,
they were far inferior in numbers and in general-
ship to their antagonist. On the 5th of July a
battle was fought at Tiberias, which, in consequence of Guy's utter weakness and incompetence,
and Saladin's energetic dispositions, resulted within
the first hour in the total destruction of the Christians. The greater part of their knights lay dead

on the field, the Count of Tripoli escaped with a few
followers by rapid flight only to die in a few days
conscience-stricken and broken-hearted. King Guy,
Reginald of Chatillon, and many of the principal
barons, were taken prisoners. Saladin received them
in his tent, and with consolatory words offered a refreshing drink to the wearied King; but when Count
Reginald reached out his hand for the cup, he clove
the head of the forsworn breaker of treaties with his
sword, so that he fell with a groan and died on the
spot. The terrific news of the defeat spread through
the land, destroying all remaining strength or courage. Towns and castles opened their gates wherever
the victorious troops appeared; Tyre alone was defended by the opportune arrival of an Italian fleet
under the Marquis Conrad of Montferrat. Jerusalem, which, as a holy city, Saladin wished to take
by treaty, capitulated on the 3rd of October, after
an investment of three weeks. Saladin's career of
victory did not yet extend as far as Tripoli and
Antioch, but the kingdom of Jerusalem, the pride
and centre of the Christian rule, was destroyed.

CHAPTER IV.

ALTHOUGH after the failure of the Second Crusade the interest felt by the Western nations in the king-dom of Jerusalem had greatly diminished, still the news of the loss of the Holy City fell like a thunder-bolt on men's minds. Excitement, anger, and grief were universal; once more before its final extinction the flame which had kindled the mystic war of God blazed high in the hearts of men. "What a dis-grace, what an affliction," cried Pope Urban III., "that the jewel which the second Urban won for Christendom should be lost by the third!" He ve-hemently exhorted the Church and all her faithful to join the war, worked day and night, prayed, sighed, and so wore himself out with grief and anger that he sickened and died in a few weeks. His suc-cessor, Gregory VIII., and after him Pope Clement III., were inspired by the same feeling, and exerted themselves for the great cause with untiring energy.

At the time of the First Crusade, Pope Urban II.
had, as we have seen, preached but once, and then
left the ardour of visionary enthusiasm to take its own
effect; but now Gregory VIII. sent legates through
every country, and through them watched the progress of arming, made arrangements for the cost of
the expedition, imposed a universal tax, called Saladin's tithe, on all classes of the European population, had the plans laid before him, removed political
difficulties, and allayed dissensions, which might have
hindered the departure of the armies,—in a word,
he acted as though he had been the monarch of a
large, warlike, and well administered kingdom. The
effect was wonderful. In 1185 a number of English
barons had put on the cross, on hearing of Saladin's
menacing progress; towards the end of 1187 the
heir to the throne, Richard, followed their example;
some months later, King Henry II. had a meeting
with his former enemy, Philip Augustus of France,
at Gisors, where they vowed to abandon their earthly
quarrels, and to become warriors of the everlasting
God. Nearly the whole nobility, and a number of the
lower class of people were carried away by their
example. In Italy, Genoa had long been urging on
the Pope, who in his turn succeeded in gaining over
Pisa,.which had always been hostile to the Genoese;
King William of Sicily fitted out his fleet, and was

only prevented by death from joining it himself. From Denmark and Scandinavia pilgrims thronged to Syria both by land and by water; in Germany, now as formerly, the zeal was not so great, until in March, 1188, the Emperor Frederick Barbarossa, at the age of near seventy, put on the cross, and by his ever firm and powerful will collected together a mass of nearly a hundred thousand pilgrims. All the Western nations rose to arms.

The news of this enormous movement reached the East, where at first it was hardly believed, but grew louder and more threatening every day, and the ferocious war-cry of Europe was answered by a voice of defiance quite as eager. Saladin had studied his antagonists with the eye of a true statesman, and had organized his dominions almost according to the Western system. Under an oath of allegiance and service in war, he granted to each of his emirs a town on feudal tenure; its surrounding land they again divided among their followers; the Sultan thus attached those wandering hordes of horsemen to the soil, and kept those restless spirits permanently together. He then invoked the religious zeal of all Mahomedans with such success that, partly from fanaticism and partly from love of plunder, volunteers flocked to his standard from every quarter, from the depths of the Arabian desert, from

H

the country between the Euphrates and the Tigris,
from Persia and Kurdistan. The warlike robbers
and hunters of the Caucasus joined his camp at
the same time as the nomads of Bulgaria, with their
cattle and camels; from the frontiers of Nubia came
crowds of Negroes, "a people of fiends and devils,"
said the Franks, "about whom nothing is white but
their eyes and teeth." These masses dispersed, it
is true, at the beginning of every winter, and the
Sultan was then left for a few months with only his
feudal troops; but on the return of fair weather
they again collected in ever-increasing numbers
round that nucleus. The arming of the East was
not even confined to the territories of Islam. Saladin well knew the mutual hatred which divided
the Greek Byzantines and the Latin Franks, and
kept so skilfully alive in the Emperor Isaac
Angelos the fear of the insolence of the Western
soldiers, that he concluded an offensive and defensive alliance with Saladin against those who.
shared his own faith. On the island of Cyprus
Isaac Comnenus had founded a separate kingdom
in open revolt against the Emperor, and although
he was on terms of bitter hostility with the Greek
Emperor, Saladin won them both over to his policy,
so that the ships of Cyprus joined the Egyptian
fleet in guarding the coasts of Syria. Even the

Armenians of Cilicia and the Euphrates, whose very
existence had been saved by the First Crusade, he
contrived to attach to his side.   The whole East,
from the Danube to the Indus, from the Caspian Sea
to the sources of the Nile, prepared with one intent
to withstand the great invasion of Europe.   Amid
cares and preparations which had reference to three-
quarters of the globe, Saladin neglected his nearest
enemy, the feeble remnant of the Christian States in
Syria, which, although unimportant in themselves,
were of great consequence as landing-places for the in-
vading Western nations during the approaching war.
The small principalities of Antioch and Tripoli still
existed, and in the midst of the Turkish forces, the
Marquis Conrad of Montferrat still displayed the
banner of the cross upon the ramparts of Tyre.   It
seems as if in this instance Saladin had abandoned
himself too much to the superb and easy carelessness
of his nature.   Hitherto he had not shrunk from the
most strenuous exertions ; but he was so certain of
his victory, that he neglected to strike the final blow.
Not until the autumn of 1187 did he begin the
siege of Tyre ; and for the first time in his life found
a dangerous adversary in Conrad of Montferrat, a
man of cool courage and keen determination, whose
soul was unmoved by religious enthusiasm, and
equally free from weakness or indecision ; so that

under his command the inhabitants of the city repulsed every attack with increasing assurance and
resolution.   Saladin hereupon determined to try
starvation, which a strict blockade by sea and land
was to cause in the town; but in June, 1188, the
Sicilian fleet appeared, gave the superiority by sea
to the Christians, and brought relief to Tyre. The
Sultan retreated, and marched through the defence-
less provinces of Antioch and Tripoli, but there too
he left the capitals in peace upon the arrival of the
Sicilian fleet in their waters. The following summer
he spent in taking the Frankish fortresses in Arabia Petræa, the possession of which was important
to him in order to secure freedom of communication
between Egypt and Syria.   Meanwhile the reinforcements from the West were pouring into the
Christian seaport towns.   In the first place the two
military and religious Orders, the Templars and the
Knights of St. John, had collected munitions of war
of every kind from all their European possessions,
and increased the number of their mercenaries to
fourteen thousand men.   King Guy also had ran-
somed himself from captivity and had gone to Tripoli,
where by degrees the remnant of the Syrian barons,
and pilgrims of all nations, gathered round him.
They took the right resolution, to remain no longer
inactive, but, with the gigantic preparations in

Europe in prospect, to begin the attack at once. On the 28th of August, 1189, Guy commenced the siege of the strong maritime fortress of Ptolemais (St. Jean d'Acre). A fleet from Pisa had already joined the Sicilian one; in October there arrived twelve thousand Danes and Frisians, and in November a number of Flemings, under the Count of Avesnes, French knights under the Bishop of Beauvais, and Thuringians, under their landgrave, Louis. Saladin, roused from his inactivity by these events, hastened to the spot with his army, and in his turn surrounded the Christian camp, which lay in a wide semicircle round Ptolemais, and was defended by strong entrenchments within and without. It formed an iron ring round the besieged town, which Saladin, spite of all his efforts, could not break through. Each wing of the position rested upon the sea, and was thus certain of its supplies, and able to protect the landing of the reinforcements, which continually arrived in constantly increasing numbers,—Italians, French, English and Germans, Normans and Swedes. "If on one day we killed ten," said the Arabs, "on the next, a hundred more arrived fresh from the West." The fighting was incessant by land and by sea, against the town and against the Sultan's camp. Sometimes the Egyptian fleet drove the Christian ships far out to sea; and Saladin could then succour the garrison with provisions and fresh troops, till new Frankish squadrons again surrounded the harbour, and only a few intrepid divers could steal through between the hostile ships. On land, too, now one side and now the other was in danger. One day the Sultan scaled the Christian entrenchments, and advanced close to the walls of the city, before the Franks rallied sufficiently to drive him back by a desperate attack; but they soon took their revenge in a night sortie, when they attacked the Sultan in his very tent, and he narrowly escaped by rapid flight. Against the town their progress was very slow, as the garrison, under an able and energetic commander, Bohaeddin, showed itself resolute and indefatigable. One week passed after another, and the condition of the Franks became painfully complicated. They could go neither backwards nor forwards; they could make no impression on the walls; nor could they re-embark in the face of an active enemy. There was no choice but to conquer or die; so preparations were made for a long sojourn; wooden barracks, and for the princes even stone houses were built, and a new hostile town arose all around Ptolemais. In spite of this the winter brought innumerable hardships. In that small space more than a hundred thousand men were crowded together, with insufficient shelter, and uncertain supplies of wretched food; pestilential diseases soon broke out, which swept away thousands, and were intensified by the exhalations from the heaps of dead. Saladin retreated from their deadly vicinity to more airy quarters on the adjacent hills; his troops also suffered from the severe weather, but were far better supplied than the Christians with water, provisions, and other comforts, as the caravans from Cairo and Bagdad met in their camp, and numbers of merchants displayed in glittering booths all kinds of Eastern wares. It was an unexampled assemblage of the forces of two quarters of the world round one spot, unimportant in itself, and chosen almost by accident. Our own times have seen a counterpart to it in the siege of Sebastopol, which, though in a totally different form, was a new act in the same great struggle between the East and the West. Happily the Western nations did not derive their warlike stimulus from religious sources, and they displayed, if not their military, at any rate their moral superiority, in the most brilliant manner.

Although in the fight around Ptolemais, this superiority was doubtless on Saladin's side, there was a moment in which Europe threatened to oppose to the mighty Sultan an antagonist as great as himself. In May, 1189, the Emperor Frederick I. marched out of Ratisbon with his army for Syria. He had

already ruled thirty-seven years over Germany and
Italy, and his life had been one of war and labour,
of small results, but growing fame. He was born a
ruler in the highest sense of the word; he possessed
all the attributes of power; bold yet cautious, coura-
geous and enduring, energetic and methodical, he
towered proudly above all who surrounded him,
and had the highest conception of his princely calling. But his ideas were beyond his time, and
while he tried to open the way for a distant future,
he was made to feel the penalty of running counter
to the inclinations of the present generation. It
seemed to him unbearable, that the Emperor, who
was extolled by all the world as the defender of the
right and the fountain-head of law, should be forced
to bow before unruly vassals or unlimited ecclesiastical power. He had, chiefly from the study of the
Roman law, conceived the idea of a state complete
within itself, and strong in the name of the common
weal, a complete contrast to the existing condition of
Europe, where all the monarchies were breaking up,
and the crowned priest reigned supreme over a crowd
of petty princes. Under these circumstances he appeared, foreshadowing modern thoughts deep in the
middle ages, like a fresh mountain breeze dispersing
the incense-laden atmosphere of the time. This discrepancy caused the greatness and the misfortune of

the mighty Emperor. The current of his time set full against him. When, as the representative of the State, he enforced obedience to the law, he appeared to some an impious offender against the Holy Church; to others, a tyrant trampling on the general freedom; and while conquering in a hundred fights, he was driven from one position after another by the force of opinion. But so commanding was the energy, so powerful the earnestness, and so inexhaustible the resources of his nature, that he was as terrible to his foes on the last day as on the first, passionless and pitiless, never distorted by cruelty, and never melted by pity, an iron defender of his imperial rights.

We can only guess at the reasons which may have induced a sovereign of this stamp to leave a sphere of domestic activity for the fantastic wars of the Crusades. Once, in the midst of his Italian feud, when the deeds of Alexander the Great were read aloud to him, he exclaimed, "Happy Alexander, who didst never see Italy! happy I, had I ever been in Asia!" Whether piety or love of fame ultimately decided him, he felt within himself the energy to take a great decision, and at once proceeded to action. The aged Emperor once more displayed, in this last effort, the fullness of his powerful and ever-youthful nature. For the first time

during these wars, since the armed pilgrimages had
begun, Europe beheld a spirit conscious of their true
object, and capable of carrying it out. The army
was smaller than any of the former ones, consisting
of twenty thousand knights, and fifty thousand
squires and foot-soldiers; but it was guided by one
inflexible, indomitable will. With strict discipline,
the Imperial leader drove all disorderly and useless
persons out of his camp, he was always the first to
face every obstacle or danger, and showed himself
equal to all the political or military difficulties of the
expedition. The Greek Empire had to be traversed
first, whose emperor, Isaac, as I have before mentioned, had allied himself with Saladin; but at the
sight of these formidable masses, he shrank in terror
from any hostile attempt, and hastened to transport
the German army across into Asia Minor. There
they hoped for a friendly reception from the Emir
of Iconium, who was reported to have a leaning
towards Christianity; but in the meantime the old
ruler had been dethroned by his sons, who opposed
the Germans with a strong force. They were destined to feel the weight of the German arm. After
their mounted bowmen had harassed the Christian
troops for a time with a shower of arrows, the Emperor broke their line of battle, and scattered them
by a sudden attack of cavalry in all directions, while

at the same moment Frederick's son unexpectedly
scaled the walls of their city.   The Crusaders then
marched in triumph to Cilicia; the Armenians already yielded submissively to a cessation of hostilities; and far and wide thoughout Turkish Syria
went the dread of Frederick's irresistible arms.
Even Saladin himself, who had boldly defied the
the disorderly attacks of the hundreds of thousands
before Ptolemais, now lost all hope, and announced
to his emirs his intention of quitting Syria on Frederick's arrival, and retreating across the Euphrates.
On this, every highway in the country became alive,
the emirs quitted their towns, and began to fly with
their families, their goods, and chattels, and hope
rose high in the Christian camp.   This honour was
reserved for the Emperor; that which no other
Frankish sword could achieve, he had done by the
mere shadow of his approach : he had forced from
Saladin a confession of inferiority.   But he was not
destined to see the realization of his endeavours
here, any more than in Europe.   His army had entered Cilicia, and was preparing to cross the rapid
mountain torrent of the Seleph.   On the 10th of
June, 1190, they marched slowly across the narrow
bridge, and the Emperor, impatient to get to the
front, urged his horse into the stream, intending to
swim to the opposite shore.   The raging waters

suddenly seized him, and hurried him away before
the eyes of his people. When he was drawn out, far
down the river, he was a corpse. Boundless lamen-
tations resounded throughout the army; the most
brilliant ornament and sole hope of Christendom
was gone; the troops arrived at Antioch in a state
of the deepest dejection. From thence a number
of the pilgrims returned home, scattered and dis-
couraged, and a pestilence broke out among the
rest, which was fatal to the greater number of
them: it seemed, says a chronicler, " as though the
members would not outlive their head." The Emperor's son, Duke Frederick of Suabia, reached the
camp before Ptolemais with five thousand men, instituted there the Order of the Teutonic Knights,
—who were destined hereafter to found a splendid
dominion on the distant shores of the German
Ocean;—and soon afterwards followed his father
to the grave.

The highest hopes were destroyed by this lament-
able downfall. It seemed as if a stern fate had resolved to give the Christian world a distant view of
the possibility of victory; the great Emperor might
have secured it, but the generation which had not
understood him, was doomed to misery and defeat.
A second winter, with the same fearful additions of
hunger and sickness, came upon the camp before

Ptolemais, and the measure of misfortune was filled
by renewed and bitter quarrels among the Frankish
princes. King Guy was as incompetent as ever;
and so utterly mismanaged the Christian cause, that
the Marquis Conrad of Montferrat indignantly opposed him. Queen Sibylla, by marriage with whom
Guy had gained possession of the crown, died just
at this juncture. Conrad instantly declared that
Sibylla's sister Eliza was now the only rightful heir,
and, as he held every step towards advancement to
be laudable, did not for a moment scruple to elope
with her from her husband, to marry her himself,
and to lay claim to the crown. Amid all this confusion and disaster, the eyes of the Crusaders turned
with increasing anxiety towards the horizon, to
catch a glimpse of the sails which were to bring to
them two fresh leaders, the kings of France and
of England. Their preparations had not been very
rapid. Henry II. of England had, even since his
oath, got into a new quarrel with Philip Augustus of France, which only ended with his death, in
1189. His son and successor, Richard, whose zeal
had led him to put up the cross earlier than the
rest, instantly began to arrange the expedition with
Philip. In his impetuous manner, he exulted in the
prospect of unheard-of triumphs; the government of
England was hastily and insufficiently provided for

during the absence of the King; above all, money was needed in great quantities, and raised by every expedient, good or bad. When some one remonstrated with the King concerning these extortions, he exclaimed, "I would sell London itself, if I could but find a purchaser." He legislated with the same inconsiderate vehemence as to the discipline and order of his army: murderers were to be buried alive on land, and at sea to be tied to the corpses of their victims, and thrown into the water; thieves were to be tarred and feathered; and whoever gambled for money, be he king or baron, was to be dipped three times in the sea, or flogged naked before the whole army. Richard led his army through France, and went on board his splendid fleet at Marseilles, while Philip sailed from Genoa in hired vessels. Halfway to Sicily, however, Richard got tired of the sea-voyage, landed near Rome, and journeyed with a small retinue through the Abruzzi and Calabria, already on the look-out for adventures, and often engaged in bloody quarrels with the peasants of the mountain villages. When he at last arrived in Sicily, his unstable mind suddenly underwent a total change; a quarrel with the Sicilian king, Tancred, drove the Holy Sepulchre entirely out of his head. Now fighting, now negotiating, he stayed nine months at Messina,—hated and feared by the inhabitants, who called him the lion, the savage lion,—deaf to the entreaties of his followers, who were eager to get to Syria, and heedless and defiant to all Philip Augustus's representations and demands. At last, the French king, losing patience, sailed without him, and arrived at Ptolemais in April, 1191. He was received with eager joy, but did not succeed in at all advancing the siege operations; for so many of the French pilgrims had preceded him, that the army he brought was but small, and though an adroit and cunning diplomatist, a tried and unscrupulous statesman, he lacked the rough soldierly vigour and bravery, on which everything at that moment depended. At length Richard was again on his road, and again he allowed himself to be turned aside from his purpose. One of his ships, which bore his betrothed bride, had stranded on the Cyprian coast, and in consequence of the hostility of the king of that island, had been very inhospitably received. Richard was instantly up in arms, declared war against the Comneni, and conquered the whole island in a fortnight; an impromptu conquest, which was of the highest importance to the Christian party in the East for centuries after.

Still occupied in establishing a military colony of his knights, he was surprised by a visit from King

Guy, of Jerusalem, who wished to secure the support of the dreaded monarch in his party contests at home.   Guy complained to King Richard of the matrimonial offences of his rival, informed him that Philip Augustus had declared in favour of Conrad's claims, and on the spot secured the jealous adherence of the English monarch.   He landed on the 8th of June at Ptolemais; the Christians celebrated his arrival by an illumination of the camp; and without a moment's delay, by his warlike ardour, he roused the whole army out of the state of apathy into which it had lately fallen.   Day after day the walls of the city were energetically assailed on every side.   On the 8th July, Saladin made his last attempt to raise the siege, by an attack on the Christian entrenchments; he was driven back with great loss, whereupon he permitted the besieged to capitulate.   The town surrendered, with all its stores, after a siege of nearly three years' duration; the heroic defenders still remaining, about three thousand in number, were to be exchanged, within the space of forty days, for two thousand captive Christians, and a ransom of two hundred thousand pieces of gold.   The war, according to all reports, had by this time cost the Crusaders above thirty thousand men.

Those among the pilgrims who were enthusiastic

and devout, now hoped their way would lead straight to the Holy Sepulchre. But it soon became manifest that the feeling which had prompted the Crusades was dead for ever. The news of the fall of Jerusalem had awakened a momentary excitement in the Western nations, but had failed to stir up the old enthusiasm. On Syrian ground, the ideal faith rapidly gave way before substantial worldly considerations. Richard, Guy, and the Pisans, on the one hand; Philip, Conrad, and the Genoese, on the other, were already in open discord, which was so embittered by Richard's blustering fury, that Philip Augustus embarked at the end of July for France, declaring upon his oath that he had no evil intentions towards England, but determined in his heart to let Richard feel his resentment on the first opportunity. Meanwhile negotiations had begun between Saladin and Richard, which at first seemed to promise favourable results for the Christians, but unfortunately the day fixed for the exchange of the prisoners arrived before Saladin was able to procure the whole of the promised ransom. Richard, with the most brutal cruelty, slaughtered two thousand seven hundred prisoners in one day. Saladin magnanimously refused the demands of his exasperated followers for reprisals, but of course there could be no further question of a treaty, and

the war recommenced with renewed fury. Richard
led the army on an expedition against Ascalon,
defeated Saladin on his march thither at Arsuf,
and advanced amid incessant skirmishes and single-
combats, into which he recklessly plunged as though
he had been a simple knight-errant. Accordingly
his progress was so slow that Saladin had destroyed the town before his arrival and rendered its
capture worthless to the Christians. Again negotiations were begun, but in January, 1192, Richard
suddenly advanced upon Jerusalem, and by forced
marches quickly reached Baitnube, a village only
a few miles distant from the Holy City. But there
the Sultan had thrown up strong and extensive
fortifications, and after long and anxious delibera-
tions, the Franks returned towards Ascalon. Meanwhile Conrad of Montferrat had placed himself
in communication with Saladin, proposed to him
point-blank an alliance against Richard, and by his
prudent and consistent conduct, daily grew in favour
with the Sultan. The Christian camp, on the other
hand, was filled with ever-increasing discord; and
the differences between Richard and Conrad reached
such a height, that the Marquis went back to Ptolemais, and regularly besieged the Pisans, who were
friendly to the English. Into such a miserable
state of confusion had the great European enter-

prise fallen for want of a good leader and an adequate object.

In April news came from England, that the King's brother, John, was in open rebellion against him, and in alliance with France; whereupon Richard, greatly alarmed, informed the barons that he must prepare for his departure, and that they must definitively choose between Guy and Conrad as their future ruler. To his great disappointment, the actual necessities of the case triumphed over all party divisions, and all voted for Conrad, as the only able and fitting ruler in the country. Nothing remained for Richard, but to accede to heir wishes, and as a last act of favour towards Guy, to bestow upon him the crown of Cyprus. Conrad did not delay one moment signing the treaty with Saladin, and the Sultan left the new King in possession of the whole line of coast taken by the Crusaders, and also ceded to him Jerusalem, where however he was to allow a Turkish mosque to exist; the other towns of the interior were then to be divided between the two sovereigns.

What a conclusion to a war in which the whole world had been engaged, and had made such incalculable efforts! After the only competent leader had been snatched from the Christians by an angry fate, the weakness and desultoriness of the others

had destroyed all the fruits of conquest. The host
of devout pilgrims had beheld Jerusalem from
Baitnuba, and had then been obliged to turn their
backs upon the holy spot in impotent grief. Suddenly a nameless, bold, and cunning prince made
his appearance in this great war between the two
religions in the world, a man indifferent to religion
or morality, who knew no other motive than selfishness, but who followed that with vigour and consistency, and had already stretched forth his hand
to grasp the crown of the Holy Sepulchre.

But on the 28th April, Conrad was murdered
by two Saracen assassins; many said, at King Richard's instigation, but more affirmed it was by
the order of the Old Man of the Mountain, the head
of a fanatical sect in the Lebanon. Everything was
again unsettled by this event. The Syrian barons
instantly elected Count Henry of Champagne as
their king; five days after Conrad's death he married his widow Eliza, and was perfectly ready to
succeed to Conrad's alliance with Saladin, as well
as to his wife. But King Richard, with his usual
thoughtlessness, allowed the scandalous marriage,
but prevented the reasonable diplomatic arrangement. As he had a certain liking for Henry, who
was his nephew, he wished to conquer a few more
provinces for him in a hurry, and to win some

fresh laurels for himself at the same time; and accordingly began the war anew against Saladin. A Turkish fortress was taken, when more evil tidings arrived from England, and Richard announced that he could not remain a moment longer. The barons broke out in a general cry of indignation, that he who had plunged them into danger, should forsake them in the midst of it, and once more the vacillating King allowed himself to be diverted from his purpose. Again the Christians advanced upon Jerusalem, and again they remained long inactive at Baitnuba, not daring to attack the city. The ultimate reason for this delay was illustrative of the state of things: the leaders knew that the great mass of pilgrims would disperse as soon as their vows were fulfilled by the deliverance of the Holy Sepulchre; this would seal the destruction of the Frankish rule in Syria, should it happen before the treaty of peace with Saladin was concluded. Thus the ostensible object of the Crusade could not be achieved without ruining Christianity in the East. It is impossible to give a stronger illustration of the hopelessness and internal conflict of all their views and endeavours at that time. They at last turned back disheartened to Ramlah, where they were startled by the news that Saladin had unexpectedly assumed the offensive, attacked the

important seaport town of Joppa, and was probably
already in possession of it. Richard's warlike impetuosity once more burst forth. With a handful of
followers he put to sea, and hastened to Joppa.
When he came in sight of the harbour, the Turks
were already inside the town, plundering in every
direction, and assailing the last remains of the
garrison. After a short reconnoitre, Richard drove
his vessel on shore, rushed with an echoing war-
cry into the midst of the enemy's superior force,
and by his mighty blows actually drove the Turks
in terror and confusion out of the place. On
the following day he encamped with contemptous
insolence outside the gates, with a few hundred
horsemen, when he was suddenly attacked by as
many thousands. In one instant he was armed,
drove back the foremost assailants, clove a Turk's
head down to his shoulders, and then rode along
the wavering front of the enemy, from one wing
to the other; "Now," cried he, "who will dare a
fight for the honour of God?" Henceforth his
fame was such that, years after, Turkish mothers
threatened their children with "King Richard is
coming," and Turkish riders asked their shying
horses if "they saw the Lion-hearted King."

But these knightly deeds did not advance the
war at all. It was fortunate for the Franks that

Saladin's emirs were weary of the long strife, and the Sultan himself wished for the termination of hostilities in consequence of his failing health. The favourable terms of the former treaty, more especially the possession of Jerusalem, were of course no longer to be obtained. The Christians were obliged to be content, on the 30th of August, 1192, with a three years' armistice, according to which the seacoast from Antioch to Joppa was to remain in the possession of the Christians, and the Franks obtained permission to go to Jerusalem as unarmed pilgrims, to pray at the Holy Sepulchre. Richard embarked directly, without even taking measures for ransoming the prisoners. As may easily be imagined, the Christians were deeply exasperated by such a peace; the Turks rejoiced, and only Saladin looked forward with anxiety to the future, and feared dangerous consequences from the duration of even the smallest Christian dominion in the East. The most active and friendly intercourse, rarely disturbed by suspicion, soon began between the two nations. On the very scene of the struggle mutual hatred had subsided, commercial relations were formed, and political negotiations soon followed. In the place of the mystic trophy which was the object of the religious war, Europe had gained an immense extension of worldly knowledge, and of wealth, from the struggle of a hundred years.

Saladin did not long survive his triumph over the combined forces of Europe; he died on the 3rd of March, 1193, at Damascus, aged fifty-seven. "Take this cloak," said he on his death-bed to his servant, "show it to the Faithful, and tell them that the ruler of the East could take but one garment with him into the grave." He was a man who has often been idealized beyond his deserts; he was ambitious, and disdained no means to gratify his love of power; a strict Mussulman, fanatical even to cruelty where religion was concerned, but otherwise of enlarged mind, great heart, generous and gay, accessible to every mental stimulus or social impression, sometimes thoughtless in trifles, but determined and vigorous in every great undertaking. His kingdom and its institutions depended on his single person, and after his death the same disorganization and disunion broke out in the Turkish Empire that we have already observed among the Christians.

I have already asserted, and I think the facts will have convinced my readers, that the spirit of the Crusades was dead and gone. The war itself did not therefore end directly, but continued for nearly a century with various intermissions. We may designate the Crusades,—in opposition to the earlier

Wars against Islam, at the head of which stood the Frankish and Greek Emperors, and to the later, which was led by the great powers of Europe,—as the foreign policy of the Papal supremacy. So long as the throne of the Vatican predominated over and led the temporal powers of Europe, the occupants of that throne strove to direct the forces of our hemisphere upon the Syrian coast. But the change that was now beginning manifested itself at that point earlier than in the interior of the Western countries. The Popes here experienced only failures, or results contrary to their wishes. A large army of pilgrims slipped from the grasp of the most powerful of all the Popes, Innocent III., and, in the pay of the Republic of Venice, directed the force of its arms against Constantinople. For a short time the Greek Empire was overrun with Latin knights; but the only lasting gain was an enormous extension of Venetian commerce. The most dangerous enemy the Papacy ever had, the Emperor Frederick II., undertook another pilgrimage in fulfilment of a vow made in his youth. He sailed to Syria pursued by the excommunication of Pope Gregory IX.; and while the clergy of Palestine shut their churches in his face, he obtained for the Christians, by a masterly stroke of diplomatic policy, and without drawing the sword, the possession of the Holy

Places; but he was forced to return home before he could complete the negotiation, in order to defend his kingdom of Naples against an attack from the Papal troops. Twenty years later, the Curia once more beheld a Crusade after its own heart, when St. Louis, burning with holy ardour, led a French army against the Sultan of Egypt. But after a brief success, he allowed himself to be surrounded by his opponents in the flooded valley of the Nile; and the campaign ended, without glory or advantage, in the capture of the whole crusading army. After this defeat, the Pope failed in all his endeavours to excite any enthusiasm for the Eastern war; one Syrian fortress after the other fell into the hands of the victorious Mussulmans, until at length and last of all, the dearly won Ptolemais was captured, after an obstinate resistance, in the year 1292; just at the time when Pope Boniface VIII., took the first steps towards his great conflict with King Philip the Handsome, of France, which resulted in the deepest humiliation of the Papal power. The system of Gregory VII. declined simultaneously in Europe and in Asia.

It must have struck all my readers, that although during the whole period of the Crusades, the hostility between the East and the West was more violent, the difference between them was far less

marked than in our own days. At the present time
Europe, in its absolute superiority of arms, of culture, and of manners, looks down upon the Eastern
world much as it does upon the perishing red
men of the West, or the falling empire of China.
The interval that separates European nations from
the Turks has come to be almost that between
civilization and barbarism. But in the thirteenth
century the relations between the two were totally different. Both East and West were then
under similar conditions as to government and intellectual culture; they were engaged in an active
contest for superiority; and we may fairly doubt
which excelled the other in intelligence. If on the
one hand a whole swarm of Turcoman horse was
scattered by the Frankish chivalry; on the other,
there was no doubt that the Turkish system of
warfare and strategy was very superior to the
Christian. Municipal administration and police,
security and order, external comforts and luxu-
ries, were on a higher level in Cairo and Damascus
than either in Paris or in London. Science and
art were cultivated in Syria and Persia with at least
as much success as in Europe. In the former as
well as in the latter, Aristotle was studied, juris-
prudence and theology were reduced to a science,
and poetry flourished in youthful freshness. To

turn to the domain of religion: while by the influence of politics and philosophy, the original
barbarism of Islam was softened and enriched,
contrariwise, out of the deepest feelings of Christianity were evolved the lust of dominion and the
most aggressive fanaticism. In Asia both the power
of the state and the religious feelings of individuals had by this time freed themselves in a
great degree from the spiritual dominion of the
Caliph, while in Europe the Papacy took every measure to destroy the power of the sovereigns and.
the very existence of heretics in as determined a
manner as Mahomet had once done in the East.
In short, in spite of all inherent differences, we find
a decided tendency to union and assimilation, and
a strong mutual influence of each nation upon the
other, in the very midst of their hatred and warfare.

It was therefore the greatest tragedy which our
historical knowledge records, when the highly cultivated Eastern world was devastated and destroyed for ever, a few years after Saladin's triumphs, by an overwhelming flood of barbarians. The
savage Mongolian hordes swept down from their
high central plains, laying waste and destroying,
throughout Persia, Asia Minor, Turkistan, and
Russia. It was no revivifying flood, like that which
enriched the Roman soil when the Germans in-

vaded it. Gengis Khan's hordes knew no joy beyond building huge heaps of the skulls of the slain,
and marching their horses over the ruins of burnt
cities. Wherever they passed, there was an end to
all culture, to all the joys of life, and to the future
prosperity of nations; a dreary savage barbarism
pressed upon countries which but a century before
could have rivalled in civilization the very flower of
Europe. Here and there, perchance, Islam could
still enter the lists of military prowess with the
Western nations, but her intellectual vigour was
broken, and the dominion of the earth was thus for
ever secured to the more fortunate nations of our
hemisphere.

It has however taken them centuries to comprehend and to solve the problem thus set before them.
We may add that they have deserved to solve it,
not only because Islam became weaker, but also
because Christianity has grown stronger; and it has
grown stronger because it has more of the nature
of inward conviction, and less of an aggressive character. We have seen what caused the Crusades to
fail; not Zenki's impetuosity, Noureddin's firmness,
or Saladin's joyous valour. In the great streams of
history, none hopelessly sink but those who destroy
themselves. It was the heat of religious excitement
which called the Crusades into existence, and then

irresistibly hurried them to perdition. We have seen how over-excitement, thirst for the miraculous, and contempt for the world, rendered any regular and consecutive plan of conquest in the East impossible from the very beginning. The Crusaders despised all the earthly resources of the human mind, and thus their mystical transports led them into every other miserable passion. With the Frankish States the very existence of the Christian religion perished in the East. In modern times, men no longer travel over the world, or found colonies, or make conquests, for religion's sake; they neither trade nor fight nor found colonies according to ecclesiastical principles. It is enough if their own faith affords the inward impulse towards justice and morality, and leaves them free to conduct the various affairs of life according to their own several laws. They no longer see, as in the Middle Ages, an inveterate hostility between heaven and earth, or expect religious perfection from the renunciation, but from the right use of earthly things. Thus it is that this age, apparently so lukewarm in religion, has succeeded in attaining an object which the zeal of Urban and the power of the Baldwins in vain strove to effect. There no longer exists on earth a hostile religion which can venture to threaten Christianity with impunity. Wherever Christian power and Christian civilization appear, the world at once recognizes, sometimes with joy and sometimes with anger, but always powerless to resist, the presence of the conqueror and ruler. Jerusalem, for whose conquest millions once shed their blood in vain, could now be torn from its Turkish ruler by a protocol of five lines, if only our generation took any interest in the matter. But we now say, with St. Bernard, "It is better to struggle against the sinful lusts of the heart, than to conquer Jerusalem."

PART II.

LITERATURE OF THE CRUSADES.

CRITICAL ACCOUNT

OF

THE ORIGINAL AUTHORITIES AND THE LATER

WRITERS ON THE CRUSADES.

LITERATURE OF THE CRUSADES.

THERE are more materials for a history of the First Crusade than for any other event of the early Middle Ages. They consist of official reports, of private communications from individual pilgrims to their friends at home; of many current histories written by eye-witnesses; all these, again, were amplified by writers in Western Europe, who were not present themselves, but who drew their statements from eye-witnesses; and finally, after a lapse of eighty years, these documents were collected by one eminently fitted for the undertaking. It might well be imagined that such ample materials would have secured for all times a true appreciation of the course of events. In fact, whosoever becomes familiar with all these narratives, is astonished at the fullness of the life therein depicted, and may hope

K 2

from all these materials to obtain a competent knowledge and a thorough comprehension of the truth
they contain.

The variety of the materials requires judgment
in selection and arrangement. The most cursory
examination discovers a great difference in the nature and endowments of the various authors. Every
conceivable impulse is at work within them; but
that dispassionate frame of mind alone capable of
producing a useful history is almost wholly wanting. In contemporaries we have to guard against
a distortion of facts from personal bias. Later
historians again may be influenced by subsequent
events. Great care, therefore, must be taken to lay
a good foundation, and to have some standard by
which the various discrepancies can be reconciled.

I. OFFICIAL REPORTS, AND LETTERS FROM INDI-
VIDUAL CRUSADERS.

The number of letters and original narratives
written by those actively engaged in the First Crusade is not large, nor do they constitute the most
mportant sources of our knowledge of those times;
but they must not be disregarded. They throw
considerable light upon many special and doubtful
points. We will mention these authorities in their
regular order, in so far as we can.

1. *Letter from the Emperor Alexius to Count Robert of Flanders.*[1]

The Abbot Guibert, in his history of the Crusades, is the first to mention this letter.[2] He gives a tolerably detailed account of its contents. Martene's collection contains another version of this letter, agreeing in the main so much with Guibert, that doubt has been thrown on the authenticity of the whole document. The silence of Greek authors, and Guibert's known carelessness, have increased the suspicion that this document in Martene's collection might be one of the usual monkish manufactures of the Middle Ages, or a free version of Guibert's text. Much that is singular in this document could not be denied. There is an absence of the high-flown official style of the Greek Empire. The praise of the Eastern women as an inducement for Christian Crusaders was considered unbecoming and childish, in the mouth of a Byzantine monarch.

Without taking upon myself to defend this document as genuine, it may be asked why an intelligent Western author should be disbelieved because a Byzantine passes over in silence the fact that his Emperor begged for assistance from a Count of

[1] Martene, Thesaur. p. 266 *et seq.*
[2] Lappenberg, in Pertz, Archiv, vi. 630.

Flanders.[3] It is very probable that Guibert received the communication from the Count Robert of Flanders himself.

2. *Letter from Urban II. to Alexius.*[4]

In the summer of the year 1096, Urban II. wrote a letter to Alexius, which has been frequently printed in the Collection of the Councils. In it the Pope recommends the Crusaders to the care of the Emperor. The letter contains little of importance.

3. *Stephen of Blois to his Wife.*

The Count of Blois, as far as we can learn, wrote three times to his wife Adela in the course of the Crusades. The first of these letters is lost, and is unimportant towards a knowledge of the Crusades, as it merely gives details of the journey to Constantinople. The second letter was written from the camp at Nicæa, shortly after the capture of that town.[5] It throws but little light upon the battles that had taken place up to that period, but gives a good picture of the respective qualities of the Greek Emperor and Count Stephen of Blois shown in their relation to each other. Stephen betrays the vanity of

---

[3] See further, under Guibert.
[4] Frequently printed in the Collection of the Councils.
[5] In Mabillon, Mus. Ital. ad Calc. Histor. Belli Sacri.

a weak nature delighted with trifles, and manifesting itself most plainly in an assumption of humility. He admires the Emperor and his riches; the Emperor behaves to him like a father, and is even pleased with the absence of the Count from his court, on learning that he is at the camp.

The third letter, written from the camp before Antioch, and shortly previous to the capture of that city, is in many respects the most instructive.[6]

At the very beginning it is stated that, for a time, Count Stephen had been chosen by all the princes as commander-in-chief, a circumstance we find mentioned elsewhere, but which requires some such confirmation as this. We are left totally in the dark as to the manner and importance of the command, and in what manner he exercised his influence. No events of any consequence followed this nomination; so that but for the Count's own testimony, the whole affair would be involved in considerable doubt. In the battle of Dorylæum, for example, the army was divided into two parts, and Stephen of Blois was with the Normans, who were exposed to the first assault of Kilidje Arslan; but there is no mention here of his issuing orders; on the contrary, Bohemund at once took the command, and won the day.

[6] In D'Achery, Spicileg. iii. *et seq.*

"We learned," continues Stephen of Blois, "that there dwelt in Cappadocia a Turcoman prince, by name Assam, whose lands we seized; we left one of our princes, with many knights there, to complete the conquest." It is not quite clear who was intended by this; whether it is a mutilation of the name of Kilidje Arslan,[7] then strange to the Latins, or whether Stephen meant some insignificant prince of the neighbourhood.

But still more interesting, spite of its brevity, is the narrative of the defeat of the second attempt to raise the siege of Antioch made by the princes who dwelt around it. In this passage, the seat of the war, and the number of the combatants on both sides, are mentioned with greater distinctness than elsewhere. We also obtain further information as to the condition of the Christian host from the statement which has hitherto been overlooked, that the troops were distributed far and wide in the neighbourhood, as they held a hundred and sixty-five places and fortresses in Syria *in proprio dominio*.

4. *Letter from Anselm of Ripemont to the Archbishop of Rheims.*[8]

Anselm, one of the most illustrious of the Lorraine barons in the army of the Crusaders, corre-

[7] As the earlier Byzantines call Alp Arslan.
[8] D'Achery, p. 431.

sponded with Manasses, Archbishop of Rheims. We shall find more about him in the ' Gesta Dei,' of Guibert. One only of his letters has come down to us, written soon after the capture of Antioch, and giving short but distinct sketches of the occurrences before and in this city. The agreement of the statements in his letters with those of other eye-witnesses, such as Raymund the author of the ' Gesta Francorum,' etc., in contradistinction in the narrative of Albert of Aix, is very remarkable. As an example I would select what occurred during the time of the fast, in 1098,—the decisive victory of the Christians and the consequent erection of the fort in front of the bridge-gate of Antioch. It is distinctly stated here that Bohemund and Raymond of Toulouse went to St. Simeon's Haven to fetch workmen for the building of the fort, that they were attacked and suffered a severe loss on their way back, and that this was subsequently avenged by a splendid victory gained by the whole army, after which the fort was completed with little difficulty. According to Albert's account, the army was in perfect repose when Godfrey of Bouillon received intelligence of this unfortunate skirmish, and immediately prepared for battle.[9]

Count Stephen of Blois relates that the princes

---

[9] Albert, iii. 64 *et seq.*

rode without suspicion of danger to meet the people
coming from St. Simeon's Haven, and fell among
enemies; that by the time the latter came up, the
princes had got all the army under arms.   Anselm's
narrative fully confirms this, and completely refutes
Albert of Aix's statement.   The princes had ridden
out with a settled purpose, at the desire of Bohemund, to secure their safe return by a movement
of the whole army.   The intention was that the
whole army should march, and it was only some
accidental delay that stopped the advance of all the
detachments.   The 'Gesta Francorum' agree with
this; and even some apparent discrepancies serve
to confirm this view, when we call to mind the
personal position of the author.   He was, as we
shall see, a common soldier, or at any rate what we
should now call a non-commissioned officer.   We
can therefore easily understand that he knew nothing
of Bohemond's general orders to the princes; he
only knew that the army stood ready for action when
Bohemund arrived.   At that moment, says he, "nos
congregati eramus in unum;" we, that is the Normans.[10]   This does not contradict what Count Stephen says, that Bohemond arrived "dum adhuc
convenirent nostri;" for Count Stephen means the
whole army.

[10] Gesta.

It is true that these are mere trifles, but they illustrate the quality of a narrative, and the relation it bears to other reports. It will not be difficult for us hereafter to show, on a larger scale, the agreement among the eye-witnesses which is here obvious, and the contradiction which they thus unanimously give to Albert of Aix; and this will completely change our view of some of the most important transactions.

5. *Letter from the Princes to all the Faithful.*[11]

This report is signed by Bohemund, Raymond, Godfrey, and Hugo. Martene gives the date as 1097, but it evidently was written in July 1098. The whole is short, and told in a summary manner. There are statements of the loss of the army before Nicæa and Antioch, which appear exaggerated. The notice at the end, that the King of Persia had threatened them with a new war after Kerboga's defeat, and that, conjointly with the Egyptians, he would attack them, is quite new.

6. *Letter from the Princes to Pope Urban II.*[12]

The date of this letter is not given by Fulcher; he has however inserted the whole of it into the

---

[11] Martene, p. 272.
[12] In Fulcher, p. 399, and Reuber, Cur. Johannis, p. 399.

body of his narrative, as well as a postscript by
one of the party, and many valuable variations,[13]
which are noticed in the edition given by Reuber.
The writers are Bohemund, Raymond, Godfrey, the
two Roberts, and Eustace of Boulogne. That Hugo
is not mentioned, seems to prove that he had already
gone on his mission to Constantinople. The greater
part of the narrative relates to the battles against
Kerboga, and gives the most important and decisive
details on this subject. The scanty chronological
notices, which can be obtained from the 'Gesta
Francorum,' are completely confirmed. The same
may be said of the narrative of the last great battle
against Kerboga. These statements substantiate, in
the most remarkable manner, the trustworthiness of
the eye-witnesses. Albert of Aix, on some special
information, asserts that the capture of Antioch
by the Christians was effected by Godfrey and not
by Bohemund. The contrary assertion made in the
.' Gesta' receives the most ample confirmation from
the words of this document, subscribed by the two
princes,—"Ego Bohemundus scalas parum ante
diem muris applicui," etc.

[13] Fulcher, for example, has for Dorylæum *in campo florido;*
Reuber calls it *in valle Doretillæ.* We see here how with the
Europeans the corruption arose of *in valle Ozellis.*

7. *Letter from the Princes, after the battle of Ascalon.*

Dodechin has handed this down to us. What little is to be said about this document will be mentioned in the account of Ekkehard, who made use of it.

8. *Letter from the Patriarch and the Princes, to the Churches of the West.* [14]

The contents of this letter are unimportant. The writers state that they have captured ten capital cities, two hundred castles, and still have one hundred thousand warriors, not counting the common people and the assistance of the Saints. But their trust in the Saints appears but small, for this jubilation is followed by an earnest appeal for help,—"Come hither, ye faithful; come hither: wheresoever only two men are gathered together in one house, let one of the twain come to the Holy Sepulchre."

II. RAYMOND OF AGILES. [15]

In the retinue of the Count of Toulouse and of the Bishop of Puy, were two Crusaders, the one a

---

[14] Martene, p. 271.

[15] Bongars thus gives the name. In the preface he gives the reading De Arguillers: in manuscripts we find it written De Agilles and De Aguilers (Pertz, Archiv, vii. pp. 56, 61, 81). I can nowhere find any reference on which he relies.

brave and worthy knight; the other an ecclesiastic, uneducated, but well disposed. These two men were intimately bound together by friendship.[16] The knight Pontius, Lord of Baladun, was desirous that the memory of so many great exploits should not perish for want of a chronicler. He was constantly pressing his friend to write down, in the quiet of his tent, the events that had occurred in the battle-field, to edify and stir up all the faithful, and especially their friend the Bishop of Vivars. The ecclesiastic Raymond was easily moved thereto: he wrote down day by day what he had seen, always with the help and encouragement of his friend, until Pontius found an honourable death in battle, before the castle of Arkas. Nevertheless he did not leave off the work begun in common with his friend. "My best friend," said he, "died in the Lord; but love dieth not, and in love will I finish this work; so help me God."[17]

Raymond only received consecration as a priest on his way to the Holy Land,[18] and then became one of the immediate personal followers of the Bishop of Puy and the Count of Toulouse. He was present at the discovery of the Holy Lance,[19] carried this

---

[16] Bongars has collected in his preface the notices of Pontius.

[17] These dates are taken partly from the preface of the book; partly from p. 163; the former was dictated by Pontius.

[18] Page 163.   [19] Page 152.

relic in the battle against Kerboga,[20] and read the formulary at the ordeal by which Peter Bartholomew proved the identity of this instrument of the Passion.[21] There is no doubt, therefore, as to the opportunities he had of observing; and his capacity to judge events may be gathered from his works. Above all things, Raymond is simple and straightforward; he states, in the strongest and coarsest manner, what he thinks. We may have some doubt as to the correctness of his facts, but never as to the truth of the impression they make on him. Then he is Provençal to the backbone. He is not highly gifted, but thoroughly enthusiastic for the success of the undertaking, and, whenever there is an opportunity, for his countrymen and their leader. The manifestations of his character are not always of the pleasantest: they display an extravagant belief in miracles, and a fierce hatred of all who are opposed to him, and a vile way of connecting divine things with the lowest motives; when to this is added a very rude manner of expressing himself, it is obvious that in the course of his narrative there must be many things to shock the reader. For instance, he mentions as a glorious deed of the Count of Toulouse, that once when hard pressed by the Dalmatians, he caused the eyes of six of the pri-

[20] Page 155.   [21] Page 163.

soners to be torn out, and their noses, arms, and legs to be cut off, in order to inspire the rest with terror.[22] At the taking of Antioch, he says,— "Something pleasant and diverting occurred after their long tribulations. A troop of Turkish horse, more than three hundred in number, hard pressed by the Crusaders, were driven over a precipice; a pleasure to see, much as we regretted the loss of the horses."[23] It is true that in this war little regard was paid to humanity, but it would be difficult to find a second example of such excessive virulence.[24] Thus he goes on, expressing delight and rapture with the same eagerness, and is completely carried away when a supernatural apparition manifests itself within his immediate circle. When the point of the Holy Lance projected above the earth, he says, "Then I, Raymond the chaplain, sprang forward to kiss it."[25] The narratives of subsequent visions occupy about one-fourth of the whole book.[26] In one word, his was a vigorous but vulgar nature, thrown by a great impulse into an extraordinary course. The book would soon excite disgust, were it not so guilelessly written, and did it not so thoroughly show the personal character of the man.

[22] Page 139. [23] Page 149.

[24] That is to say, in trustworthy histories. Albert has some additional particulars.

[25] Page 152. [26] Nine or ten folio sides, in Bongars' edition.

It is obvious that his judgment is only to be trusted in certain cases: he can be followed when once he is known. He may be depended upon as to matters of fact, which he narrates with the strictest accuracy. He is rich in detail, but not in anecdote. A few cases, unimportant in themselves, may be found in which we are forced to reject his statements; on the other hand, he gives conclusive accounts of the most important events, and, in comparison with others, he must be looked upon as a guiding authority. On some points his narrative is essential to a right view of events, *e.g.* the battle with Kilidje Arslan, before Nicæa—the siege of Antioch—and, above all, the quarrel between Bohemund and the Count of Toulouse. He agrees perfectly in the main points with the 'Gesta Francorum;' the discrepancies are few, and those only on special matters, quite independent of the general view of affairs. Moreover, the two works are quite independent of each other, although, from their similarity, it has been supposed that they had a common origin,[27] and that Raymond had only ampli-

[27] Such an assertion might appear true, when we compare some of the longer and more connected narratives, such as the siege of Antioch, or of Jerusalem, with the totally different account given of the same occurrences by Albert of Aix. We must make up our minds to leave the false and unfounded statements quite on one side; if we attempt to connect the false with the true, it leads us to wrong conclusions.

L

fied the 'Gesta.' Each author tells the exact truth as far as he knew it, the one as to what occurred among the Normans, the other among the Provençals. The events were neither secret nor involved, and the similarity of the statements of the two authors is therefore by no means wonderful. Identity of expression, even in isolated passages, nowhere occurs; in two places, pointed out by critics, it is only apparent: but at the end of the book, which has not come down to us in its perfect form from Raymond himself, passages have been added from the 'Gesta' by a foreign hand.

The question is, when and by whom the interpolations were made. In all manuscripts which have hitherto been found, the passages in question invariably occur. It is still more important that Tudebod, who in this instance follows Raymond, found these words, and copied them into his text, perhaps comparing them with the 'Gesta.'[28] It is probable, indeed, that Raymond himself made the interpolations, that he felt the omission in his own narrative, and endeavoured to fill it up with the fragment from the 'Gesta.' This circumstance is important, as affording the most convincing proof

[28] It is singular that the text in Tudebod is more like that of the 'Gesta' than that of Raymond. However, he clearly took the passage from Raymond, as is proved by the words that immediately follow it.

of the contemporaneous composition of the ' Gesta,' even if the book did not contain sufficient internal evidence.

We have dwelt at some length on this apparently trifling circumstance, for various reasons. First, in order to establish the date of the ' Gesta,' and next for those which relate to the subject itself. We hear on all sides that it is impossible to form an exact or authentic picture of the occurrences in Constantinople from the original authorities.[29] This is mainly owing to the confusion that prevails in Albert's narrative,[30] which renders it impossible to combine the Latin authorities with the Alexiade. But if we can succeed in extracting from the eye-witnesses clear and unanimous statements, if we have the courage upon their authority to pronounce a strict judgment on Albert of Aix, the apparent discrepancies which exist in Anna Comnena's works offer no further difficulties.

To sum up our judgment on the work of Raymond of Agiles, we should say it was full of ample and trustworthy details, the value of which is somewhat impaired by the passion and superstition of the otherwise veracious author. As a writer, Raymond, in spite of his violent, zealous, and super-

---

[29] See Wilken's History, i. 116, 117. Michaud, Hist. i. 191.

[30] We have treated this subject further on.

stitious nature, takes a correct view of things, and with all the vulgarity of his mind he is a true representative of his time and of his country. He is genuine and outspoken, and no one who enters into his spirit can read his work without benefit.

III. GESTA FRANCORUM ET ALIORUM HIEROSOLYMITANORUM.[31]

Besly, in the preface to Tudebod's 'History of Jerusalem,'[32] positively asserts that the 'Gesta Francorum,' edited by Bongars as a genuine and authentic narrative, and frequently used as such by former writers, was nothing more than a plagiarism of the grossest kind, the anonymous author being entirely indebted to Tudebod for his facts, and thinks it his duty to expose such a wholesale plagiarism. Besly grounds this assertion chiefly upon three passages,—one in which Tudebod speaks of himself, and two wherein he mentions the death of his brothers. In these cases, Tudebod, he says, speaks as an eye-witness, and the anonymous author of the 'Gesta Francorum' has carefully omitted all mention of these occurrences in his narrative.[33] Besly's views met with general concurrence, and have been

---

[31] In Bongars' Gesta Dei, p. 1 et seq.

[32] Du Chesne, iv. 773 et seq.

[33] Pages 810, 811, and 796, 803.

followed by all subsequent historians of the Crusades.[34]

I must confess that the reasons urged for this opinion appear to me thoroughly unsatisfactory, and, that there is evidence of exactly the reverse. In the case in point, Tudebod narrates an unlucky event which occurred at the siege of Jerusalem; "the author," he adds, "Tudebod, a priest of Sivray, was present, and was an eye-witness." The whole narrative, to which this statement is appended, is omitted in the 'Gesta Francorum,' and I can conceive nothing unlikely in the supposition that Tudebod, having got so far in his transcription of the 'Gesta,' should have inserted in this place something he had himself witnessed. There is nothing to disprove that he and his brothers were present with the army, but there are many objections to looking upon his narrative as the original source of the 'Gesta Francorum.'

First of all, the anonymous author invariably speaks in the first person; Tudebod, sometimes in the first, at other times in the third person.

Further, the anonymous author, as we shall presently see, was a knight. Tudebod was a priest. The

---

[34] Since the decision, which agrees with Bongars, given in the Hist. Littér. de la France, viii. 629, no one has had a doubt on the matter.

first remains true to his character, whereas Tudebod introduces himself sometimes as a warrior, at others as a priest,[35] which can easily be accounted for, if we consider him only as the secondary author.

In both works passages occur which are wanting in the other. Those which Tudebod alone has are anecdotes, traits of individual character, etc., which can be easily inserted or omitted, without interfering with the narrative. But it is not so in the other case. It clearly appears that Tudebod, from a mistaken endeavour at compression, has omitted passages essential to the meaning. His narrative of the conquest of Nicæa has faults inexcusable in an eye-witness, but easily understood as the errors of a transcriber. It is impossible not to see that the 'Gesta Francorum' is the source from which he draws.

This leads me to the last and most important point, which Besly passes over lightly, but which appears to me conclusive. Tudebod makes use of Raymond's work, as well as of the 'Gesta.' He has inserted several passages from the former, word for word, in his compilation. Had the author of the 'Gesta Francorum' followed Tudebod, it would be impossible that some passage from Ray-

---

[35] Pages 782, 788. The cavalry is mentioned in contradistinction to the infantry. Tudebod quietly copies the distinctive passages.

mond should not have slipped into his text. Precisely
the one passage which is to be found both in Raymond and in the anonymous author of the 'Gesta
Francorum,' makes the matter quite clear. Tudebod
follows first the 'Gesta,' then Raymond, and then
repeats the last sentences from the 'Gesta' for a
second time.

But the originality of the 'Gesta Francorum' has
been attacked from another quarter, and it has been
traced to the 'Historia Belli Sacri' in Mabillon.
But in this the character of a compilation comes
out still more strikingly. Besides the anonymous
author of the 'Gesta,' Tudebod, Raymond, and Rodolph of Caen, have been extensively laid under
contribution.[36]

In short, in every way, and as yet against all
comers, we are disposed to defend the originality of
the 'Gesta Francorum ;' and, considering the value
of the work, the question is not an unimportant
one.

Our knowledge of the life of the author is but
slight. The work was anonymous, even to those contemporaries who made use of his text ;[37] nowhere do
we find any certain notice of the writer. We only

---

[36] See further on.
[37] Robert, Baldric, and Guibert, all speak of a small anonymous document, which they wished to work up.

know that he quitted Amalfi with Bohemund in 1096, and remained with him until the victory over Kerboga. He served there among the knights,[38] and had the good fortune to take part in all the important actions. For instance, he was one of those who assaulted Antioch ; he likewise joined the band which in the summer of 1098 joined Robert of Normandy and Raymond of Toulouse, in their attack upon Mara and Tripoli.[39] This is the last notice which we can find of the author.

His personal character does not come out so strongly in connection with the matters which he relates, as it does in Raymond of Agiles, but it shows itself sufficiently to inspire confidence in his narrative. In the first place, the author is thoroughly imbued with the general feeling of the Crusades. He attributes them immediately to Divine inspiration, and in many passages calls God himself their true leader and protector. "Almighty God, just and merciful, who letteth not his host to perish, sent us very present help. Thus were our enemies overcome by the power of God and of the Holy

---

[38] This appears from pp. 7 and 17.

[39] Page 25. "Exeuntes quatuordecim ex nostris militibus,—ex exercitu vero Raimundi comitis," etc. Tancred was also with this army, according to Rad., c. 96 ; nevertheless it is not to be understood that the author accompanied it, as he does not once name him.

Sepulchre. We, however, wandered securely in the fields and mountains, glorifying and praising the Lord." With such sentences he begins and ends nearly every account of each single deed and skir- mish. We can but read such expressions with pleasure; indifference on such subjects in a con- temporary would darken and disturb the picture. Moreover, his enthusiasm is restrained within due bounds, and is never blindly violent against worldly considerations or polemical against hostile opinions. He shows an equal interest in human affairs, as in Heaven and all its Saints. He relates that at Dorylæum, when the anxiously expected succour came, they all exclaimed,—" Let us fight valiantly in the faith of Christ; if it be God's pleasure, we shall all gain riches."[40] And thus throughout. His passion for war, for its own sake, is as strong as his religious impulse. "Tam mirabiliter," says he frequently, had they attacked the Turks, or the latter the pilgrims. Occasionally, but very seldom, he is struck by the individual heroism of one of the Crusaders; he then describes the act with quiet pleasure, and we may be sure that it de- serves mention. He then speaks of the difficulties and hardships they had to encounter, in the simplest manner, how they had nothing either to eat or to

[40]. Page 7.

drink, for days, and then satisfied their hunger
with the bark of trees, and their thirst with water.
He makes no exclamations, no reflections; at most
he adds that they endured such plagues and necessities for the sake of Christ, and the Holy Sepulchre. What would have filled others with a high
idea of the value of the sacrifices in question, viz.
the holy object of the enterprise, appears to him
precisely what excludes any claim to admiration or
pity.

I cannot refrain from noticing one point especially, as marking his sentiments, and this is the terms
in which he speaks of his opponents the Turks, and
the conduct of the pilgrims towards them. He does
the Turks full justice. "Who," says he, "can describe
the prudence,[41] the warlike glory, the bravery of
the Turks? I will tell the truth, which none can
gainsay. Were they but steadfast in the holy faith
of Christ, it would be impossible to find greater,
stronger, or abler warriors." Now it is a well-known
fact, that this war was carried on with savage cruelty; there was no question of quarter being given
or taken; the heads of the slain were hewn off, the
dead were mutilated. All this is mentioned with
delight by the historians of the age. The author of
the 'Gesta Francorum' is a remarkable exception to

[41] Page 7.

the rule. He passes over such subjects on numerous occasions; and when he does allude to them,
he does it with quiet indifference, never with exul-
tation or unction. It is obvious that his is the indifference of the soldier, who passes his life amid
blood and wounds, and who considers such horrors
as of everyday occurrence, not worth mentioning,
and certainly not deserving praise, or matter of edi-
fication.[42] His position in life, and his own nature
give the clue to the method and general intention
of his narrative. His is the report of an eye-witness,
not in the very highest position, nor always acquainted with the leading motives of events. So
far as he can see them, he traces them clearly, and
reproduces them in a correct and simple narrative.
It is not by any means a mere diary of the personal
life of the author; he records with minuteness only
the most important events. He has great skill in
distinguishing between various facts, and selecting
the best. He is never carried away by what is
strange, wonderful, poetical, or personally interesting, but continues the even tenor of his narrative.

Michaud complains that it is impossible to re-
construct the plans of battles, the orders of march,

[42] He only mentions the murders in Antioch, because of the
offensive stench from the dead bodies; and the carnage at Jerusalem, because it took place against Tancred's orders.

and so forth, out of the unskilful writers of the twelfth century;[43] the rest of the modern historians of those events, if we may judge from their works, would appear to have attained the same resignation.[44] With regard to the works of Albert of Aix and William of Tyre, the reproach, is perfectly well founded; but I must deny that it applies to the 'Gesta Francorum,' which in this respect affords ample materials for the history of the First Crusade. The 'Gesta,' in general, is rich in details, in so far as they concern the matter in hand. All the events which the 'Gesta'. relate are duly set forth and com- plete in all their parts. The battles, sieges, and all that appertains to those subjects, are easy to trace. For instance, all the measures of defence taken by Bohemund at Dorylæum, the position of the whole army, the application of the several arms, are accurately set forth; then, when the remaining forces have arrived, the formation of the line of battle, and lastly the movement of the Bishop of Puy, which decided the battle, are explained.[45] In like manner, but still better, the siege of Antioch is brought before us: how the Christians, in an unpro- tected position, and attacked on all sides, first of all

---

[43] Hist., t. i. pp. 187, 475.

[44] See, for example, in Wilken, i. p. 156, the battle of Dory- læum; p. 223, the battle of Antioch; in Raumer, the siege of Antioch, etc.   [45] Page 7.

cleared the immediate neighbourhood, then placed themselves in communication with the sea, at length completely surrounded the town with a line of forts.[46] Each individual encounter in the course of the siege, the victory over Kerboga, the measures taken against Arkas and Jerusalem, are developed in the same manner. The reader feels he is on safe ground, and soon learns to place implicit confidence in his author.

It is not often that he permits himself to judge of persons, or to indulge in general reflections; where it does occur, he is rough and vigorous, but, *præmissis præmittendis*, unprejudiced and correct. He always says whatever is best and fittest for a man in his position to say.[47] I only know of one instance in which he treats of matters of universal import, and I never read it, rough and unpolished as is his style, without pleasure. I allude to the introduction to his book:—" When the time was fulfilled," says he, " which Christ showed to his apostles, speaking daily and especially in the Gospels, Whosoever will follow me, let him deny himself, and take up his cross: then a great movement took place throughout France: That whoso-

[46] Page 9 *et seq.*

[47] This may be said also of the few expressions concerning Aléxius and the Greeks. They are crude, but by no means false.

ever wished to follow the Lord with his whole heart, and to carry his cross after him in faith, he should not delay quickly to begin and walk in the way of the Lord. And straightway the Pope, with his archbishops, bishops, priests, and abbots, crossed the Alps, and began to teach wisely and to preach, and spake thus: Whosoever will save his soul alive, let him not hesitate to walk in the way of the Lord. Whosoever lacketh money, he will, by God's grace, be plentifully provided therewith. And when these words were bruited abroad, the Franks who heard them sewed red crosses on their shoulders and said that they would follow with one accord the footsteps of Christ, who had loosed them from the bonds of hell," etc.

If we consider that the author had no intention of giving a connected narrative of the Crusades, but solely meant to describe what he himself saw, this opening leaves little to be desired. Short as it is, it places us in the clearest and truest manner, in the midst of the beginning of the enterprise. It gives the source from which it originated—the religious impulse of the West; it names the individual, Urban II., who gave expression and life to this impulse; it tells the manner in which the army was collected and organized by the personal enthusiasm of the individuals. The anecdote of Peter the

Hermit is happily suppressed. Christ, the Pope, the whole of Western Europe, are the worthy actors in this great enterprise.

I believe that what I have said justifies my assertion that we have here to do with the most important authority for a true history of the First Crusade. A character like that of the author of the 'Gesta Francorum' is peculiarly fitted to give a true picture of great events. Devoid of personal pretensions, strong in will; without any adventitious interests, but inspired with a great purpose and full of religious enthusiasm, which, however, does not preclude him from feeling an interest in human affairs, he shows a meritorious industry in making use of the rich materials at hand to give a picture of the important events in which he himself had been an actor. It is likewise interesting to find in him the purest expression of national character. He exemplifies the Norman type, in that mixture of the temporal and ecclesiastical, in the freedom with which he handles all subjects, keeping every part of his picture in subordination to the whole. In Raymond of Agiles, we saw the Provençal, full of zeal, forgetting the future and the past in the immediate present, and pressing forward step by step in impetuous passion. In small things there is the same antagonism, upon which the most important events of the Cru-

sades depend, that antagonism which from the very
first disagreement about Antioch separated Bohemund and Raymond of Toulouse more and more,.
until the activity of the one was extinguished in the
chains of Danischmend, and that of the other in the
deserts of Phrygia.[48] Even now both these chiefs
speak to us in their own tongues, each one of his
own nature, of his deeds, and of their mutual contention. By this means, if we understand their
words rightly, scarce any important point can remain obscure to us.

1. *Tudebod.*

I have already mentioned Tudebod, the priest of
Sivray. We know but little of his life. Besly asserts
that he was with the army of Poitou, commanded
first by Hugo of Lusignan, and then by Gaston of
Béarn. But there is no positive proof of this.[49]
Besly was led to this conclusion because Hugo was
then Lord of Sivray.[50] The book copies the ' Gesta
Francorum,' nearly word for word; many of the

[48] Their effectual action was then at an end, at least as far as
concerns the East.

[49] Although the Hist. Litt. de la France, i. c., cites Tudebod
himself, pp. 173 and 809 in support of it.

[50] If we allowed this to hold good, it would afford an additional argument in favour of the originality of the 'Gesta.'
Why should a native of Aquitaine, devote himself so exclusively
to the history of the Normans?

interpolations are mere episodes, and of little importance. He gives some details concerning the capture of Jerusalem, which may serve partly as an amplification, partly as a rectification of the 'Gesta.'

2. *Guibert, Abbot of Nogent.*

Guibert was born in the year 1053, at Beauvais, of noble parents.[51] His youth was passed in those times when the Roman Church began to bring the world under its dominion. Many circumstances concurred to subject Guibert altogether to these ecclesiastical influences, his mother was enthusiastically pious, and lived only in the mortification of the outward senses, and in the cultivation of the inward and spiritual perceptions. Before his birth his parents had vowed to devote their son to the service of the Church,[52] and long before manhood he assumed the monk's cowl at Flavigny.[53] As he grew up, the lusts of the world awoke within him : he became a poet and learned music ; he attempted imitations of Ovid and of Virgil's Bucolics. But his teacher was

[51] De Vitâ suâ, i. 3. 14. Cf. Bongars in præf. and Hist. Litt. x. p. 439.

[52] Vita, i. 4.

[53] Mabillon, Ann. i. 62, n. 65, gives the year 1064. I see no positive testimony for the exact date ; the assumption of the cowl by no means took place later.

M

warned in a vision, and the lad himself saw how
he sinned against the rules of his Order.   In this
frame of mind he met with Anselm, Abbot of Bec,
afterwards primate of the English Church, whose
powerful influence at once directed him into the
strict path of the Church.   Gifted as Guibert
was, he soon attained fame by his eloquence and
learning, and at an early age became abbot of No-
gent on the Seine.[54]   He remained there, respected
by a large circle, and distinguished in politics and
literature,[55] until his death, in 1124.[56]

The results of such a career are visible throughout his writings; he was not without abilities, and
for the times in which he lived, he was well read.
The advantages of his birth and of his ecclesiastical dignity were of great service to him in writing
a history of the Crusades.   His acquaintances and
connections extended over all France;[57] he was
indebted for many valuable hints to Count Robert

[54] Vita, i. 17, 19.

[55] The third book of his autobiography gives an account of his
outward life; the Hist. Litt. i. c., gives his writings.   He himself
speaks frequently enough of their effect.

[56] Mabillon, Ann. i. 74, n. 71.

[57] But not further.   His notices on the French nobility, pp.
486-501, are very useful, as well as his statements as to the consequences of the Council of Clermont, and on the Crusades especially, pp. 481, 508, 552.   But Godfrey and Bohemund are out
of his circle.   He adduces the most fabulous accounts of both,
pp. 485-438.

of Flanders;[58] Archbishop Manasses of Rheims allowed him to consult the letters of Anselm of Ripemont[59] and he was himself present at the Council of Clermont. As a man of learning he affects a cultivated style and artistic form, but he only selected the Crusades as his subject, in order to make the 'Gesta Francorum,' in his paraphrase, more agreeable to cultivated readers. It is true that he has succeeded very ill: the simple tone of his original is overwhelmed by his inflated and pompous style; he appears, conscious of his own high position, to disregard the opinion of others; and frequently intimates that those who do not approve his manner of writing may seek some other. Valuable as his work is, in his literary character, full of pedantry and conceit, he is most offensive.[60] The dignified servant of the Church, the man with whom everything has succeeded, the ecclesiastic who belongs to a ruling party, is too conscious of a proud position. He feels all his power when he attacks Fulcher of Chartres, as to his doubts

[58] He was his personal friend; pp. 521, 535, 548. The frequently noticed letter of the Emperor Alexius to Robert appears to me to be thoroughly trustworthy, p. 474.

[59] Pages 543, 553–4. We have before mentioned an original letter which has come down to us (in the third volume of D'Achery's Spicilegium, edit. 2).

[60] Compare his preface and the procemium of almost all the separate books of his history.

with respect to the Holy Lance, and reproaches him with credulity and superstition as to other miracles.[61] It was not in vain that Guibert had studied the science of demonology, that he had himself seen visions, and had everywhere found the doctrine of apparitions and wonders flourishing.[62] Nor was it either doubt or enthusiasm that stirred Guibert to anger against Fulcher. The pride of superior learning, the consciousness of belonging to a dominant orthodox party, made him look down with contempt on his rival.[63]

The close of his work is remarkable;[64] hard as he had worked at the historical form of his book, he could not master his mass of learning. He had come to the end of the 'Gesta Francorum,' which was his guide, and he still had on hand a variety of unused materials, too good to be lost to posterity.

[61] Page 552.

[62] De Vitâ suâ, i. i. c. 20 et seq., i. ii. in extenso. We can conceive nothing, however extravagant, that is not here stated as true and defended as reasonable. We see in this instance how little we can trust the judgments of modern authors, who sometimes call him the most credulous, and sometimes praise him as the most philosophical of all the authors of that time. Compare, for example, Gibbon, pp. 1069, 1072 (London edition, 1836), and Michaud, Bibl. i. 124.

[63] What Neander quotes of St. Bernard, p. 309, from his work 'De Pignoribus Sanctorum,' appears to me to suit very well the picture here given. It is the same belief in prodigies, reduced to a system; the unmistakable influence of Anselm of Canterbury.

[64] From p. 530.

He determined to use them at all events, and strung fragment upon fragment, digression upon digression, important and useless matter in utter confusion, until his store of knowledge was exhausted. These stories extend as late as the middle of the reign of Baldwin I., and it is easy to conceive how they vary in value and credibility; the most ordinary and the most unexpected matters are mixed together; occasionally we find individual notices on points but little known, which throw new light on familiar subjects. Such are the details as to the government of Robert of Normandy in Laodicea, which Lappenberg has made use of,[65] and which are important as correcting a widely spread statement by Albert of Aix,[66] and the account of the Crusade of the year 1011.[67] Of more special subjects we would also mention the death of Anselm of Ripemont and the end of Baldwin of Hennegau; the former serves to supply deficiencies in the narratives of Raymond and Radulph,[68] the latter is remarkable for its accurate agreement with the local history of Giselbert of Bergen.[69]

The book was begun in the year 1108 or 1109, and certainly not finished till 1110. Guibert says

[65] Page 554, Lappenberg's Geschichte von England, ii. p. 224.
[66] Albert, p. 290.   [67] Ibid., p. 527.
[68] Raymond, p. 164; Rad. c. 106.
[69] In Bonquet, vol. xiii. of the Recueil.

that he is writing two years after the death of
Manasses, Archbishop of Rheims,[70] which occurred
on the 17th September, 1106,[71] and in another
place he mentions the death of Bohemond,[72] which
is known to have taken place in the year 1110.

3. *Baldric, Archbishop of Dol.*

Baldric was born at Meun, near Órleans.[73]   He
was first a monk, and then became Abbot of Bour-
gueil in 1079, and in 1107 was appointed Archbishop of Dol in Brittany.   His personal character
was a complete contrast to that of his contemporary
Guibert.   I dwell with the greater pleasure upon
it, as it forms an agreeable relief to that of Guibert,
and also because Baldric represents a more common
though, at that time, an oppressed type.

The ascetic zeal which pervaded the hierarchy of
the eleventh century, was as hateful to the nature
of Baldric as it was congenial to the Abbot of No-
gent.   Baldric saw no impediment to a Christian
life in secular learning and art; the mortification
of the senses was not to his mind; sullen looks and
strict fasts—in short, the whole pomp and ceremony
of holy works—appeared to him not sufficient to

---

[70] Page 537.   [71] Bonquet, xiii. p. 497.
[72] Page 483.
[73] Baldric, Carmina apud Duchesne, vol. ii. p. 268.

fill up human life. He enjoyed the quiet of his cloister, the smiling garden, the clear running stream, the budding groves, while in his own room there were books, manuscripts, and all the appliances of learning. "This is the spot," writes he to a friend, "in which peace can be found."[74] There he wrote his verses; nothing remarkable, but unpretending, and a labour of love.[75] There also he applied himself to severer studies, and interchanged letters with friends of similar tastes. They carefully discussed their works, among others the History of the Crusades.[76] They allowed the ecclesiastical contests to be settled elsewhere; it concerned them but little that a new hierarchy had conquered and remodelled the world; not that they neglected their duties,[77] but their true life lay in their books, in their gardens, and in their meadows. They were not always able to defend their peaceful existence from the incursion of a hostile element; their ideas were peculiar and too much opposed to

---

[74] Baldric, p. 269.

[75] He re-wrote an epitaph of six lines on William I. of England three times.

[76] His correspondence with Peter, Abbot of Maillezais, is given by Bongars, before the History of the Crusades.

[77] He zealously maintained his metropolitan rights against the claims of Tours, and obtained the pallium from Paschal II. All the documents concerning the quarrel are in Martene, 'Thesaurus,' iii. 857 *et seq.*

the dominant party. Baldric writes to the Bishop of Ostia : "My vessel sails only by stealth, for pirates of all sorts swarm around me; they hem me in on every side, gnashing with their teeth because I do not quit my books, because I do not go about with eyes cast on the ground. Thus am I flagging in my work. May your hand protect me."[78]

As bishop, he remained true to himself and to his nature. He was very religious, but gentle and mild. It is true this did not always succeed in his diocese, with his fierce Bretons.[79] He was not fit to hold ecclesiastical power. He quitted Brittany, and sought a more peaceful asylum at Bec, Fecamp, and finally in England.[80] Men like him would never have gained honours and triumphs for the hierarchy; but it is a pleasure to meet with a nature so pure, so cheerful, and so gentle, in times so full of energy, war, and austerity.[81]

[78] Carmina, p. 275.   [79] Orderic Vitalis, p. 718.

[80] The Hist. Litt. xi. 96 *et seq.*, gives more particulars.

[81] As may be conceived, the judgment of the Benedictines on him is different. Mabillon, in the Annals, accuses him of worldliness and lukewarmness. In the main he supports this opinion by those passages of Baldric's poems, and he quotes a letter of Ivo of Chartres, wherein he is reported to have said that Baldric had tried every method of bribery in order to become Bishop of Orleans; but it is only stated in this letter (No. 66. 5, in Duchesne), that Baldric's rival was preferred "quia animadversi sunt plures et pleniores sacculi nummorum latere in apothecis amicorum istius, quam apud abbatem."

His history of the Crusades breathes the same
spirit. He is exact and trustworthy in his use of
the 'Gesta;' he has not made many additions to
its contents, but the views and opinions which he
expresses are in keeping with his character. He
does not withhold praise, even from the Turks;[82] he
omits the word "faithless," as applied to the Emperor Alexius, which constantly occurs in the 'Gesta.'[83] He endeavours to excuse Count Stephen of
Blois, who is generally styled *impudens et abomina-
bilis*, on the score of the general weakness of human
nature.[84] The additions he makes are mostly taken
from oral testimony, and generally well selected.[85]
Of course it is only in few instances that he can be
called an eye-witness; he undoubtedly is so where
he mentions the effect caused by the beginning of
the Crusades in France.

Baldric died before 1130, as his death was
known to Pope Honorius II. His work on the
Crusades seems to have been widely known. Ordericus Vitalis made use of it, and William of Tyre
in many instances took it as the groundwork of his
own history.

---

[82] Prooemium. [83] Pages 92, 93.
[84] Page 118.
[85] Praises of the chastity of the Crusaders, p. 96: rather a
doubtful statement. Page 137 gives a good account of the Battle
of Ascalon.

4. *The History of the Holy War.*

The anonymous book bearing this title is a compilation from the 'Gesta,' from Tudebod, Radulph, and Raymond. All these works have evidently been used, as we find passages taken from each which are wanting in all the rest.[86] But there are numerous original additions, from which we may gather some idea of the author. These mostly have reference to Bohemund and his affairs, so that we may fairly surmise that the author was a Norman, and apparently one of humble origin.[87] After the war he most likely lived in Antioch, as while he speaks in indistinct terms of the election of the King of Jerusalem, he gives original accounts of Tancred's rule, from 1100 to 1103, and ends his work with a short review of Bohemund's life and adventures.[88] This gives the measure of his trustworthiness. His narrative is lively, and

[86] The narrative about Nicæa is from the 'Gesta,' and is not to be found in Tudebod. Chapter 17 is not in the 'Gesta,' but is in Tudebod (Tud. p. 781). Chapter 55 (p. 792), c. 69, 70 (p. 789), c. 5, 16, 17, init. 24, 30, are from Raymond, pp. 140–142. The chapters 107, 109, 129, 131, 132, 135, and 136, are out of Radulph, c. 106, 110.

[87] Such are c. 37, 45, 66, 67, 83, 90, 93. The 'Gesta,' p. 5, shows that the Count of Roussillon, whose death is mentioned in chapter 45, was in Raymond's army. Most of these statements can also be confirmed by Raymond and Radulph.

[88] Chapters 130, 138, 139.

very like that of the 'Gesta.' It was written later than that work; probably about the year 1131, as the death of Bohemond is mentioned.

Mabillon has given a complete edition of this work in the second volume of his 'Museum Italicum.'[89]

5. *Henry of Huntingdon.*

According to a frequent custom of his times, Henry of Huntingdon has inserted a history of the Crusades in his larger work. But it is without importance, and was most probably derived entirely from the 'Gesta.' I should have scarcely noticed it here, were it not for allusions to the work in Lappenberg's History of England. He has not made much use of it.[90]

6. *Fulco, Gilo, and the Monk Robert.*

I mention these authors together, as Gilo cannot well be separated from Fulco, whose continuator he is. But Gilo, although in the first part of his narrative he is as independent of the 'Gesta' as Fulco, still belongs to the same category, as the last

---

[89] Muratori, Scr. Rer. Ital. t. iv. It is said in the notes to the passage here referred to, that this chapter was taken from a special manuscript in Monte Cassin. Pertz reports that this manuscript only contains that edited by Mabillon (Archiv, v. 157); their identity is easily verified by comparing the two.

[90] History of England, ii. 221.

four books of his work are taken word for word
from the ' Gesta ;' and lastly, it is only in connection
with the two others that we can give our judgment
on Robert the Monk.

We know nothing more than his book tells us as
to who Fulco was, where and when he lived, and
whence he gained his information. The title of
his work, ' The History of the Crusades of Our
Times,' proves that he lived during the period of
the Crusades. The concluding sentence of his poem :
" Cætera describit Gilo,"[91] shows that he was a contemporary and probably wrote from the same place as
Gilo, and this is the utmost that we can learn of him.

Fulco's work treats of the first events of the Crusades until the siege of Nicæa ; it is in three books,
and in hexameters.   His verses are heavy and over-
laden with quotations and illustrations ; he lays no
claim to poetical skill, and the only question is whether his work is worth examining historically : but
it is easy to prove the contrary ; it contains, with
scarcely an exception, nothing but what is perfectly
well known, utterly confused, and altogether useless.

Instead of the usual examination, I will briefly
review his narrative of Godfrey's adventures in the

[91] The Hist. Litt. xii. 84, is wrong also when it maintains
that Fulco has composed his book as a continuation of the work
of Gilo.

Greek Empire; this will be sufficient, without entering into any elaborate comparison with original
authorities, to give us the measure of his work. Godfrey, he says,[92] while in Thrace, learnt the approach
of the other armies, and determined to wait for
them at Constantinople. Alexius alarmed and angry, prepared to drive the Duke away by force of
arms. In the first place he refused to supply him
with provisions ; whereupon Godfrey plundered the
land, seized upon two thousand swine, which were
collected for the Imperial kitchen, and eventually
completely routed the Imperial troops. The latter,
during their retreat, fell in with a body of Lorrainers, who, posted in Adrianople, had not been
aware of the outbreak of hostilities, persuaded
them to accompany them to Constantinople, and
easily made them prisoners. In order to release his
companions-in-arms, Godfrey agreed to the Emperor's terms and crossed over into Asia.

All these occurrences are purely imaginary. A
certain interest which they possess, lies entirely
apart from their representing any historical facts.
Godfrey did not yield to the Emperor, as has
generally been represented, from any motive of
princely generosity, nor out of regard to the Christianity of Alexius, nor yet from eagerness to prose-

[92] Page 896.

cute the war against the Saracens; he was forced, much against his will, by the superiority of the Greek arms, to do homage to the Emperor. We see that this general result lies at the root of Fulco's narrative; the facts are strangely misrepresented and added to; intense hatred to the Greeks is quite obvious; and the author's grand object is not only to save the personal honour of the Duke, but to glorify him even in his defeat. He can point to no written authority for his statements; it is not probable that he possessed any other sources of information than his continuator Gilo, and it appears most likely that the latter trusted to oral tradition.

Gilo,[93] who came from Toucy, in the province of Auxerre, lived for a time at Paris, then entered the monastery of Clugny, and was made Bishop of Frascati, and Cardinal by Calixtus II.[94] He was subsequently employed on important missions;[95] lastly he was sent in 1134 into Aquitaine, as legate from the rival Pope, Anaclete, which naturally exposed him to the most violent abuse from the opposite side.[96] When he gave in his adhesion to the

[93] The Hist. Litt. xii. 81, gives a review of his life and works.

[94] Martene, Præf. ad Ekkeh. (Coll. Ampl. v. 508).

[95] 1127, to Palestine. William of Tyre, p. 827, calls him Ægidius.

[96] Bibl. Cluniac. pp. 720, 767, contain violent letters of the Abbot, Peter of Clugny, to him. In the notes to this passage, p. 127, André Duchesne has given a biography of Gilo.

victorious Pope, Innocent, is unknown; and we are
not informed of the date of his death.

When he wrote his history of the Crusades, he
was still living in Paris. The work is in hexameters,
and consists of seven books; it was written after
the year 1118, as the author speaks of Baldwin I.
as having *formerly* reigned at Jerusalem. The three
last books follow the ' Gesta ' word for word, with
the exception of three brief original additions.[97]
The four first books are more independent, and differ
in numerous points from the ' Gesta,' but afford
few emendations on it. For example, let us compare the beginning of Gilo's narrative, namely, the
account of the siege of Nicæa, with that given by
eye-witnesses.[98] The town was surrounded, and the
whole army of the Crusaders united before the
walls, from the very beginning. But we know from
Raymond, who was himself present, that the Provençals only arrived there on the fifteenth day of
the siege. We learn from Fulcher, who was with
Robert of Normandy, that the northern French,
with the exception of Hugo, reached the camp
several weeks after the Provençals. At the very be-

---

[97] Page 251: a number of new pilgrims flocked together to
Antioch. Page 261: the mention of Rambaud at the storm-
ing of Jerusalem (compare likewise Rad. c. 119). Page 263:
Guichu, the lion-slayer, was the second to scale the walls of Jerusalem.   [98] Gilo, p. 214.

ginning of the siege, says Gilo, the pilgrims saw that
it was essential to cut off the water communication
from the besieged ; for this reason a fleet was built,
which compelled the besieged to offer to surrender.
Such an offer was certainly made, not •to the Crusaders, but to the Emperor Alexius, and took place
before the pilgrims thought of occupying the water
of the lake.[99]   Gilo has it that the attempt
made by the Sultan to succour the town followed
upon this.   On its failure, the inhabitants lost all
heart, and gave up the town to the Greek Emperor.
It is however well known that this skirmish occurred quite at the beginning of the siege, on the
same day on which Count Raymond reached the
Christian camp, and that Nicæa offered a resistance that lasted four weeks longer.   We see the
gross errors in facts and dates contained in this
narrative : how ill such a beginning promises for
the rest of the narrative ! And indeed in the course
of the work there is little to induce us to alter

[99] The manuscript from which Duchesne had the work printed,
contains an interpolation which is not without interest for
the dissemination of these statements.   The negotiations are
broken off, war is renewed; at night the Christians capture
a messenger, who was to announce the approach of the Sultan,
and so on, as we may read the story in Albert of Aix; only it
is written in hexameters instead of in prose. It is an addition
entirely void of sense, as Raymond's absence is noticed, and the
Count is at the same time named as one of the attacking party.

our judgment. Wherever the author does give more accurate accounts, such for instance as that of the occurrences before Antioch, and elsewhere, his narrative, if not exactly a copy of the 'Gesta,' follows that authority very closely.[100]

That Gilo drew largely from oral tradition is obvious in itself, but still more so when we consider the work of the monk Robert. The connection between Gilo and Robert is evident on the slightest comparison; but, as far as I know, Michaud was the first to point this out. He does not hesitate to consider Robert's narrative as the source whence Gilo took his history.[102] According to Michaud, Robert inserted into the text of the 'Gesta,' which was his original, a number of events which he himself witnessed. These were again borrowed by Gilo, who made fresh additions to them, of very little value. But if we take any subject from these three authors, for instance, the siege of Nicæa, we shall perceive that Gilo and the 'Gesta' give two completely different versions; and that Robert has attempted to combine the two with a very bad result.[103] We can follow Robert step by step in this process, and can see how the

---

[100] Compare the single combats before Antioch.
[102] See his Bibliothèque des Croisades, article Gilo.
[103] Gesta, p. 5. Gilo, p. 218. Rob. p. 39.

attempt to combine two such different accounts involves him in hopeless contradictions, and how he tries to reconcile them.

If we cut out the information derived from the 'Gesta Francorum' and from Gilo, there remains but a small amount of original matter belonging to Robert the Monk, at the very most about five passages, and those not very credible;[104] we thus see that the position of this writer, who has been placed on an equality with the author of the 'Gesta,' and with Raymond of Agiles, and far above the other copiers of those two eye-witnesses, is a very unimportant one.

According to common report, the monk Robert became abbot of the convent of St. Remy, at Rheims; here he was subjected to severe censure by the abbot Bernard of Marmoutiers, who was his superior. This resulted in his deposition, by the Archbishop Manasses of Rheims. Robert appealed

---

[104] The history of a Provençal apostate who joined Kerboga, which is to be found with some variations in other authors. Page 66: countless numbers of heavenly warriors fight with the Crusaders against Kerboga. Page 70: the remark that Raymond was quite in the right in the quarrel with Antioch; and further, the account of the last consultation of the princes in Kafertah. Page 73: the notice that Anselm of Ripemont had been a zealous protector of the church at Anchin, which is confirmed by Sigeb. Gemblac, A.D. 1099. Lastly, page 75: the totally unfounded assertion that Baldwin had been with the forces before Jerusalem.

to Pope Urban II., received a favourable judgment in Rome in the year 1097, went to the Crusades, and was present at the capture of Jerusalem. Spite however of the Papal judgment, he could never obtain a restoration to his former dignity; but he was made instead the prior of Senuc, where he wrote his history of the Crusades. He lost the latter preferment by a judgment of Pope Calixtus II. and died in 1122. For all these circumstances we have contemporary authority. There are the acts of the Council of Rheims[105] which deposed him, letters from himself, from two archbishops concerning him,[106] the acts of the Council of Poitiers which acquitted him; but for his participation in the Crusades, and the most important of all, the composition of his history, we can discover nothing of the sort. In all those documents there is no mention of these facts, and no other writer alludes to them. The most ancient author who mentions his pilgrimage is, I believe, Blondus, in his 'Decades';[107] Marlot, in his 'Metropolis Remensis,' is the first to speak

---

[105] In Mansi, in the supplement to 1097, as well as in Marlot, in a passage we shall give.

[106] His letter to the Bishop of Arras in Baluze, Miscell., iv. 315. A letter of Hugo of Lyons, in Martene, Coll. Ampl., in the Chron. Adag. p. 998. A letter of Baldric of Dòl, in Duchesne, iv. 276.

[107] Decad. ii. i. 4. Bongars cites him in his preface.

N 2

of him as an author "in cellâ Senucensi;"[108] but, until proof is afforded for both these assertions, I see no certainty, either of the identity of the abbot of St. Remy with the author of the history by the monk Robert, nor of the pilgrimage of the one or the other to the Holy Land, whether they be one, or two different persons. If we examine the writings before us with reference to these points, the evidence is doubtful rather than affirmative. The author calls himself only a monk, not an abbot: he speaks of St. Remy, and not of Senuc, as the spot where he wrote his work.[109] But the work was written after 1118,[110] when the abbot Robert had long lived at Senuc. There is only one passage which leads one to suppose the author ever to have been in Jerusalem, and that by no means proves his participation in the Crusades.[111]

Be this as it may, the question is unimportant, considering the small value which we attach to his

[108] Tom. ii. 221. Mabillon, Ann. iv. 347, quotes from it, the Gallia Christ. Nova, ix. 230. The Hist. Litt. de la France follows him (x. 323); also Oudin, de Script. Eccles. ii. 862, quotes Marlot, and Joannis follows him in his statement. From the Hist. Litt. it has passed into all modern histories. Trithem and Fabricius give no further particulars.

[109] In præf. apol.   [110] As Gilo is used.

[111] He says, p. 78,—"A quodam Turco qui hæc" (on the battle near Ascalon) "postea in Jerusalem retulit habuimus." I believe that he, like Ekkehard, was at Jerusalem at some later period.

work, which is a compilation without any peculiar interest, even supposing it to have been composed in the camp of the Crusaders.[112]

IV. FULCHER OF CHARTRES.

The ' Gesta Peregrinantium Francorum,' by Fulcher of Chartres, may be divided, according to its method and its value, into several parts. A brief account of the author's life will furnish the best clue to a criticism of his work.

Fulcher, a chaplain from Chartres, took the cross in the year 1095, and joined the army of Count Robert of Normandy and Stephen of Blois, with which he marched through Apulia and Greece, and reached the camp before Nicæa in June, 1097. He remained with the bulk of the crusading army until its arrival in Meerasch, and went thence to Edessa with Count Baldwin, who then commenced his enterprise against that town.[113] Up to this point his information is good, and frequently most important ; both on particular facts and on the general aspect of affairs. I allude more particularly to his account of the journey through Italy and Greece.[114] He here

[112] His account of the Council of Clermont is however in a better style : here he speaks as an eye-witness.
[113] Pages 383, 389, 400, in Bongars.
[114] Pages 384, 385.

shows the incorrectness of the impression that the armies had met together in the west of Europe, and that great masses of them had marched towards the East in regularly organized bodies. "We wandered," says Fulcher, "as we could, in April, May, June, until October, wherever we could obtain supplies." Adhemar had appointed Constantinople as the general rendezvous.[114] Moreover Fulcher's narrative of the march from Dorylæum to Eikle is important, and very attractive, from the great descriptive powers of the writer. His account of the occurrences in Edessa is conclusive, as he was the only eye-witness.[115] It agrees in the main with that of Matthew Eretz of Edessa, who is the next best authority; whereas both Albert of Aix and Guibert have followed quite different reports.[116]

Unfortunately Fulcher breaks off here, and turns his attention to the main body of the crusading army, which then seemed the point of most interest. It is scarce credible that a contemporary, living at the distance of only a few days' journey, should receive such absurdly false accounts. What reliance can be placed on these traditions, when even in a

---

[114] Chron. Podiense, in the Hist. Gen. de Languedoc, ii. 8.

[115] Fulcher, pp. 388, 389.

[116] Fulcher, p. 389; Matthew Eretz, in the Notices, etc., de la Biblio. du Roi, ix.; Alb. p. 222 *et seq.*; Guibert, 496.

few score years they circulated in the distant West in such wild and uncertain forms? The chronological sequence of events is lost; the accuracy of the narrative disappears, and a blind enthusiasm finds vent in miraculous stories. Even here however some few passages are important: such as the account of Tancred's conquest of Bethlehem, which checks a different report given by Albert of Aix; Tancred's plundering of the Temple, and the subsequent negotiations, which are supported by the testimony of Radulph against Albert.[117]

Fulcher remained in Jerusalem, after a short absence, until the death of Godfrey of Bouillon at Edessa. He then accompanied Baldwin I. to Palestine, and remained there with the King in the same capacity as he had previously been with the Count.[118] From this time his work is most important. Here, where all other eye-witnesses fail, his account is trustworthy, and often full. Let us attempt from this point to determine its general character.

It is obvious, in the first place, that the author by no means intended to write a history: the work is in reality a diary of his own life, with all the circumstances as they happened; in which state Guibert saw it in the year 1108 or 1110, in the West;

---

[117] Alb. p. 281; Rad. c. 135 *et seq.*
[118] Pages 400, 403.

though it does in fact come down to 1127. He records what personally concerns himself, and devotes to it more or less space, according to his own individual taste. I will select the first example that occurs to me (to which many might be added); the passage in which he relates Baldwin's taking possession of Jerusalem. He begins with a vivid description of the march from Edessa: "Collegit exercitulum suum,"—two hundred knights and seven hundred infantry; they go from city to city; the Prince of Tripolis sends bread, wine, wild honey, and mutton to their tents; at the same time he tells them of an ambush prepared for them near Berytus. This they found terribly confirmed, for the narrow and wild passes were occupied by the Saracens. He then describes the battle, and how the Christians were at first unsuccessful. "We were ill at ease," says he; "we affected courage, but we feared death. I wished myself home again at Chartres or Orleans." Luckily, however, they fought their way through, and Fulcher devotes many pages to a description of the happy manner in which they brought this adventure to a close. They subsequently reached Kaiphas, which then belonged to Tancred, who, as is well known, was one of the leaders of the opposition against Baldwin's succession. Fulcher enters into no explanation of

the relations between the two princes. He only
says shortly: "We did not enter Kaiphas, because
Tancred was then at enmity with us; but," he continues, "Tancred being then absent, his people sold
us bread and wine outside the walls, for they considered us as brothers, and were anxious to see us."
And a little further on: "As we approached Jerusalem, the clergy and the laity came forth to meet
the King in solemn procession; likewise came the
Greeks and the Syrians, with crosses and candles,
who received him with joy and honour and loud
shouts, and escorted him to the Church of the Holy
Sepulchre." After this the narrative again becomes
very meagre. "The Patriarch Dagobert was not
present; he had been slandered to Baldwin, and
bore him a grudge; wherefore he sat apart on Mount
Sion until his malice was forgiven." Not one word
explaining the cause and purport of this quarrel.
No one could suppose that the whole existence
of the Christian kingdom in the East was at that
moment at stake; nor does he bestow more attention upon the King and his peculiar talent for government. He proceeds:—"We remained six days
in Jerusalem, rested ourselves, and the King made
his first arrangements; then we started again."
Then follows a detailed and most lively journal of
his travels through the whole southern portion of

the kingdom. Later we find a short narrative of the Second Crusade. He was in 1102 with the King during an expedition against Ascalon in Joppa. "There," he says, "he met several knights who were waiting for a favourable wind, in order to return as speedily as possible to France. They had lost their horses the year before, together with all their baggage, during a march through Rumania."[119]

Fulcher's work has been much used, both by his contemporaries and by subsequent writers. We have already mentioned that Guibert knew the book. Spite of his obligations to Fulcher, Guibert speaks contemptuously of him, without however bringing any specific charge against him. Bartholf de Nangiejo was more grateful: he compiled the 'Gesta Expugnantium Hierusalem,' distinctly acknowledging his authority.[120] Many passages are taken from the 'Gesta Francorum,' not exactly word for word, but they betray their origin. Others, again, are evidently fabulous tales, having no pretence to authenticity. The work is in no way important.[121]

---

[119] There are many similar accounts of other things that happened, of the products of the country, foreign customs, etc. ; page 401, on the water of the Dead Sea ; page 407, on the church music in Jerusalem, etc.

[120] In Bongars, p. 561. The name is in Barth. p. 500.

[121] It reaches from 1095 to 1106.

We must also here only mention the 'Secunda Pars Historiæ Hierusalem,' by Liziard, of Tours, embracing the years 1100–1124;[122] its contents are of no value.

The work of William of Malmesbury is mixed up much more with foreign and even fabulous matter.[123] It is instructive only as regards the family of Godfrey of Bouillon, and the early and subsequent career of Robert of Normandy.[124] The rest of his book, where he ventures to quit Fulcher, does not belong to an historical account of the Crusades.

The ecclesiastical history of Ordericus Vitalis is beyond measure more important. He compiled the history of the Crusades partly out of Fulcher, partly out of Baldric ; but added a number of curious details, which are not all equally authentic, but are nevertheless interesting and important.[125] This part of his work, and indeed the whole of it, contains a vast mass of local information. The several facts are characteristic and life-like ; and, when taken as a whole, are of the greatest value towards

[122] In Bongars, p. 594.

[123] In his ' Gesta Regum Angliæ,' p. 131 et seq., in Savile.

[124] Page 142, 151, and in other places.

[125] Lappenberg, in his History of England, ii. 337, gives the most instructive account of his work. In comparison with this the earlier statements in the Hist. Litt. de la France, are very unimportant.

obtaining a knowledge of the state of things at that
time. He gives the most valuable information concerning Peter the Hermit,[126] Otho of Bayeux, and
his death,[127] and many noblemen of Normandy and
of the north of France.[128] No one shows more completely what view the people who lived in those
times, took of the whole Crusade.[129] Capefigue says
of him,[130] that he was "le conteur d'anecdotes ; il
règne dans toutes ses pages un esprit romanesque,
qui se ressent déjà des trouvères et de la poésie."

This applies only to some part of his book : the
reports which came to him from the East bore
that impress. They tell of pagan princesses who are
unable to withstand the charms and merits of the
celebrated Christian heroes :[131] the pilgrims give
battle not only to Turks and Saracens, but to
hosts of lions and tigers :[132] the Lord blinds the
eyes of the unbelievers, so that the Christians may
destroy them at their ease.[133]   In the midst of such
stories we suddenly meet with facts of real import-

[126] Page 723.
[127] Pages 646, 660, 664.
[128] Concerning the Grantmenils, p. 707.
[129] Pages 700–701 ; above all, pp. 718–719.
[130] Hugues Capet, iv. 232.
[131] In Edessa, p. 745. The Daughter of Dalmian, p. 796.
The daughter of Bagi-Sijans, who was willing to become a
Christian for the sake of eating pork.
[132] Page 790.   [133] Page 758.

ance, which could only come from well-informed eye-witnesses, and which throw light on the most important events of the Crusades.[134] In short, we see that the author made inquiries in all directions; much of his information was undoubtedly derived from men who took part in affairs; truth and fable flowed in upon him; all of which he reproduces faithfully, and without comment. Instructive as this author is, when properly used, his narrative would mislead those who are not capable of distinguishing these two elements.

In conclusion, I will mention in this place the fragment of French history in the four$_{th}$ volume of Duchesne :[135] though the narrative is too general to be traced entirely to Fulcher. It gives some details as to the conquest of Jerusalem, which are only to be found in Bartholf.[136] The statement, that Godfrey refused the name and ensigns of royalty in a city where his Saviour had been crowned with thorns, is first mentioned in this fragment. Moreover, the merit of this humility is given, not to

[134] On the strength of the Christian army against Kerboga, p. 741. On the negotiations before Ascalon, p. 758. On the Anglo-Saxons in the East, pp. 725, 778.

[135] Page 85.

[136] E. g. that Tancred had stormed the town solely for his own purposes. According to the general acceptation, he was with Godfrey on the tower.

Godfrey himself, but to the barons who surrounded him.[137]

There are three authors of the twelfth century who have made use of Fulcher; but, from their entire want of original matter, it is scarce worth while here to enter into their merits. Stenzal gives extracts from a work compiled from that of the monk Robert, with additions from Fulcher;[138] secondly, there is the Chronicle of Richard of Poitou,[139] who has taken his materials from Raymond of Agiles and from Fulcher, and often in a very confused manner.[140]   Lastly, there is the Chronicle of Bishop Sicard, of Cremona,[141] which contains some original but worthless notices concerning Peter the Hermit;[142] in other respects, it follows Fulcher word for word.[143]

[137] The usual version is to be found in William of Malmesbury, p. 143. Histor. Belli Sacri, c. 130. In the preface to the Assizes of Jerusalem, and in William of Tyre.

[138] Archiv für Deutsche Geschichtskunde, iv. p. 97. But it mentions Martene, in præf. ad Ekkehardum. It is of the date of 1145. I have seen a copy of it at Bonn.

[139] Muratori, Antiquit. Ital. vol. iv. p. 1058 et seq. The Hist. Litt. vol. xiii. p. 530, gives sufficient information on the author.

[140] It gives the most contradictory accounts of the Holy Lance, one by the side of the other, without remark.

[141] Murat. Script. vii. 586 et seq.

[142] Ad annum 1084, ex cod. Ertensi.

[143] Pertz, in his Archiv, vii. 543, gives a copious account of a copy in Lambert Florid.

The true, primitive sources, the narratives of eye-witnesses, here cease. We possess narratives written by individual members of the three nations which formed the main body of the crusading army. The parallel which we drew between the Normans and the Provençals, may be extended to the Lorrainers. Raymond of Agiles is important for Provençal matters, but is far inferior to the 'Gesta' as regards a right understanding of the Crusades; and the heroes of the two works, Bohemund and Count Raymond of Toulouse, may be said to stand in the same relation towards each other as the works themselves. In the same manner, Fulcher's value rises and falls with the position occupied by the Lorraine princes. During the march, he gives only a few details which are of any interest, but afterwards, with regard to Baldwin I., he takes the first place. Bohemund was then a prisoner, Raymond of Toulouse was involved in difficulties with the Greeks, and thus the King of Jerusalem found himself the undisputed head of all the Christian possessions in the East.

V. Rodolph of Caen.

The two authors whom we shall next mention, Rodolph and Ekkehard, were not themselves actually present at the Crusades. Nevertheless, we may class them among the original sources, in the proper sense of the word, since they describe, of their own knowledge, that which immediately preceded and followed the Crusades, and since both of their works contain accounts of men who bore a part, and an important part, in those enterprises.

Rodolph was born at Caen about the year 1080, entered Bohemund's service in 1107, and was present at the siege of Dyrrachium. Soon afterwards he went into Asia, and accompanied Tancred on his march to relieve Edessa.[144] He remained attached to Tancred's person, and wrote his book between the years 1112 and 1118, from information given to him orally by that prince.[145] The chief topic is Tancred, and his great qualities. Rodolph is an enthusiastic admirer, but he is not a partisan. His narrative is absolutely essential to a knowledge of Tancred's character. Moreover, Rodolph has a strictly historical feeling, in spite of the poetical form which his work occasionally assumes. His eloquence carries him away: he revels in images, antitheses, and climaxes, but for all this

[144] The quotations appertaining to this stand together in the prefaces of Marténe and Durand. That which is there mentioned relating to his subsequent fate, notwithstanding it has been so constantly repeated, cannot be proved.

[145] He writes after Tancred's death in 1112, and dedicates it to the Patriarch Arnulf, who died in 1118.

he does not lose sight of the real character of events.

We shall sooner judge of the individual importance of his work, when we consider how it was written. Rodolph himself tells us in his preface,[146] that Tancred had never expressly desired him to write his history, nor had he ever given him information with that view. What we find in Rodolph, therefore, can only have been obtained from the chance recollections of the Prince, as conversation brought them out; the anecdotes were naturally mere fragments, and the connecting them together was entirely Rodolph's concern. As far as regards the sequence of events, or a perspicuous view of affairs in general, Rodolph's work can have no claim to be considered as an immediate authority We must also distinguish between these fragments All those which immediately concern Tancred, his views and his actions, are entirely worthy of belief. To the latter, Rodolph was an actual eyewitness, and there is no reason to doubt the truth of his statements with regard to the former. We wish we could say the same, of the rest of his narrative. The events recorded are of two kinds; those which Tancred had no better means of knowing than any soldier in his army;—the visible progress

[146] In præf.

of a battle, the spot where a combat took place, the date of any occurrence; or those which Tancred's rank and position in the army gave him peculiar opportunities of learning;—the plan of an attack, negotiations among the princes, and the like. For this latter class of facts, Rodolph is clearly again a perfectly trustworthy authority; the only regret is, that they are not more numerous. The rest of his narrative cannot be placed in the same rank with that of the 'Gesta' or of Raymond, as his information is always at second-hand. Each fact must be subjected to a searching criticism.

Let us endeavour to explain our meaning by an example; for instance, the siege of Antioch.[147] He first describes the position of the Christian army and its several bodies. His statements have received no attention, since they disagree with those of Albert of Aix and William of Tyre; and excite our mistrust by being mixed up with subsequent events. Notwithstanding this, I do not hesitate to prefer the report of a commander on such a subject to all others. This opinion is justified by the extreme care with which Rodolph explains his plan of attack, without regard to the chronological sequence of events. When he describes the several battles fought by his hero, I look upon his account of them as equal

[147] Chapter 46.

to that of an eye-witness. Then follows a whole
series of events, all probably very correct and accurate, but for us utterly useless, since we cannot
reduce them to the same order as that in which
they are given by other authorities. As to the capture of the city, his testimony is decisive. No one
can lay claim to higher credibility as to the treachery of Firuz and the negotiations that preceded
it, than the cousin of Bohemond, who derived his
knowledge immediately from that prince.

Rodolph himself is quite conscious that the
manner in which he got his information, and the
order in which he places events, have no reference to each other. During the whole course of
his book there is a want of historical proportion.
Some events and characters are described with excessive diffuseness, while an important measure, or
a whole period, is dismissed with a few words. In
many cases he appears altogether to lose the thread
of his narrative, either in elaborate and dull descriptions or in long-winded discussions; while he
deals in the most arbitrary way with the detail of
facts. As an example of this we may compare his
account of the quarrel between Bohemond and St.
Giles about Antioch, with that of the other authorities.[148] His details, and above all the order in

[148] Chapter 99.

which he relates them, differ entirely from those of
Raymond and of the 'Gesta;' but we soon perceive
that he paid no attention to details ;—that he wished
to represent one general feature,—the antagonism between the natures of the Normans and the Provençals; and that he selected and arranged his materials with that view. We are obliged to him for
the principle thus indicated, but we know where to
get our facts.from better sources. It is the same
with the speeches which he places in the mouths of
his heroes, and with the letters which he inserts;
they are one and all, as is clearly proved by their
style, his own invention, and merely give us an insight into the author's mode of thought.

The only copy of this book, that I know, is that in
the 'Historia Belli Sacri;' taken, according to the
opinion of the editor, from the manuscript of the
author. This is important on account of some
marginal notes, which thus acquire the same authority as the text.[149]

VI. Ekkehard of Urach.

The productions of Ekkehard as an historian, as
well as his connection with the Chronicle of Auersberg and the Saxon annalists (hitherto quite pro-
blematical),[150] have lately been made perfectly clear

[149] Pertz, Archiv, p. 524, confirms this.
[150] The extracts belonging to this are to be found in Eccard,

by the researches of Pertz.[151] We may likewise, on
the same authority, form a safe judgment on Ekkehard's 'History of Jerusalem.'

Among the works of Ekkehard, concerning which
Pertz has given us information, we will first allude
to his 'Chronicle of the World,' down to the year
1106. At first it only came down to the year 1100,
but after the author's pilgrimage to the Holy Land,
he enriched the original work with many additions,
and continued it down to the year 1106. These
additions have reference entirely to the history of
the Crusades, and were partly made by the author
while he was in Palestine.[152]

Some years afterwards Ekkehard remodelled this
work for Abbot Erkembert of Corvey, with a special
view to the instruction of the Abbot concerning the
Holy Land. The account of the Crusades was extracted from the continuous narrative of the Chronicle, and, with some alterations, appended to the
end of the work.[153]

Lastly, there was a new edition of the Chronicle in 1125; the work was brought down to that
year, and the text in many places altered. We

Corpus Hist. Medii Ævi, n. 10. Martene, Coll. Ampl. t. iv. præf.,
n. 1-5, t. v. p. 512. Also in the Archiv für Deutsche Geschichtskunde, i. 397, ii. 309, iii. 590, v. 158.
[151] Archiv, vii. 469.   [152] Archiv, p. 473.
[153] Archiv, pp. 482-484.

therefore possess four different versions ;[154] that of
1100, that of 1106, the version arranged for Erkembert, and lastly that of 1125. All of them are
open to our inspection and comparison : the first,
in the copy of the Saxon chronicler ; the third, in
Martene's collection and in the copy of the Saxon
annalist ; the fourth, in the copy of the Chronicle
of Auersberg. Let us see whence they drew their
materials, and what light they severally throw upon
the Crusade.

The information given by the Saxon chronicler[155]
is far inferior in minuteness and importance to all the
others. The origin of the Crusade is only slightly
indicated, and the narrative is singularly meagre
until we come to the siege of Nicæa. From this
time it is somewhat more detailed, but no measure
is observed. Some of the statements are to be
found nowhere else; while many others want only
confirmation to be of the greatest value towards a
knowledge of what really took place. Fortunately
this confirmation is possible. The source whence his
statements are taken word for word, has come down
to us, and is in the highest degree authentic. It is
the Report or letter addressed to Pope Paschal II.,

---

[154] Archiv, p. 499. Further remarks are in Riedel, Nachrich-
ten von Havelberger Handschriften, pp. 7, 11.

[155] Ad annum 1096.

on the progress and issue of the Crusades, down to August, 1099, by Godfrey, Raymond, the two Roberts, and Archbishop Dagobert. This Report was preserved by Dodechin, and has been often quoted, but has never, so far as I know, been applied in this manner. Ekkehard has neither omitted nor added anything, he has scarcely altered a single word. I see not the slightest reason to doubt the authenticity of this document. Ekkehard himself quotes it in his work,[156] and Dodechin inserts it, after repeating Ekkehard's annals of the preceding years. If we examine the several statements, we find them quite unprejudiced, and exempt from official exaggeration, omission, or misrepresentation; always excepting the exaggerated statement of the numbers at the battle of Ascalon. The contents are therefore most important.

The edition of the year 1106 differs but little, according to Pertz, from the work written for the Abbot Erkembert. The time when it was composed does not appear to me so certain as Pertz and Martene think. It was clearly written after the year 1108, since the author calls himself the Abbot of Urach; but it is doubtful whether it was so late as 1117,[157] for Ekkehard speaks of the taking of Accon

[156] "Sicut epistola docet, à Comite Ruperto delata." Ursp. copies this; the Ann. Saxo omits it.

[157] The ground for this assertion is, that Erkembert, for whose

and the marriage of Baldwin I., as having just occurred.[158] The history of the Crusade in this copy
is much enlarged. Ekkehard has also shown much
research both as to the preparations for the First
Crusade, and its commencement. It is evident that
he drew his information from those who were actually
present,[159] and he may be considered as a leading
authority for the enterprises of Peter, Volkmar, Gottschalk, and Emicho. In the year 1101, a book fell
into his hands at Jerusalem, which, as he says, accurately described both time and place of the three
years' war.[160] He introduced into the text of the
Report or letter above mentioned, numerous fragments from this book, the original of which is lost.
We must deplore its loss, as the quotations he gives
prove it to have been a wholly independent and
useful addition to our other sources of information.[161]

information as to the pilgrimage he contemplated this book was
written, started on his journey in 1117. This, it is evident, is not
conclusive; Erkembert might have expressed his intention some
years before he actually set out on his pilgrimage.

[158] Page 533.

[159] As he also expressly asserts in one passage.

[160] Page 520. "Legimus Ierosolymæ libellum à loco præsenti
totam hujus historiæ seriem diligentissime prosequentem, pluri-
mos populi Dei per triennium labores in captæ Jerusalem lætis-
sima victoria concludentem."

[161] Compare p. 521, for Godfrey's battles in Constantinople;
p. 522, for the negotiations between Christians and Saracens.
Regard must also be had to his characteristic of Godfrey as
the ruler of the conquered land.

The most important new matter, however, is the latter portion of his work, in which the author gives an account of his own pilgrimage in the year 1101. He went part of the way with the main body of the army which met so calamitous an end in the summer of that year, in Asia Minor; his account of which is indispensable. On this matter he is to be considered in the light of an eye-witness; his descriptions are lucid, his judgment clear and free from passion; there is nothing brilliant and nothing deceptive.

Pertz mentions[162] that this chronicle contains fragments from Sigebert of Gembloux. I know not whether this applies to the rest of the work, but I do not see it in the part relating to the history of the Crusades. Sigebert has clearly much that is similar in his narrative, but only in fragments of the letter of the princes to Pope Paschal. As the whole of the subsequent narrative widely differs, it appears to me more probable that they both drew from the same original authority.[163] Extracts from Sigebert are also to be found in the fragment of the History of Jerusalem, which Martene has published *ad calcem Ekkehardi.*

The connection between the Saxon annalist and

[162] L. c. p. 483.

[163] Here, as in the following passages, I spare myself the trouble of quoting the texts. The identity is too obvious not to be seen at once.

this compilation of Ekkehard is still more evident.
The discrepancies between the two are very small,
and thoroughly unimportant. That which Ekkehard tells in a continuous narrative,[164] is divided by
the Saxon annalist according to years. Some few
things which Ekkehard assumes or repeats are corrected as to dates.[165] Peter the Hermit receives his
letter of credentials from Heaven, and the catalogue
of the princes is enriched with some new names.[166]

We now come to the fourth compilation of Ekkehard. It would appear, so far as we can judge
from the Chronicle of Auersberg, that little has been
altered in the history of the Crusades; at any rate,
nothing that can in any way modify the real view of
events. We must observe, in reference to the Auersberg Chronicle, that indications of a double compilation are obvious. In the years 1096–1097, the

---

[164] It is not quite clear in Pertz whether the history of the
Crusades, even in this copy directed to Erkembert, was taken
out of its regular place and transferred to the end. He says so,
in general terms, of the amended copy of the 'Chronicle of the
World,' p. 482; but at p. 484, he calls the 'Hierosolymita' a
somewhat altered repetition of the history of the Crusades. My
account refers only to Martene's edition.

[165] For instance, the Catalogue of the Princes, the Embassy of
the Egyptians before Antioch.

[166] The narrative of the devastations of the pilgrims in Bohemia
is added, from Cosmos, Prag. ad annum 1096. We also find here,
as in the Chron. Ursperg., the statement that Archbishop Rot-
hard had protected the Jews in Mayence.

narratives of the Saxon chronicler are repeated; German affairs occupy the year 1098; in 1099 the author briefly mentions the conquest of Jerusalem, and adds:—" Concerning this divine undertaking I intend to add some matter." He then repeats the whole book of Ekkehard, as contained in Martene's edition : a circumstance which does not raise our opinion of the Chronicler, as the two compilations of Ekkehard contain contradictions which are here carelessly left side by side.[167]

Ekkehard's work has been frequently used and copied during the Middle Ages. I shall here mention the transcripts made in the twelfth century alone, without attempting to explain their connection with each other. There are sundry short notices from annals, which state only that, at the instigation of Peter the Hermit, a countless mass of people flocked to Jerusalem, and wrested that city from the hands of the heathen, after having forcibly converted the Jews. These are the *Annales Wirciburgenses, Brunvilarenses,* and *Hildesheimenses.*[168] They all communicate the same facts, and Pertz has called attention to the use made of Ekkehard.[169]

---

[167] Concerning the destruction of a host of pilgrims in Hungary.

[168] The two first in the Monum. t. ii. ; the last in t. v.

[169] In præf. We see the origin clearly enough, when we compare the Annal. Saxo ("Petrus in finibus emersit Hispaniæ," etc.) Dodechin, who is somewhat shorter, and these Annals.

Otto of Friesingen, in the seventh book of his Chronicle,[170] has extracted largely from Ekkehard, making however many alterations as to order, (which are not always improvements) and many additions. The best known is the frequently quoted but erroneous statement, that Urban II. had been reinstated at Rome by the aid of the Crusaders.[171]

The Chronicle of St. Pantaleone likewise copies the narrative of the Crusades entirely from Ekkehard, with some variations which show that the Ursperg Chronicle had been likewise used.[172] Nothing more need be said of this, nor of the German translation.

Godfrey of Viterbo also follows Ekkehard in his 'Pantheon.'[173] He also has made no additions worth mentioning.

The narrative of Helmold, in his Hist. Slav., deserves somewhat more notice.[174] It is quite clear

[170] vii. c. 2.

[171] Even Stenzel, Fränk. Kaiser, ii. 160, accepts this; so does Gieselar Kirchengeschichte, ii. 2, p. 45, and quotes Fulcher as well as Otho as authorities; the two latter, however, state the real facts correctly.

[172] It contains the passage, "non modica quippe multitudo," etc., before the proposition, "legimus Hierosolymæ libellum," etc.

[173] Pages 338, 339, in Pistori, ii. I will remark here, that the work which Pertz found appended to the Nuremberg Codex of the same author must, according to the words given at p. 558 of Pertz, Archiv, vii., be Albert of Aix's, or an excerpt from him.

[174] Hist. Slav. i. 29 et seq.

that in his history of the Crusades he has followed Ekkehard, or one of his imitators. He, like Otto of Friesingen and Godfrey of Viterbo, condenses his original.

Lastly, we must mention Dodechin, who also abridges Ekkehard's narrative.[175]

On reviewing this series of copiers, we recognize a similar leaning in all of them, especially as regards Godfrey of Bouillon and Peter the Hermit. Their method of condensing is nearly identical. They copy the whole passage about Peter the Hermit *in extenso*,[176] and then compress into the smallestlimits what they have to say on the Crusade. They do not mention Godfrey of Bouillon, as Ekkehard does, as the Chief chosen in Jerusalem, but generally, as the leader of the army.

[175] Ad annum 1096 *et seq.*

[176] The only exceptions are Otto of Friesingen and Godfrey of Viterbo. They speak of Urban II. as the originator of the Crusade; in this they follow Ekkehard, who places Peter and Urban in their proper connection.

CHAPTER II.

ALBERT OF AIX.

BUT little is known of the remarkable Chronicle which now engages our attention.[1] The author is named on the titlepage Albert, or Alberich,[2] Canonicus Aquensis Ecclesiæ, but it is not quite certain whether Aix in Provence or Aix-la-Chapelle is intended. It has been much discussed, but in truth no progress whatever has been made towards a solution of the question.[3] Latterly, and as I think with justice, the opinion is in favour of Aix-la-Chapelle.[4] At the very beginning of his book the author calls France the Kingdom in the West, which would

---

[1] I may perfectly dispense with noticing the early researches concerning Albert of Aix. None of them contain any description either of his person or of the sources from which he drew. But the sum of all the traditional opinions about him was the utmost veneration.

[2] See Bongars, in præf.

[3] The Hist. Litt. de la France, x. 277, contains something on this subject.

[4] For example, Michaud and Capefigue.

seem to point more to Aix-la-Chapelle than to Aix
in Provence.[5] There is one apparent piece of local
information, which has been considered as decisive,
but upon which I do not lay so much stress as upon
the general tendency of his views of affairs, which
admits of no doubt.[6] The traditions and interests
of Germany and Lorraine predominate through the
whole book. Godfrey of Bouillon is avowedly the
hero of it,[7] and we shall have frequent occasion to
mark the influence of this circumstance on the tone
of the narrative. It is true that all this merely affords a greater probability, but no real proof, of the
German origin of Albert.

The same uncertainty prevails likewise as to the
period when Albert lived and wrote his work. The
last events he describes relate to the year 1121. The
only matter that can be maintained with any certainty is, that the work must have been begun shortly
after that date, as the author in many places refers to
the direct information he received from eye-witnesses.
For other questions of importance, such as the nation of the author, and the credibility of his book,
we have no evidence, save that afforded by the

---

[5] 1, 2: "Amiens, quæ est in occidente de regno Francie."

[6] vi. 36.

[7] "Incipit liber primus expeditionis Hierosolymitanæ urbis, ubi
Ducis Godefridi inclyta gesta narrantur, cujus labore et studio
Civitas Sancta sanctæ Ecclesiæ filiis est restituta."

work itself.   Let us therefore examine into the
origin of the narrative, so as, if possible, to come to
some conclusion concerning it.

On many occasions Albert himself quotes the oral
testimony of eye-witnesses which altogether forms
a considerable mass of authorities.[8]   He repeatedly
speaks of several persons who communicated these
facts to him.   They touch upon the most various
circumstances; one refers to the progress of Gottschalk through Hungary; six relate to events which
befell the great crusading army; and the last describes the defeat in the year 1101, in Asia Minor.
The character, however, of all, is similar; the author
relates the strangest and most wonderful things,
for the truth of which he appeals in the most
express manner to his authorities.   In the first,
unheard-of cruelties;[9] in two others, the wonderful prowess of Godfrey of Bouillon;[10] further, the
frightful distress of the army in the Phrygian desert,[11] and at Antioch;[12] the splendour of the Temple at Jerusalem;[13] the miraculous preservation of
the Christians at Ascalon;[14] and lastly, the fabulous
circumstances that occurred at the defeat of 1101,
when for miles round, the earth was covered with

[8] Bongars, præf., mentions some, but not all.
[9] i. 24.   [10] ii. 33; iii. 65.   [11] iii. 2.
[12] iv. 55.   [13] vi. 24.   [14] vi. 50.

gold and silver vessels, while the blood of the slain flowed in mighty streams.[15] Such are the narratives which he particularly calls upon us to believe, and which he details with the profoundest conviction of their truth. They are not exactly miracles, or proofs of the direct interference of God; but the perfection of human heroism, and the display of extraordinary splendour mixed with extreme misery. Such are the things which especially interest him, and stimulate him to seek for information from all quarters.

These sentiments invariably appear wherever the author's book is opened. That all human virtues were developed to the highest degree by the Crusades; that it was impossible to conceive greater heroes and more extraordinary deeds; such were his convictions, such the chief motives to his researches. "For a long time," says he,[16] "was I filled, by the singular and wonderful things that I heard, with a longing passion to be one of this expedition, and to worship the Saviour at the Holy Sepulchre. But as this desire was not gratified, I will at any rate set down some things which

[15] viii. 21.

[16] "Diu multumque his usque diebus, ob inaudita et plurimum admiranda sæpius accensus sum desiderio ejusdem expeditionis. . . . . Temerario ausu decrevi saltem ex his aliqua memoriæ commendare, quæ auditu et revelatione nota fierent ab his qui præsentes affuissent."

were revealed orally to me by those who were present." If such be really the case, (and there is not the smallest doubt that it is so);[17] if he has drawn his narrative solely from oral sources, the work is a very remarkable one. No one can form an idea of the amount and the variety of the materials, which succeed one another in an inexhaustible supply, with wonderful vividness and individuality. Whether he touches on the dream of Peter the Hermit, or on any period of the Crusades; whether he treats of Godfrey's or Baldwin's reign, or the events that occurred simultaneously at Antioch and Edessa; whether he narrates the general march of events, or enters into endless digressions, there is ever the same wealth of materials, the same graphic power of description. There is not a line of reflection; nor does he ever attempt to shorten or condense his narrative. The mass of the army hurries on, the armour gleams in the sunshine, the crimson banners wave; he distinguishes the several nations and their princes, and describes them in succession. Godfrey, Bohemund, the Bishop of Puy, and others, lead their hosts with a wise discipline. And now the enemy show themselves at a distance, on the brow of the mountain range, mounted on fleet horses and

---

[17] I need not go into details to show that he is not in perfect accord with any author that has come down to us.

galloping wildly about. Immediately ten Christian knights spring out of the ranks, and with inde-
scribable courage disperse sixty of the enemy; suc-
cours arrive to both parties; on both sides the numbers and the excitement increase. Lances are splin-
tered; the horses snort and foam; clouds of steam
hang over the battle-field; here a Provençal, there
a Lorrainer distinguishes himself; who knows not
the approved valour of the one, the early deeds of
piety of another, the strength of a third, renowned
at home and abroad? At length the Turkish ranks
are broken. Then follows the pursuit through
mountain and valley, over field and flood; gold
and silver, camels and horses, all that is precious,
becomes the spoil of the warriors of Christ.[18]
There is an unbroken series of incidents throughout
the book; the princes hold council together, the
ecclesiastics pray, the warriors fight, everything
is brought, with epical vividness, before our eyes.
The talent of the author in this respect is marvellous; no passage seems to be made up for
the occasion, or taken at second-hand; there is a
rapid flow of lively and pertinent descriptions. It
is impossible to deny that in this book we come
in contact with a host of people, who saw, suffered,

---

[18] Almost verbatim from several passages: *e. g.* the battle of
Dorylæum, the siege of Antioch, etc.

and acted as they describe; the voices not of one but of many nations, speak to us with a thousand tongues; we possess the picture of united Christendom, shaken to its foundations by an event which occupied the minds of all, from the highest to the lowest.

So far the work is admirable and worthy of all praise; though indeed very little is said that can determine the value of his testimony as an historian. The question, whether this profusion of details throws much light on the main object, whether the author can lay claim to trustworthiness himself, remains wholly untouched. If we examine Albert's mode of collecting and working up his materials, strong doubts will arise, which we shall find confirmed, not alone by instituting a comparison of this writer with other authorities, but by an examination of his own statements.

In every historical narrative, we require that the facts should be accurate as regards time and place; and that it should not destroy its own value by contradiction. Now it cannot be said of Albert that he fulfils this indispensable condition; he is regardless both of the external connection and internal consistency of his facts. The same free and easy method which aids his descriptive powers, hurries him along carelessly in the composition of his book,

and accident alone seems to determine whether the
separate narratives to which he gives currency, agree
one with the other, or are totally incompatible.
This consideration does not strike Albert; in a
hundred passages such discrepancies are obvious,
and it is worth our while to expose some of them.

For instance; he states that the Emperor Alexius
and Godfrey of Bouillon had waged war against
each other far into the month of January of 1097,
and only suspended hostilities during Christmas,
out of respect for that holy festival.[19] He connects
this with a second notice, in which he says, with
the most perfect indifference, that the Greek Emperor sent presents daily to the Lorraine knight,
from Christmas, when peace was concluded between
them, until Whitsuntide.[20]

He further relates that Robert of Normandy,
Stephen of Blois, and Eustace of Boulogne, were
with Alexius at Constantinople, while Godfrey was
laying siege to Nicæa.[21] Shortly afterwards he
states, from some other authority, that among various Crusaders, Stephen, Eustace, and others, had
assisted at the first attack on Nicæa.[22]

Again, after the battle of Dorylæum, which is
well known to have taken place on the 1st of
July, 1097, Albert proceeds in the following man-

[19] ii. 10.   [20] ii. 16.   [21] ii. 21.   [22] ii. 22.

ner :[23]—"When the hostile attacks ceased, the
Franks, at daybreak of the fourth day, proceeded
further, and passed that night on the summit of the
Black Mountain. When it was day, the whole army
descended into the valley Malabyumas, where the
day's march was brought to a close by the narrow-
ness of the pass, the number of the troops, and the
heats of *August*. As there was still another Sunday
of the same month, the thirst of the army increased,
and so forth." The utter indifference to all chronology is here too obvious to require any further examination.

He gives two totally different accounts close
upon each other, of the celebrated accident to Duke
Godfrey while hunting. According to one account,
Godfrey was wounded by a bear near Antiochetta,
and was only cured some months later; meanwhile,
his illness had a baneful effect upon the whole army.[24]
According to another version, the Turks immediately
attacked the Christian host. "Cædem et strages
operantur Boemundus et Godefridus : præterea illus-
cente die, dux Godefridus, Boemundus, et universi
capitanei, exurgentes armis loricis induti, iter in-
termissum iterare jubent,"—whereas Adhemar arranged the order of march, and Godfrey is named
as taking the command of the rear-guard.[25]

[23] iii. 1.   [24] iii. 3, 4, 58.   [25] iii. 35, 36.

He introduces the history of Sweyn, the son of the King of Denmark, in the following manner:— It must be observed that Sweyn followed in the wake of the main army, which was then carrying on the siege of Antioch. "After the capture of Nicæa, he had delayed his march a few days, was well received by the Emperor Alexius, and then went right through Rumania."[26] It appears to me obvious that here he follows two totally discrepant accounts; from the one the mention of Nicæa, from the other that of the Emperor is taken. As a whole, as the passage now stands, the statement is devoid of sense.

The author then proceeds to state that Sweyn was killed at Iconium by Kilidje Arslan. But subsequently it is related in detail how the Sultan, during the whole of the siege of Antioch, had remained in that city, or was with Kerboga at Mosul, in order to strengthen the opposition against the Christians.[27] It is manifest that the presence of the Sultan, as the chief enemy of the Christian pilgrims, was considered necessary everywhere; just as Godfrey, their best defender, was represented as fighting in spite of his wounds.[28]

Baldwin obtains dominion in Edessa; he so distinguishes himself, says Albert, that a brother

[26] iii. 54.   [27] iv. 2.   [28] iii. 31.

of Prince Constantine, of the name of Taphnuz, gives him his daughter to wife. It is subsequently mentioned, evidently from some other source, that he took to wife the daughter of the deceased Prince of Edessa.[29]

The embassy of Kilidje Arslan to Kerboga again involves Albert in remarkable chronological contradictions. Bagi-Sijan sends the former, some time in March, to ask for succour.[30] Kerboga says :— "Before six months are passed, I shall have exterminated these Christians from the face of the earth."[31] It is obvious that Albert follows some other authority when he subsequently says, that at the appointed day the Turkish army assembled ;[32] that it advanced, and in June arrived before Antioch.

In his account of the siege of Jerusalem he again gives accounts that do not agree. This is evident from a circumstance otherwise unimportant. During the siege the Christians draw a line of posts over the Mount of Olives. A little further on he describes the Mount of Olives as open, and the besieged as having free passage over it, which is obstructed only after some long subsequent occurrence.[33]

A Flemish pirate named Guinimer, altogether a

[29] iv. 6.

[30] iii. 62. The fight *in capite jejunii*, in February ; then another fight, and then the embassy.

[31] iv. 7.   [32] iv. 10.   [33] v. 46 ; vi. 12.

secondary personage, is mentioned several times in Albert's history. But even concerning him we have conflicting accounts. Guinimer takes Laodicea. In one place we are told that while the Christians besiege Antioch, the Greeks take Guinimer prisoner, and only release him at Godfrey's request. In another passage he was still ruling at Laodicea, when Antioch had become a Christian city, and delivered up Laodicea to Count Raymond of Toulouse.[34]

At the siege of Arsuf by Duke Godfrey, it is said that Gerhard D'Avesnes, who had fallen into the hands of the besieged, was tied to a mast, and thus exposed to the arrows of his co-religionists. Afterwards mention is made of the influence of the Christians in Ascalon: it was so great, says Albert, that the Emir, of his own accord, sent back to Jerusalem the two brothers Lambert and Gerhard D'Avesnes;—the very same whom we have seen tied to the mast.[35]

In the history of the Crusades of the year 1101, cases of this sort occur so frequently, that I cannot venture to determine whether they are to be attributed to discrepancies in the original reports, or only to Albert's carelessness. The dates also are full of contradictions. He says that the army of Anselm of Milan left Constantinople

[34] iii. 59; vi. 55.   [35] vii. 2, 5.

on the 9th of June, and encountered the Turks for the first time on the 23rd.[36] Immediately afterwards we find it stated that it marched for three weeks in perfect tranquillity.[37] It is related of the Count of Poitou that eight days after the reverse of the Count of Nevers,—that is, in the last days of August,—he reached the Bulgarian frontiers.[38] According to this he would have been in Constantinople towards the middle or the end of September; but in another place it is said that he spent five weeks in Constantinople, and then passed over into Asia at *the approach of harvest-time.*[39]

He is not more accurate in his topographical, than in his chronological statements. Anselm marches, in the two or three weeks above mentioned, from Nicomedia to Ancras (which means Ancyra[40]), then to Gargara (Gangra in Galatia, not far from Halys), after that many days "through Flagania;" at length Meraasch is mentioned, two days before the defeat, from which the fugitives escape to Synoplum.

---

[36] Lib. viii.: when Whitsuntide drew nigh (9th June), they first negotiated for some time with the Emperor, they then departed. Cap. 8: they stormed Ancras on the day before St. John's day (23rd June). • [37] Cap. 8, init.

[38] Cap. 31: "Actæ sunt hæ strages" (of the Count of Nevers) "mense Augusto." C. 34: "Modico dehinc intervallo, dierum scilicet octo, post hanc recentem stragem, Wilhelmus Comes terram Bulgarorum est ingressus."

[39] c. 36. [40] As Anna Comnena shows, p. 331.

The latter is clearly Sinope. But what lies between Sinope and Gangra is altogether fabulous; as the retreat takes place on the Pontus, there can be no question of Murasch on the Euphrates. It would not be worth while to bestow more trouble on the point; the last-mentioned place has probably slipped into the narrative from some other authority; in any case the whole scene is laid in a mythical region, like that which he describes as covered for miles round, after the defeat, with gold and silver.

We have already mentioned Anselm as having reached Ankras in three weeks. The Count of Nevers enjoys an easier march thither, and reaches Ankras from Kibotus in two days;[41] and that no one may confound this with a second town of that name (and in fact there is such a place at about two days' march distant), Albert expressly affirms its identity with the town occupied by Anselm.

But the confusion is the greatest with regard to the army of Poitou, which marches from Nicomedia to Stankona (Iconium), thence to Finimina (Philomelium),[42] then again to Recklei (Archalla),[43] in fact,

[41] Lib. viii. 27.

[42] A comparison with p. 253 clearly gives this interpretation. Alexius, it is there stated, went as far as Finimina in the summer of 1098. In the Appendix incerti auctoris ad calc. Radwici, Philomelium is called Finiminum. Ausbert calls it Vinimis.

[43] This is the present Erkle, on the borders of the then Arme-

in the most unaccountable manner, to all the points
of the compass. It is absolutely impossible to make
sense or connection out of this chaos of details.

In his eleventh book, Albert is entirely wrong by
one year, as any one may easily perceive. He places
the taking of Tripolis in the year 1108,[44] of Sidon
in 1109,[45] and the attack of Baldwin on Ascalon in
the year 1110.[46] In the same manner he mentions as
occurring in 1110, the attack of Maudud of Mosul,
against Antioch,[47] which actually took place in the
summer of 1111, as a reprisal upon Tancred for
the capture of Atsareb on Shrove Tuesday in 1111.[48]
This action of Tancred's is mentioned in another
place by Albert, from some other authority, with its
correct date. He arrives, by this means, at the
most extraordinary result; he inverts the sequence
of these events, and makes Tancred attack Atsareb
in revenge for the Turkish assault on Antioch.[49]

I think that this series of examples, taken from

nian Cilicia. This is proved by comparing iii. 3, where there is
a similar confusion.

[44] Cap. 1: " Eodem anno, quo Balduinus ab obsidione Sagittæ
rediit." This must be 1108. Cap. 3: " Eodem anno, mense
Martio," etc.; and so on to the fall of the town.

[45] Cap. 16 gives the year after the fall of Tripolis, which is
right.

[46] Cap. 35. The connection of the narrative gives us the date.

[47] Cap. 38.

[48] Kemaleddin, in Wilken, ii. 289; and Michaud, Bibl. iv. 28;
also Fulcher, p. 422.   [49] xi. 40.

various parts of Albert's book, and nearly all of them touching more or less important events which we learn chiefly from him, will be quite sufficient to show his method in the composition of his work. He himself, and we may add, the authorities of which he is the exponent, afford but little warranty for any order, connection, or unity in his work. The history is a series of countless fragments, which are wholly unconnected, and agree neither as to time nor place. When you think that you seize upon some connection, it eludes your grasp. The various and changing figures appear, and vanish again; and we are most certain to be led astray when they seem to be brought before us in the most distinct manner. If we select one particular fact out of the mass, and subject it to a critical examination, we shall at once perceive that the general character I have given is the true one. I have before alluded to the great detail, the endless particularity of his descriptions; we soon perceive how similar they are to one another, how little they assist us in coming to a knowledge of the real facts. The march of the army is described; how it advances through fruitful vales, and through trackless mountain passes; the enemy first attack, then fly, their cities are taken and plundered, and the like; but in what order the army marched, how long the campaign lasted, with what object it

was undertaken; on all these points we learn absolutely nothing, or if perchance something is said concerning them, it cannot be relied upon. The only
example which now occurs to me, is at page 227,
where Adhemar de Puy orders the army to march
upon Antioch; one part was to advance to the attack, while the other was to protect the rear. He
then proceeds to give a long list of the leaders of
both: Frenchmen and Italians, Germans and Normans, princes and knights, are so mixed together
that we need not the testimony of other authorities,
of which there is plenty, to induce us to disbelieve
the whole. It is exactly the same with the descriptions of battles, sieges, or diplomatic negotiations;
there is no lack of praise of the various heroes; the
arms gleam, the swords clash, the walls frown in
awful magnificence; but as to how the victory was
actually obtained, what was the plan of the attack
or of the defence, we are left entirely in the dark.

I purpose here, more for the sake of example than
of proof, to bring forward only a few cases :—Nicæa
has been taken, and one should imagine that an historian of such an event, especially one who enters
so much into detail as Albert, could have had no
more important object than to narrate exactly all
the negotiations with the Greeks, as to the position
of the town, and the impression it made upon

thé. Crusaders. In vain do we attempt to find even a mention of these matters; but in lieu of them we are treated to the edifying history of a nun, who, after going through a variety of adventures, was rescued from the Saracens, but, after all, could not be induced to leave her heathen paramour.

We will now follow the army in its march as far as Dorylæum. The authorities, which on this point are rare and conflicting, render any accurate cognizance of the route and halting-places difficult enough. We therefore place our hopes on Albert's well-known amplitude of detail, and we fully expect to find, by his assistance, an explanation of the names of the few places which are mentioned. He however describes with great prolixity how the army advanced for days between ravines and rocks, how it passed over a river by a bridge, and encamped in shady meadows. Not only are our expectations disappointed, but we soon learn that under all this sparkling indistinctness, we obtain no correct information whatever. If we wish to get from original sources an idea of some of the most important events of the war, such as the siege of Antioch, for instance, we must entirely discard Albert as an authority. I have mentioned how the fall of Antioch was gradually effected by the erection of

forts round the city : these important constructions
are as nothing in Albert's narrative, when compared
with the chivalrous single combats and romantic adventures which lead to no possible result.   What is
worse still, and only appears later, is, that even as to
these, Albert makes the grossest blunders in time.
and place.   I shall here again allude to Solyman's
embassy to Berkjarok and Kerboga.   I have already
mentioned it, but as giving an insight into this quality of Albert's book, it is worth further consideration.   Solyman and his retinue advance towards
Samarcand, the capital of Khorassan.   The Caliph,
sits on his throne in all his splendour.   The ambassadors rend their clothes, and bewail the sufferings they endure from the Christians.   The Caliph,
in his infatuation, laughs, and utterly disbelieves
the tale ; he ridicules Solyman, who justifies himself
by producing Baji-Sijan's petition.   Kerboga, who
holds the second place next the throne, then exclaims
that in six months this Christian host shall be exterminated, and summons his countless vassals to his
aid.   I will not reproach Albert for giving us no
satisfactory account of the state of the kingdom of
the Seljukes, and the position of the other Emirs at
Antioch ; although in many matters of detail he is
not ill informed about the East, and in this particular
passage he mentions Armenian affairs, which we look

for in vain in other Western authors.[50] But when we consider that he has made Baji-Sijan and the Caliph speak of such an embassy as occurring some four months before, the whole tale appears only a splendid scene, contradicted by previous facts; for how could the Caliph, who had already been long ago informed by that embassy, have any doubt as to the power, nay even the presence, of the Crusaders? As far as Albert is concerned, we may fairly conclude that as in the previous cases, he has carelessly or ignorantly admitted two different versions of the same occurrence. In regard to the statement itself, this picture of grim heathens in all their power, magnificence, and haughty insolence frequently occurs. It was then current over the whole world, and popular tradition gave birth to a number of similar representations.

Let us now review the subject as far as we have come. In the first place, we have hardly any indications of Albert's personal character; he has the merit of keeping his own impressions quite in the background. What we can discover of the character and tendency of our author has been already intimated; his leaning is rather against than for the miraculous and visible interposition of Heaven,

<hr>

[50] Called Kogh Basil (Corrovasilius in Albert), and Constantin, (the son of Rupeus in Matthew Eretz).

in order that he might give greater splendour and prominence to manifestations of human heroism. It is true that he begins with the glorious legend of Peter the Hermit, the heaven-sent apostle of the Crusades, but there is little else of the same kind in the whole compass of his history. The Holy Lance, which even in the East was the prolific source of many similar legends, is dismissed in a few lines.[51] This was clearly attributable to Albert, and not to those from whom he had the legend; for it is impossible to conceive that the numerous wonders and revelations attached to it could have escaped his notice. It appears to me that many of his stories must be regarded as having originally fromed part of a collection of mystical traditions, from which he borrowed them. The fact, that he wholly puts in the background the influence of the Pope on the Crusades, is a sign of a similar feeling on his part. He is not more influenced by the hierarchical than the mystical tendency of his con-temporaries.[52]

His book contains a vast mass of reports taken from eye-witnesses, active partisans, and other con-temporaries. They are given genuine and unal-tered, nor is any attempt made to invest them with the character of historical authority. They bear

[51] iv. 43.   [52] i. 6.

only on the outward form of things, and on details in their utmost prolixity, with a complete disregard of the connection or distribution of his, subject-matter. There is no attempt at generalizing. If there is any unity in the work, it is not to be sought in the authenticity of the facts, or in the logical mode of handling them. But in order to make a critical examination feasible, it will be necessary to examine these events as given by other authorities, and thus to discover whether and how far they may be regarded as agreeing. Their similarity would be the best proof of the genuineness of the representations of Albert of Aix. We have seen that this author professes to rely chiefly upon oral statements of eye-witnesses; and that though much written matter came into his hands, it was such as would be more likely to be derived from letters or conversation, than from testimony given with the knowledge that it was to be used for historical purposes. The contrast between oral and written tradition can only be considered as accidental. When we have to prove the internal agreement of testimony, we shall find it does not so much consist in the manner in which the tradition was handed down, as in the intellectual tendency of the men who represented those opinions. In many cases we think it can be proved that oral and written tradition have been, so to speak, welded together. This remark is in its place here, as it helps to explain the otherwise astonishing mass of such accounts.

Guibert mentions Fulcher's history only to append to it a severe and somewhat groundless criticism. He says, "Fulcherium quædam scabro sermone fudisse comperimus."[53] He proceeds in a subsequent passage :—"Dicitur, in sui, ni fallor, opusculi referre principio," etc. No one would suppose from this that he had the book before him, or that he had formed his judgment upon written documents. It strikes one therefore as singular, that immediately afterwards he quotes nearly word for word from Fulcher the lengthy narrative of a miracle which clearly could not have rested on oral tradition.

William of Tyre wrote the first half of his work entirely from extant authorities, viz. from the 'Gesta,' from Raymond, Fulcher, and Albert of Aix. The concordance even goes so far as to identity of words : it is so general and complete as to be obvious to the most superficial observer. Notwithstanding this, he says in his preface (where he had been previously speaking of another work derived

[53] Page 552. Fulcher's book reaches to the year 1127 (in other editions to 1124). The passage in Guibert was written between the years 1108 and 1110. In this connection of the time there is a strong presumption in favour of the supposition in the text.

from Arab sources), "In hac vero nullam aut
Græcam aut Arabicam habentes prædicam scrip-
turam solis traditionibus instructi, exceptis paucis
quæ ipsi oculata fide conspeximus." That we must
give but little importance to the "Græcam aut
Arabicam," is proved by another passage, in which
he expresses himself still more clearly on the subject of his authorities.[54] "Hactenus" (until the
year 1142), "aliorum tantum, quibus prisci tem-
poris plenior adhuc famulabitur memoria, colle-
gimus relatione—et scripto mandavimus. Quæ se-
quuntur deinceps, partim nos ipsi fide conspeximus
oculata, partim eorum, qui rebus gestis præsentes
interfuerunt, fide nobis patuit relatione." It is
clear that no one would speak of written works,
some fifty or sixty years old, as they would of the
narratives of those who still had a fresh impression of what had occurred in old times. Indeed,
apart from the contents of the book itself, subsequent passages forbid such a supposition; for he
says that he had spoken with some old men who
had gone to Jerusalem with Godfrey. He also
speaks in a totally different tone when he refers
to written sources in matters of history. He made
the proceedings of the Kings and Patriarchs of
Jerusalem his particular study, and he says concern-

[54] Præf. libri xvi.

ing them,[55]—"Hæc omnia etsi aliorum relatione comperta et etiam quorundam opera scripto mandata, presenti interseruimus narrationi." Here he places the "relatio" in direct opposition to the "scriptum."[56]

I see only one way to escape out of these contradictions. It is obvious that the narratives of Guibert and of William of Tyre were derived from the works of Fulcher and of others; but at the same time I cannot bring myself to discredit entirely the positive assertions of the first-named authors. The conjecture seems to me reasonable, that these writings were circulated sometimes in parts, sometimes as a whole,—as fragments or extracts; that narratives were framed out of them, were gradually altered by frequent repetition, and were handed down to posterity in greater or smaller portions, by word of mouth or in writing, without any acknowledgment of their original sources. Guibert might thus quote such reports with an "ut di-

[55] Lib. ix. c. 16.

[56] I do not mean by this to bind him to any strict terminology; for this and many passages in his work should be carefully examined where he mentions the 'traditiones veterum,' ix. 17; xi. 40; xxi. 26, and other places; meanwhile the passage quoted in the last shows that without something more precise we are not to think of direct written testimony. It is quite clear from the context that a similar phrase (xvii. 7) refers to contemporaneous events, and cannot therefore come into consideration here.

citur," while William of Tyre might give them as from "old reminiscences."[57] It is easy to conceive, how such a process once introduced would favour the maintenance of, and the addition to, oral tradition. The genuine narratives were split up into fragments, and made to appear similar in outward appearance to the current rumours of the day; and by this means it would not be difficult to melt the two into one.

Thus much at least appears obvious, that after half a century, William of Tyre still found himself in the midst of living traditions, whence he drew copious and varied information We do not want this explanation for contemporary authors, as we have already distinctly acknowledged a large portion of them to be indebted to oral reports. Guibert and Baldrich say distinctly, that what they did not themselves see or copy from the 'Gesta,' was told to them. Fulcher asserts the same as to the history of the three years from 1098 to 1100. The 'Gesta Expugn. Hieros.' and Orderic acknowledge it as to their additions to Baldrich and Fulcher. We

[57] We can further quote here v. 21, "Audivimus quod inter alios Dominus Flandrensis et Dominus Tancredus ascenderint;" as well as vi. 14, "clericus, ut dicitur," etc. (the history of the Holy Lance). If these passages do not distinctly prove the general diffusion of the writings of the original authors, it still shows how deeply imbued William of Tyre was with the still current traditions.

have already said that this was probable in the cases of Fulco and Gilo and the monk Robert. Among all these Guibert is the only one who had authentic historical information, besides having access to the 'Gesta.' The interpolations of all others depend solely on the credibility of some tradition handed down to them in the manner I have explained. It is therefore not difficult, with their aid, to determine the character of the authors from whom they quote.

The first thing that appears is an evident tendency to details of a purely human and, if possible, of a personal character. They have this in common with Albert,—that they omit all general considerations. Baldrich makes but one addition to the 'Gesta,' relating to the battle with Kerboga: "A refreshing dew fell during the morning, which wonderfully restored the troops."[58] We have already mentioned Orderic's taste for anecdotes and episodes. Among those we have named above, he is the author who gives the most discrepant accounts. Guibert relates Baldwin's rise in Edessa, specially quoting eye-witnesses, and describing at great length the ceremony of the adoption of Baldwin : how the actors in it stripped to their shirts, and embraced each other naked.[59] But the general position of

[58] Page 120.   [59] Page 496.

Baldwin, that he was beloved, and the old prince hated, by the people of Edessa, is involved in utter confusion. Most of the additions to the 'Gesta,' in respect to the siege of Antioch, are equally absurd and improbable; for instance, the princes work with their own hands at building a fort;[60] Tactikios wears a nose made of gold.[61] Bishop Adhemar causes the troops to be shaved, so as to distinguish them from the Turks.[62] Wherever Fulcher quits the Gesta Expugn. Hieros. we meet with the same sort of fables. Firuz, to meet with Bohemund, makes his way into the Christian camp by stealth, —"quasi aliquid empturus."[63] Fulcher relates of Baldwin how he hewed down a Turk; the 'Gesta' says that he pierced the Turk and his horse through with one stroke.[64] And so it goes on. We occasionally meet with a fact of importance in several of these authors, but it is always something which strikes their individual fancy.

But in order to see clearly the richness of invention displayed in these traditions, we must compare the descriptions of the same event given by various persons. In a number of cases we find, besides the correct account given by original authorities, another reading totally different, resting

[60] Page 499. [61] Page 501. [62] Page 561.
[63] Page 566. [64] Page 585.

solely on tradition. Albert furnishes many examples
of this mode of proceeding. Sometimes the versions are numerous. For instance, there are four
versions of the accident that occured in hunting
to Duke Godfrey;[65] three, of the death of Roger of
Barneville;[66] there are four incorrect accounts of
the treachery of Firuz;[67] and at least as many
unauthenticated of the death of Godfrey.[68] I could
easily bring forward more cases of this sort, but I
prefer to give some examples of a contrary proceeding, equally indispensable to a knowledge of these
authorities.

Ekkehard wrote, in the year 1100 or 1101, a
narrative of the defeat of Gottschalk in Hungary,
the incorrectness of which he discovered in 1106,
and rejected without hesitation. But the same
errors are found in detail in Albert's narrative, although he wrote after 1121; so that in spite of
its falsity, the tale was repeated twenty years after.[69]

[65] Albert, iii. 4; Guibert, p. 537; William of Malmesbury,
p. 144; Lupus Protosp. p. 47.

[66] Besides the correct statement in Raymond, p. 150; in Albert, p. 248; and the Hist. Bell. Sacr. c. 66.

[67] Fulcher, p. 391; Gesta Exped. Hieros. p. 566; Alb. iv. 15;
William of Tyre, p. 705.

[68] William of Malmesbury, p. 144; Guibert, p. 548; Albert,
vii. 18; Matth. Eretz.

[69] Albert, i. 25; Chronogr. Saxo, A.D. 1096; Ekkehard, c. 11;
the double-dealing negotiations of Kalmani.

Albert gives an account of the battle of Dorylæum, which Gilo had heard in Paris some years before: Radulph, who wrote in Antioch after the year 1130, had information which contradicted Albert's account: "Yet it is true," he adds, "the contrary is still very frequently related."[70] It was indeed altogether groundless; nevertheless it was spread abroad at that time in Germany and in France, as well as in Syria and in Palestine. Radulph has also an account of the well-known quarrel between Baldwin and Tancred in Tarsus, which might have been corrected by reference to the 'Gesta;'[71] yet Albert brings this forward in his history, quoting (it is easy to see) from Lorraine authorities.[72] Such is the spirit of tradition; it is bound by no rules; sometimes it rejoices in an endless multiplication of incidents and narratives,—in crowding together figures, in changing forms; sometimes it seizes particular points, and obstinately retains them: they are spread far and wide, and, after many years, they re-appear in some spot far distant from their original source. No search is made into time, place, or fact. Here, various occurrences are blended together without scruple; there, one and

---

[70] Albert, ii. 38; Gilo, p. 216; Rad. c. 21; the accidental or intended division of the army.

[71] Rad. c. 36. [72] Lib. iii. 5; for more particulars see further.

the same event is introduced in a new place, as if it had not occurred before. As an example of the former, we must read the account of Peter the Hermit in Guibert and in Fulco; there we see the expedition of Walter, Peter, Volkmar and Gottschalk, mixed together; a fabulous whole is compounded out of the beginning of the one, the middle of another, and the end of a third; some of it is pure fabrication, some of it an echo of the traditions found in Albert; in a word, it has the effect of a wild, perplexed dream. The following example is of a different nature:—Bohemund's enmity to the Emperor Alexius was notorious to his contemporaries; no one imagined that the Norman traversed the Greek Empire in the year 1097 with any peaceful intent. There were reports of incitements sent by him to other princes to make war upon Alexius. Albert is perfectly aware of this, and relates that Duke Godfrey declined this invitation.[73] Orderic has the same fact, but he states that the princes to whom appeal was made were Duke Robert and Count Stephen.[74]

These remarks are sufficient to render obvious the great extent of the circle which we are contemplating. The essential point in Albert's narrative, which is common to so many others, consists

[73] Albert, ii. 14.   [74] Page 727.

in this. We cannot look on them as the account of
one certain and known person, whose character and
position enable us at once to recognize the value
of his work: we must rather regard them all as
portions of one great tradition, current throughout
the whole of the West, the credibility of which
we must test at every step. By some accident,✓
a large mass of this tradition has come down to
us, under the name of Albert. The unscrupulous
manner in which Albert has adopted whatever was
most strange and contradictory, precluded the opportunity of selecting or recasting his materials;
as might have been expected from a single indus-
trious author. We can only look to the contents of
each individual fragment, and ask ourselves, without
reference to Albert's share in the matter, how far
the accounts of the authorities on whom he relies
can be trusted. We must do the same with regard to all the other separate narratives, the character of which we have been at some pains to
describe. We must try to discover how much
truth there is in their statements, and how much is
sheer invention.

It is quite clear that we can depend but little
upon their veracity. No one can deny that where
three or four different versions of the same occurrence are given, two or three of them must be

fabulous. With regard to the history of the First Crusade, the result of my inquiry is that Albert and all his companions seldom adhere to the truth; but their reputation has hitherto been such, that I am bound to bring forward some evidence as to the truth of my assertion, which I will do from the later portion of Albert's book. For this purpose I will select some part of the history of Baldwin's reign; in which the divergence in particulars will lead us immediately to positive contradiction in generals.

One well-known difference between Albert of Aix and William of Tyre lies in their accounts of the quarrel between Baldwin and the Patriarch Dagobert, which are totally at variance with each other. William, who professes to have made special inquiries into the subject,—and his diligence is quite obvious in this case,—clears the Patriarch of all blame. It is true, he says, that Dagobert had opposed Baldwin's accession to the throne, but he had done so only because the Lorraine party had refused the Patriarch the accustomed feudal homage. At any rate, it was entirely owing to the slanders of his old opponent Arnulf, that an open rupture took place; which, however, was peacefully arranged before Christmas, 1100. Dagobert's position remained undisputed, till Arnulf, by incessantly working on the clergy, forced Dagobert to escape into Antioch in 1103.[75] Albert gives another turn to the whole affair. He passes over in complete silence the suzerainty of the Patriarch over the crown, and thus deprives Dagobert's conduct towards Baldwin of any legitimate excuse. Hereupon Baldwin concerts his measures, after Tancred, the protector of Dagobert, had left the kingdom, and appeals to the Pope at Rome; who sends, at his request, the Cardinal-Legate Maurice. According to Albert's account, Maurice examines into the affair during the month of March, 1101, and pronounced Dagobert's suspension. At Easter, Dagobert gives Baldwin a bribe of three hundred gold pieces to reinstate him, makes friends with the Legate, and the two waste the revenues of the kingdom in secret orgies.[76]

At page 131, Albert proceeds with his history. The king is in want of money, and comes, some time in August,[77] from Joppa to Jerusalem; he asks a certain sum of the Patriarch, who denies his ability to give it. Baldwin having received infor-

---

[75] William of Tyre, pp. 780, 790, 797. [76] Page 308.

[77] The date is not quite clear. He remained in Cæsarea till the day of John the Baptist; he then went to Joppa; after three weeks he advances against the Saracens, waits some time for them, and then dismisses the army; " nec longo post hæc intervallo," he goes to Jerusalem, vii. 56–58.

mation from Arnulf, surprises the two ecclesiastics
in their cups; a violent scene ensues, when the Patriarch is forced to leave Jerusalem, goes to Joppa,
and thence to Antioch to Tancred, in March, 1102.
Baldwin remains with the Legate in Jerusalem,
paying him high honour. In the beginning of September, having received intelligence of hostile arma-
ments, he assembles his army, and advances toward
Joppa.

At page 332, we find that after Baldwin had
beaten the Saracens in July, 1102, he summons Tancred and Baldwin of Burg, in September, to assist
him against a fresh attack. They come to Joppa, and
Count William of Poitou with them. Dagobert arrives with them, and they agree to assist the King,
but only on condition of a fresh inquiry into Dagobert's case. On this being conceded, they advance
with him against Ascalon. Dagobert's deposition
was however confirmed anew, under the presidence
of the Cardinal.

Much as modern criticism has done for the history of these times, it has hitherto attempted in
vain to reconcile these contradictions. In most of
the narratives, we find both accounts side by side,
and the choice between the two is left to the reader.
It frequently occurs that William of Tyre, though
extolled for his unprejudiced description of these

events, and for his careful research, incurs suspicion ; while Albert's copiousness of detail is amusing, and he is consequently subjected to a less rigorous examination. Fulcher appears to me to pass over this matter with intentional silence ; for which reason the. information, that might have been gleaned from various notices in his diary, has been entirely disregarded. There is a notice of this sort to the effect, that in March, 1101, Tancred had gone from Jerusalem to Antioch.[78] How was it possible then for Baldwin, after Tancred's departure, to begin a quarrel with Dagobert, and appeal against him to Rome; for the Pope to name a Legate; for the latter to reach Palestine, go through the inquiry, and pronounce Dagobert's suspension; and all this, before the end of the month of March? Albert was forced to antedate the commencement of the quarrel; but even so, he cannot establish his statement; since we learn, from a thoroughly impartial eye-witness,[79] that Maurice was actually in Syria before Baldwin set foot in Jerusalem; that in the year 1099, Maurice had been sent with a Genoese fleet to the

[78] Page 407. " Eo tempore " (he had spoken of the small population in the kingdom) " contigit in Martio mense, Tancredum Cayphan oppidum suum Balduino relinquere, Tiberiadem quoque, et Antiochiam ambulare."

[79] Caffaro, ap. Muratore, vi. 249.

East.[80] The whole of the first part of the narrative therefore falls to the ground.

Albert says that Baldwin took Cæsarea on Whit-Sunday (9th June), and stayed there till the 24th (the birthday of John the Baptist). Cæsarea, however, according to the testimony of Fulcher, who was present, fell on a Friday, the 7th of June, and Baldwin proceeded, immediately after its fall, to Ramla, where he remained four-and-twenty days, in expectation of a hostile attack; as this did not take place, he returned to Joppa.[81] Fulcher then proceeds :—" Cum autem postea auribus semper ad eos intentis per septuaginta dies quieti sustinuissemus, intimatum est regi Balduino, adversarios nostros permoveri, et jam parati nos appetere accelerebant. Hoc audito fecit gentem suam congregari, de Hierosolyma, videlicet, Tyberiade quoque, Cæsarea et Caipha."[82] If we compare this with Al-

[80] He came in the autumn of 1100 with the Genoese to Laodicea; and I should think with them to Jerusalem during Lent of 1101. In Oct. 1100, Baldwin of Edessa had gone to Jerusalem by way of Laodicea. Maurice was then in Laodicea, and, as is clearly proved by Fulcher's silence, did not go with the King. That he went by himself by land in mid-winter is not at all likely, considering the troubled state of those provinces.

[81] Fulcher, p. 410 (c. 25, 26).

[82] Fulcher's chronology proves itself. The battle took place on the 7th September. If we reckon twenty-four days from the 7th June, we come to the 1st July; from that date to 7th September are sixty-nine days.

bert's account, we perceive how irrational Dagobert's flight to, and sojourn at, Joppa, would be. His wish was to avoid Baldwin, whereas in the month of September he would exactly meet with him, even according to Albert. I have no hesitation, after this, in disbelieving Baldwin's presence at Jerusalem in August, the scene at the feast, and all that followed. We cannot solve the contradiction in these two narratives, by supposing that Fulcher suppressed Baldwin's departure and return, from a desire not to touch upon ecclesiastical matters. He expressly says that Baldwin's armament took place, not from Jerusalem, but from Joppa; with which the Queen's presence in Joppa agrees.[83] She might very well be there if Baldwin remained two months; but it would be impossible to account for her stay according to Albert's version of the matter. Albert has exactly inverted the facts; he brings Baldwin to Jerusalem, and Dagobert escapes to Joppa; whereas the former was at Joppa, and the latter remained, undisturbed by any royal demands, at Jerusalem.

A similar case, the mention of the Count of Poitou, gives us some insight into the credibility of the events of the year 1102. Fulcher has on

---

[83] Compare the letter to Tancred, which Fulcher and William of Tyre give verbatim.

this subject this simple statement :[84]—" Cum prope
Pascha esset, Hierusalem perrexerunt" (viz. William
of Poitou, Stephen of Blois, and the other princes of
the crusading army of 1101, who went from Joppa),
"qui postquam cum Rege Balduino Pascha cele-
brando pransissent, Joppen omnes regressi sunt.
Tunc Comes Pictavensis navim ascendens et Fran-
ciam remeans à nobis discessit." The rest of the
princes fall shortly afterwards in a disastrous battle
with the Turks. And this same Count of Poitou,
who had sailed back to France at Easter, suddenly
advances from Antioch in September, joins the
other Crusaders before Ascalon, and disappears as
suddenly as he had appeared. Yet neither Fulcher,
the King's chaplain, nor Radulf, Tancred's companion, nor Matthias, Baldwin's subject, mentions
one word of this armament of Tancred, of Baldwin of Burg, or of William of Poitou. On the contrary, Fulcher expressly says :[85]—" Expleto bello "
(in July) " Rex Joppen reversus est. Postea quievit
terra bellorum immunis, tempore sequenti autum-
nali atque hiemali." Here again we cannot attribute Fulcher's reticence to his wish to say nothing
concerning Dagobert, as there is no question of
Dagobert, but of quite different matters.

To sum up: we see that the statements of William of Tyre agree, both in details and essentials, with what we learn of the events of those times from other sources; his dates are all confirmed, and he is never open to the slightest charge of contradiction or incongruity. With Albert the reverse is the case; in attempting to get at any connected narrative, we invariably find that his representations are at variance with all others. With regard to places and dates, as we have them from the most undoubted sources, we can by no means accept his testimony. We cannot therefore believe the sum of his facts, or the character he gives of persons or events. On the contrary, we perceive that his facts are made to bear out a foregone conclusion. The traditions upon which Albert's history rests celebrate Baldwin's princely splendour; and to support this view the numerous fictions are invented to which we have alluded. But this is not the place to pursue the subject further.

Raymond of Toulouse laid siege to Tripolis from the Pilgrim Mount in 1101 or the beginning of 1102. He took up strong positions in the neighbourhood, and occupied the lesser Gibellum in 1102: not in 1104, as Albert says; for we possess documents of the year 1103, by which Raymond made a gift of half the town,[86] and then died in 1105.

[86] Albert, ix. 26: "Proximo dehinc anno." Before that he had

The quarrel between his immediate successor, William of Cerdagne, and his son Bertrand, threatened to destroy the fruits of his labours. The latter, says Albert,[87] appealed to Baldwin for assistance, promising to do homage to the Crown in the event of receiving succour. Baldwin gladly accepted the offer. At the same time Tancred, Baldwin of Edessa, and Joscelyn of Courtenay, were at strife; Baldwin, in order to settle differences, summoned them all to meet him in the camp at Tripolis, where they appeared with splendid retinues. All the Frankish princes of Syria met together, in order that Baldwin might arbitrate between them.

To collate and sift all the narratives touching on this point, would require a severe examination. It is sufficient for our purpose to call attention to two statements which are above suspicion, and completely illustrate the point at issue. Fulcher gives a tolerably detailed account of the quarrel between William of Cerdagne and Bertrand.[88] He blames them for quarrelling about the possession of the city, even before they had taken it. "Ad nutum

reported as 1103. Caffaro (p. 253) says indeed, "Primo anno hujus compagnæ," A.D. 1104. But the connection gives the error and the correct year as 1102. The document of the 16th January, 1103, is in the Hist. de Languedoc, ii., preuves, p. 360. The history itself indeed attempts to save Albert, but by a most forced construction.

[87] xii. 9.   [88] Page 420.

Dei," he adds, "momenta transvolant et cogitationes hominum vanæ subvertuntur. Et non fuit mora : postquam Rex Balduinus ad illam obsidionem venit, causa deprecandi Januenses, ut eum juvarent eo anno ad capiendum Ascalonem et Beruthum, necnon Sydonem, et ordiebatur concordiam fieri de duobus comitibus memoratis . . . interiit Gulielmus ille Jordanus." Here we see a different reason for Baldwin's presence; he is not the highly honoured King, from whom the other princes expect judicial decision on their rival claims, but a chieftain seeking assistance, who is incidentally called in to act as a mediator. It may be said that these negotiations, important and well-known as they were, might have escaped the notice of Fulcher; but we would quote, as settling the question, a statement of Matthias Eretz of Edessa.[89] This author, whose information on Armenian subjects is always good, (ill informed as he was on matters occurring in distant countries,) relates the Tripolis events with many variations; but in another place he states, that in the summer of 1109 the Count of Edessa and Joscelyn of Courtenay had made an unfortunate expedition to Kharran in Mesopotamia, which he describes in some detail. There is no longer therefore any room for doubt ; and Matthias both ne-

[89] Notices et Extraits, ix. 325.

gatively and affirmatively destroys all idea of the
congress of princes spoken of by Albert. This is
in fact simply a proof of the opinion which had
been formed in the East, of the position, power,
and character of King Baldwin. People could not,
or would not, believe that he really had very little
influence over the rest of the princes. They had no
doubt that the Patriarch had succumbed to Baldwin's energetic assertion of his rights. Albert's
lively imagination seized upon this idea, and dressed
it out with a variety of anecdotes, the inaccuracy of
which we have here attempted to prove.

We have already stated that Baldwin was the
centre round which the most fabulous inventions
were grouped. We shall see that the same may be
said with still greater truth of his more famous
brother, Godfrey. We have already quoted the in-
troductory words in Albert's history,—" Incipit
liber primus expeditionis Hierosolymitanæ urbis,
ubi Ducis Godefridi inclyta gesta narrantur, cujus
labore et studio, Civitas Sancta sanctæ Ecclesiæ
filiis est restituta." This assertion will astonish any
one who has paid the most cursory attention to the
original sources; as he will not be able to discover
in them the slightest evidence that Godfrey bore
the chief part in freeing the Holy Sepulchre. After
this preface of Albert's, we expect to find Godfrey

the leading spirit in the crusading army. But
when we examine his work, we are astonished to
discover no confirmation of the Duke's fame. Godfrey's ability is proved by many facts; but in the
first half of the narrative he is not conspicuous
above the other princes; and as it proceeds, his
name is frequently omitted altogether in the account of the most important actions and discussions. Particular passages strike us in the course
of the narrative from the sharp and insulated manner in which they stand out. Godfrey, who, even
according to Albert's representation, contributed
little to the success of the undertaking, is all at
once represented in strong terms as the head of
the army, the most noble of the princes, the pillar
and support of the enterprise. When he was ill,
the whole Christian host was prostrate; when God
wished to raise it up, he permitted the Duke to
recover. This is repeated in various places. But, as
I have often remarked, it is vain to look to Albert for
any connection between what has been said before
and what follows; we seek in vain for any cause
of Godfrey's preponderance. From an apparent
equality with, or even inferiority to, other princes,
the Duke suddenly emerges, for no reason whatever, to this dazzling eminence. And this surpass-
ing glory vanishes, while the words which announce

it still ring in our ears. Absolutely nothing comes of this solemnly proclaimed pre-eminence, save a few chivalrous hand-to-hand encounters, productive of the most insignificant results.

The origin of Godfrey's fame, for which worldly events are insufficient to account, is thoroughly mystical and superhuman. A command proceeding immediately from God places the Duke in the midst of the enterprise—a fact as miraculous as the dream of Peter the Hermit or the apparition of the saints at Dorylæum. If it be once admitted that the Duke owes his exaltation to God's command, there is no longer any question of a worldly nature, nor does anything depend upon his individual actions. Albert, with perfect simplicity, admits the miraculous into his narrative, without caring to observe how inconsistent it may be with temporal affairs. In this manner alone was it possible to transmit to posterity a true and lively picture of the ideas then prevalent. We shall soon see a clear, critical intellect engaged on these ideas, and shall have to mark the disturbing influence it exercised on them.

The complete purport of this legend or romance cannot be gathered from Albert's work, but it was he who first gave a fixed form and a uniform character to the tradition which we have described. We must review the whole circle of this tradition to make its nature clear or comprehensible; this will give a sufficient insight into all parts of the legend. The individual elements are scattered and fragmentary, while portions are frequently illustrated by incidents which William of Tyre derives from older and long-lost authorities. But the common ground upon which these inventions have been based is perceptible, even after long years and in the remotest lands. Flitting and confused as are the outward and visible figures, the fundamental principle remains fixed and unshaken under the most various influences. The poetical vigour of nations is as remarkable for its richness as for its permanency. We are transported into times when the world was young; when religion, poetry, and a community of spirit grew up in an unconscious but intimate connection. As yet there were no artists by profession, no works of art with fixed forms or clear unity of design; but the imaginative impulse of thousands found expression in pictures full of life and variety, in the many-coloured expression of one simple idea.

Nor is it Godfrey alone who inspires his admirers with such poetical images. There are many traces of a similar glorification of Provençal and Norman heroes, but none so complete and so full. I would trace the cause of this, not so much to the deficiency of the sources of our knowledge, as to the nature of the subject itself; for Godfrey's character and the position he acquired especially favoured the invention of such legends. But as I have before stated, neither Bohemund nor the two Roberts, nor Raymond, were without a halo of poetical glory.

We have observed above, that Albert shows, in the whole tenor of his work, that his nature was essentially of the earth, earthy. He endeavours to paint in rich colours the splendour of chivalry; he disposes in few words of the main and marvellous object of his work, the glorification of Godfrey; mystical as is its character, he presents it in the form of worldly poetical splendour. If we consider that he was only a collector of current fragmentary legends, that he omitted many wonderful narratives, and that, in those which he used, he discovered a human stamp, we are compelled to look to some higher source for the origin of these legends.

When the crusading army marched to the East, animated with religious enthusiasm, the Church had already made a great advance towards the subjugation of the world. It was still involved in violent contests; especially when its ambitious tendencies encountered any attempts at reformation. Other and deeper thoughts may have influenced Gregory VIII.; but most of the clergy considered themselves the restorers of a debased morality, and liberators of the Church from the bonds of the flesh. Every aspiration after faith and holiness of life took the form of asceticism; monastic Orders of the strictest discipline arose; and the doctrine of works of mortification, came to high honour. The pleasant inspirations of art were dried up at their very sources. Poetry withered away, as its true soil—a vigorous and healthy appeal to the senses—was counted sinful. The history of literature shows the suspension which then prevailed, and how subsequently other causes gave rise to a new development of its power. But if there were few poets, the poetical element still existed; on the first great impulse given to it, it manifested all its vigour. It seized upon the subject of the Crusades, which had been in so great a degree the fruit of the zealous ascetical spirit we have spoken of. The outbreak of poetical feeling showed what force it still retained, even under the pressure of the opposing tendency.

Nor was it long before, out of this wide circle of unconscious poets, some individuals arose who invested the subject with an artistic form, and brought it within the proper province of poetry. How far the work of Gregory Bechada belongs to

this category, it is impossible to tell from the
few notices there are of him;[90] but the romance
of 'Gandor of Douay,' and some others by unknown authors, indicate their origin more clearly.[91]
Of their contents, and their relation to our history
and to other poems, I shall speak elsewhere; I will
here only remark that, in spite of greater freedom
in their treatment of particulars, and a more decided
mixture of religious colouring, these authors belong
to the same school of tradition which has hitherto
engaged our attention.

[90] Foncemagne's opinion on this subject (Hist. Litt. de la
France, t. xi., avertiss. p. 34) appears to me forced and untenable.
The text of Gauf. Vos. p. 296, by no means justifies us in re-
ceiving a double emendation, even in the improved version of
Foncemagne.

[91] Michaud (Bibl. des Croisades, p. 273,) gives excerpts. A notice of them is to be found in 'Roquefort de la Poésie Française,'
p. 162, where he calls Gandor (after Fauchet?) only the continuator of the poem begun by Renar, or Renaus.

CHAPTER III.

WILLIAM OF TYRE.

WHILE the West appropriated and developed the history of the Crusades in the manner we have described, a very remarkable man was engaged in Palestine with the praiseworthy object of giving to that kingdom a history of its past, and to Europe a memorial for the future. He wrote with a strong feeling of patriotism, and at the same time under the sad impression that he could only find solace for present sorrow in the recollection of former happiness. The means at his disposal and his personal character fitted him for the task. The strong and persistent energy with which he mastered his materials enabled him to produce one of the greatest historical works of the Middle Ages.

William of Tyre was born in Palestine, but we have no information as to the place of his birth or his parentage.[1] He was educated in Europe, most probably at Paris ; but this surmise is merely conjectural ; for he himself (our sole authority) only states that he quitted Syria about the year 1163, in order to pursue his studies. Four years afterwards we find him an archdeacon of the Church of Tyre, a friend of King Amalric, and tutor to the subsequent King Baldwin IV. Even at that time the King employed him in the most important negotiations ; he went to Greece in 1168, to ratify an offensive alliance with the Emperor Manuel against Egypt. Personal affairs carried him to Rome in 1169. On his return, at the death of the Bishop of Bethlehem, he was made Chancellor of the kingdom, and in the year 1174 Archbishop of Tyre.[2] From that time, he was naturally considered one of the most important members of the aristocracy of the land ; he took an active part in all negotiations of any importance, and his influence was felt by all ranks throughout the kingdom. The time and place of his death are involved in mystery ; the information on this point given by Hugo Plagons is unworthy of credit, and scarcely deserves mention.[3]

The idea of writing his history had occurred to

[1] Bongars (in præf.) gives all needful particulars of his life. I only quote here what appears essential to a comprehension of his personal character.

[2] William of Tyre, xxi. 9.   [3] Compare Wilken, iii. 2. 261.

William of Tyre in the year 1170. Besides his own wish, there was an additional reason in the command of King Amalric, at whose desire he had already written a history of the Arabs since the time of Mahomet. For this latter work he employed Greek and Arabic materials, above all the history of Saith, the Patriarch of Alexandria. Amalric also busied himself in procuring him materials, and doubtless much that was valuable in this book has been lost. It cannot be asserted that it would have been free from error. The work of William of Tyre which we do possess precludes such a supposition. But that work shows a more complete and scientific knowledge of Saracenic life than any of his contemporaries or co-religionists possessed. It appears that in the year 1182 he had nearly completed the collection of his materials; at all events, he then began to put them into form; and he mentions in several passages, in the first and nineteenth books, the year we have given as the time when he wrote them.[4] In 1184 he had completed twenty-two books, and brought down his narrative to the autumn of the preceding year. He was then in doubt whether to continue to portray the in-

---

[4] i. 3; xix. 21. In accordance with xxi. 26, Bongars supposes that this part was already composed in 1180; but nothing is there stated, beyond the fact that in that year William of Tyre had deposited certain papers in the archives of that town.

creasing miseries of those times, and determined to complete the history of the year 1184 in a twenty-third book.[5] But his purpose was not carried out; the work that has come down to us breaks off with the first chapter of that book.

The manner in which the author collected his materials appears to me similar to that already described. He wrote partly from information obtained from those who had still a vivid recollection of the past, partly from his own observation and the honest reports of eye-witnesses. It is an important consideration, that the materials of his first fifteen books are still, for the most part, extant in their original sources. Albert of Aix, Archbishop Baldrich, Fulcher of Chartres, Raymond of Agiles, and Chancellor Gauthier, supply him with the materials for the First Crusade, and the reigns of Godfrey, Baldwin I., and Baldwin of Burg. We shall see further on what changes he introduced; but, in general, the accuracy of the copy spares me the trouble of pointing out individual instances. Before passing, however, to the consideration of his own original contributions, I will notice a few doubtful points.

[5] Præf. i., and xxiii. In this he says that he had divided the whole of his work into twenty-three books. He wrote his preface in 1184. The preface to his twenty-third book, in which he was still undecided, must therefore have been written first.

Lib. i. cap. 8, a copious and detailed passage on the misery of Europe in the eleventh century, is taken from Fulcher (p. 381), with some rhetorical ornaments of his own added. I have no doubt that an account (cap. 13) of the contention between the Emperor and the Pope, as well as the description of France after the Council of Clermont (cap. 16), are to be traced to Fulcher (pp. 383–385).

There is a notice of the imprisonment of Hugo the Great, interpolated from Fulcher (p. 384) into the narrative of Albert. I should also attribute the origin of cap. 16 to the same author. It is easier to trace to Fulcher the origin of the statements regarding Robert of Normandy (p. 205), and to Albert the accounts of the arrival of Tatikios and Peter the Hermit.

Lib. iii. cap. 2. It is said that the pilgrims at first stormed Nicæa without forming in regular order. This is but a repetition of Albert's statement, that the Crusaders on their arrival were not daunted by the appearance of the towers, but charged the enemy at several points, at full speed, with colours flying and couched lances.

Lib. v. cap. 1–3. The battle before Antioch is compiled from Albert and Baldrich; the beginning of cap. 1 is taken from Albert; the end of cap. 1, as well as cap. 2, from Baldrich; and cap. 3 again

s 2

from Albert. That the two accounts, composed under different circumstances, contradict one another
does not seem to disturb our author.

Lib. vi. cap. 14. The story of the Holy Lance is
told as shortly as possible. Nevertheless the mention of the Apostle Andrew and other visions, shows
that the narrative was taken, not from Albert, who
is equally short, but from Raymond of Agiles.

On the whole, Albert is the leading authority in
these books up to the capture of Jerusalem. The
battle of Ascalon is related from Raymond, and
then, as far as the twelfth book, he chiefly follows
Fulcher. The end of Prince Raymond of Antioch
is taken from Gauthier, and the further the narrative advances, the more copious is the use made
of unknown authorities. Occasionally we are de-
ceived by an apparent appeal to eye-witnesses.
According to the confident assertions of those who
were present,—says he, speaking of a successful
naval fight,—the sea was stained red with blood
for some distance. But the whole narrative is only
a copy of Fulcher, who, as far as we can learn, had
never trusted himself on the sea.[6]

Although the interest of these first books is not
very great, our respect for William of Tyre in-
creases when we examine the mode and the extent

[6] Fulcher, p. 434. William of Tyre, xii. 21.

of his own researches. He has carried his inquiries in all directions; selecting with the greatest skill the original authorities for each separate fact, and eliciting with careful accuracy the substance of their statements. As he does not quote his authorities by name, it is difficult to distinguish them; nevertheless the few whom he does name give a favourable impression of his method and capacity. We observe that he made inquiries concerning Tancred's proceedings in Tiberias itself, where that prince ruled for many years. Tancred's administration of that town, he says, was so admirable that his memory was still cherished by the inhabitants.[7] He also sought information concerning Idumæa; he says that he was told such and such things by the older inhabitants of a castle that was to be built there, etc.[8] He received an account from Hugo Embricus, lord of Biblium, of the taking of that city by that prince's grandfather. We believe his statement, although he makes a wrong application of it.[9] When King Amalric was separated from his wife Agnes, on account of their near consanguinity, William of Tyre was in Europe, and was un-

[7] William of Tyre, ix. 13.   [8] xx. 20.

[9] xi. 9. He confuses it with the capture of Gibellum by Bertram of Toulouse and William Embricus, concerning which the documents in the Hist. de Languedoc, ii. pr., p. 374, and Caffaro, p. 253, give further particulars.

able later to obtain anywhere precise knowledge of the relationship in which they stood to each other. After long inquiry he applies to the Abbess Stephanie of Santa Maria Major, herself a relation of the Queen.[10] Hugo of Cæsarea, one of the first barons of the kingdom, supplies him with various details concerning his. embassy to the Egyptian Caliphs, and his negotiations with. Schirkuh, the uncle of Saladin; very probably also as to certain treaties with Saladin himself, in whose favour Hugo constantly endeavoured to direct the policy of the rulers in Jerusalem.[11] When Amalric's last enterprise against Egypt failed, William of Tyre is unable to conceal his astonishment. On his return from Rome to Syria, he sought from all the barons, and then from the King himself, the causes of this failure.[12]

These examples show, how all the sources of information then accessible were open to him, and how little he neglected his opportunities. But the number of his various authorities is still more apparent, when he treats of doubtful or remarkable events; and although he does not mention his originals by name, it is impossible not to recognize the care and accuracy of his inquiries. He continually assures us, that he had learned this or that fact from

[10] xix. 4.   [11] xix. 17, 28.   [12] xx. 20.

persons whose veracity was above suspicion,—barons who were themselves present, or old men who had themselves borne a part in the affairs. If he received contradictory accounts, he gives both versions with strict impartiality; and this throughout his work, in great and small matters, and on every occasion. The examples, which I shall take without any special selection from among a host of similar cases, will bear out my assertion.

"The first army of the Crusaders was afflicted in Antioch with a dangerous epidemic, and William of Tyre gives various accounts of the causes of the disease.[13] The losses at Edessa were attributed by some relaters of the events to the Archbishop, while others acquitted him of all blame.[14] He had reports of the expedition of Louis and Conrad from eye-witnesses, who told him the numbers of the army, and gave him various opinions as to the relations subsisting between Louis and Raymond of Antioch.[15] He does not trust himself to speak with certainty of the corrupt practices which brought the siege of Damascus to such a fatal termination in 1148; but he brings together many and very discrepant accounts.[16] He speaks in the same manner concerning the capture of Paneas in 1165, of the strength of the army with which Amalric waged

[13] vii. 1.   [14] xvi. 5.   [15] xvi. 21, 27.   [16] xvii. 7.

war in Egypt, and of the origin of the last rupture between Amalric and the Fatimites.[17]   After the victory of Baldwin IV. on Mount Gisard, he says : " I know not how many we lost ;" and adds, " Audivimus à quibusdam fide dignis, quod centum viderant loricas extrahi." Concerning the strength of the enemy, he states that he had formed his opinion after careful inquiry from the most trustworthy sources.[18]   At this period, as chancellor and metropolitan bishop, he took part in the most important affairs, but even then he did not neglect to prosecute his inquiries.   It was he who had to conduct the odious negotiations in 1175 with Count Philip of Flanders.   After quoting speeches and counter-statements, he adds, that he had obtained a clue to the motives of the Count, partly from various narratives, and partly from the Count himself.[19]

We are thus introduced to as many authorities as Albert of Aix-la-Chapelle can produce.   The latter has united in his narrative the rumours of the West ; William of Tyre lays before us a host of Syrian authorities.   It remains now to determine where they agree and where they differ.   At first sight the preference would appear to be on the side of William of Tyre.   He moves in the highest ranks

[17] xix. 10, 24 ; xx. 5.   [18] xxi. 22.   [19] xxi. 14.

of the world which he describes; he numbers among his authorities the most honourable names; the care he takes to prove and sift his evidence is quite manifest. But as a favourable impression is apt to deceive, and praise requires proof, we will inquire whether he understood the right mode of using his carefully collected materials, and to what end he employed them.

General Character of the Work.

One circumstance which will strike even the most superficial reader, and must be mentioned here, is the undeniable merit of the style of William of Tyre. The language is naturally the Latin of the Middle Ages, mixed with Southern French and Italian elements. But, together with the influence of classical studies, we can trace a thorough command of this mixed language, and evidences of general cultivation. The clearness of his narrative also is deserving of praise, and he possesses the talent of selecting the most striking passages from those of inferior value. His pictures are remarkable for detail, without being overcharged; his language is to the purpose and dignified; his thoughts are thoroughly well expressed. The same treatment is maintained throughout with no apparent effort. The whole is a work cut, as it were, out of one block;

we feel at once that William of Tyre displays the faculty, not of a chronicler, but of an historian; otherwise he could not have attained such ripeness and evenness of style.

The more we examine the work in question, the more clearly we perceive the author's mastery of his materials. He has a quick eye for grouping his objects, so that he can class them according to their affinity. Before entering into any new subject, he completely disposes of the consequences of the first. The subject of his history shows the value of this treatment. A feeling for order and clearness is the most important quality in an historian, who has to describe the complicated intercourse between four Christian and ever-varying Saracenic empires, to show where they acted singly or in alliance, where Greek and European elements are at work, and where several distinct autonomies pursue their various interests. On most occasions we must award the highest praise to William of Tyre. No complication of circumstances, however tangled, disturbs him; he finds the best way of unravelling it, without affecting the other portion. For instance, in his fourteenth book, he has to narrate the dissensions which originated in the arrival of the Emperor John at Antioch. The subject was an embarrassing one. The personal character of John, and of Prince Raymond,—the political position of Antioch towards Constantinople,—the relation of Raymond to his own vassals,—all had to be considered. John had vast plans against Antioch, as well as against Noureddin. King Fulco and the Count of Tripolis shared the interests of Raymond, and notwithstanding this, it was the defeat of the two by Noureddin which immediately forwarded the views of the Emperor. William of Tyre explains all this with the fullest detail, and is so little embarrassed by the number of his subjects, that he goes out of his way to insert into his narrative the part which the kingdom of Jerusalem played in the matter. The whole is developed in so clear a manner, that even Wilken has closely followed William of Tyre in the disposition of his subject.

The introduction of the work gives us a remarkable example of the same quality. I have already made favourable mention of the preface to the 'Gesta Francorum.' But the stamp is very different. In the latter work the mystical element of the First Crusade is strikingly expressed; indeed, the great merit of the passage consists in its showing so clearly the existence of the feelings which prompted that enterprise. William of Tyre, as he was not an actor in the Crusades, but speaks only from an historical point of view, embraces a far wider range. He begins with Mahomet, the originator of the quarrel: he then enumerates three violent attacks on Christianity, each of which called up important counter-effects, the last of which was the First Crusade: and so he comes to his subject. He clothes this subject with details, and developes his theme quietly and broadly. In most of the modern authors we find a more ornamented style and a greater abundance of materials, but they are inferior in the power of recognizing and appreciating essential points.

On the other hand, it cannot be denied that this very attempt to separate his materials has led the Archbishop in many cases too far, and involved him in obvious errors or want of tact. We frequently notice, that to preserve the regularity he has prescribed for his work, he changes the chronology, or at any rate makes it incomprehensible. We learn from Fulcher, that during the captivity of Baldwin II., Eustace Grenier was named viceroy of the kingdom; and that the Venetian fleet arrived shortly before Eustace's death: whereupon William of Buris was made viceroy, and was present at a successful sea-fight. William of Tyre depends solely on the authority of Fulcher, but his great object was to tell the deeds of the Venetians in a consecutive narrative. He therefore states the death of Eustace and the election of Buris as his successor;

after which he reports the arrival of the Venetians [20]
The city of Paneas was betrayed in the year 1129
by one of the tribe of the Assassins into the hands
of the Christians; three years afterwards it was
given as a fief to the Knight Rainer of Brus. William of Tyre, who relates with great detail the war
of Damascus which occurred in 1129, omits to
mention the capture of Paneas until Rainer takes
possession of it. No one would guess from his context that three years had intervened between the
two events.[21] We might quote many similar instances, and many where, for the sake of the form
of the narrative, the chronology, although indicated,
is inverted. For us it is sufficient to have discovered his mode of proceeding, and that even facts
are occasionally made to bend to it.

That the chronology of William of Tyre is the
weakest part of his book, has been proved in
many passages by Wilken, who corrects his errors
by appealing to Arabic authorities.[22] Frequently,
however, the error is clearly the transcriber's, in
cases where William of Tyre marks the time by
giving the date of the year and that of the reign
of the ruling prince. There will always, however,

[20] Fulcher, p. 434. William of Tyre, xii. 20, 21.
[21] William of Tyre, xiv. 19.
[22] I will only mention Wilken, iii. 1, p. 239; 2, pp. 4, 17, 139,
by way of example.

remain a considerable number of errors of which we cannot acquit him. He is not devoid of a feeling for accuracy, but he is not sufficiently careful in minor details. But, what is most remarkable, we often find no dates at all, as for instance in the account of the reign of Amalric. Wilken proves here beyond a doubt, that without the aid of Arabic authorities, it would be impossible to restore the chronology by a reference to William of Tyre.

We are however convinced that the defect we have indicated is rather an exception to, than a consequence of, his general mode of proceeding. The accuracy, even in the more trifling details, which we should have expected from his industry, is confirmed in the fullest manner by the Oriental authorities. These latter are, generally speaking, ampler in detail and frequently full of anecdotes; they care only for the single fact which engages them for the moment; the utmost they do is sometimes to give a very general view, as in the instance of the religious zeal of Noureddin or of Saladin.[23] William of Tyre, on the contrary, has always his subject fully in view. He frequently breaks off a digression which would have led him too far; for brevity's sake, he suppresses many details, and

[23] Reference to the "excerpta" in Reynaud will easily convince any one.

there is no question but that his views are much larger than any to be found in Kemaleddin or Abu Yali. We are therefore the more pleased at the agreement between these authors, which often appears in unimportant trifles, is seldom disturbed by patriotic or religious prejudices, and is even occasionally confirmed by their very discrepancies. We should have been surprised had William of Tyre received less uncertain accounts of the march of Saladih upon Mosul; on the other hand, it is very surprising that, amidst some obvious errors, he should bring together so much that was true about the Egyptian Fatimites. Still more striking are some passages where, in contradiction to all European authorities, he gives a statement which is only to be found in Arabic or Syrian writers; *e.g.* that of the battle of Harran, in the reign of Baldwin I., which he describes in a manner similar to Kemaleddin, and quite differently from Radulph and Albert. The only native historian, Matthias Eretz, of Edessa, attests the justice of his choice.[24]

I should dwell longer on this point were I writing a general history of the Crusades. But in this

[24] William of Tyre, x. 29. Radulf and Albert are directly at variance with him on the cause of the war. Both give a completely false version of the defeat of the Armenians, and Albert makes Tancred carry on a war of revenge, which falls to the ground merely from its dates.

monograph I must be content to indicate the fact, and refer for proofs to Wilken's third volume, where they will be found in great number. It must be remembered that the history of William of Tyre is written with unity of design, and also that, with a few trifling exceptions, he has not anywhere had recourse to Arabic or Greek authorities. When the Emperor John was besieging Schaisar on the Orontes, he had to fight several important battles before the Franks arrived. William of Tyre does not mention this, and only makes the war begin on the arrival of the Frankish princes.[25] The facts therefore for which he had not the authority of the Latins, were to him as if they did not exist. The fullness and truth of his account of Arabian affairs depend entirely on their close contact with the Christian powers. He tells us nothing new concerning the descent of Zenki, or of Noureddin, or of Schirkuh; but he characterizes them admirably as soon as they come to close quarters with the Franks. Whenever he investigates matters which we can test by Arabic authorities, he so far agrees with them, as we have before observed, as to leave no doubt of the accuracy of his narrative. But we can always easily recognize the totally different origin of the accounts. It is impossible

[25] Wilken, ii. 632.

to think that a person of his experience should have had such religious pride as to despise learning something from Arabic sources. He himself says, that for his history of the Arabs, he had consulted and used Arabic writings. It was clear therefore that for other reasons he rejected such authorities. The solution appears to be, a dislike to mix up with his own narrative elements so dissimilar. This would suppose no very high idea of his own critical power; but the very unskilfulness shows his power, and his wish to carry out his work diligently. This remark takes us back to the character of his work, which, in comparison with those before alluded to, springs from a totally different soil. It represents a complete whole, marked by great unity of thought, and independence both in material and form.

Character of William of Tyre.

After the preface to which we have alluded, William of Tyre follows Fulcher in his report of the condition of the Holy Land. The manner in which he enlarges on the materials of his original is here seen clearly. Fulcher bewails the excesses of the robber chiefs, the desolation of fruitful provinces, the oppression of the poor and helpless. William of Tyre, on the other hand, from the same materials draws a picture of universal demoralization, arising not from mere rude lawlessness, but from positive wickedness.[26] Fulcher is oppressed and afflicted by the universal misery around him.   To him the advent of the Crusades is a Divine interposition, a miracle in the strictest sense of the word.   William of Tyre asserts that, as matter of history, the Crusades really did produce some moral good; but he assigns to them a human instead of a miraculous origin, and attributes them to the general guidance of divine Providence.

The train of thought which lay at the bottom of this different view of events is apparent throughout the book.   The author believes in a living personal God, but in all human matters feels the necessity of a temporal foundation; whereas the author of the 'Gesta Francorum' immediately refers to some prophecy of the Bible.   William of Tyre advances no step in his work until he has satisfied himself on all points of time and place.   In relating the setting out of the first band of Crusaders on their march, he takes occasion to give concise but excellent observations on the kingdom of Hungary.   Before Godfrey reaches Constantinople, our author endeavours to give a correct view of the condition of the Greek empire, and after-

[26] Fulcher, pp. 381, 385.—William of Tyre, i. 8, 16.

wards of the state of Dalmatia, Bulgaria, and Ser-
via. He then enriches the narrative of the Crusade
with a description of Constantinople, Nicæa, and
Antioch. Edessa and Jerusalem are described, and
the most important events in. the history of those
places are brought under review. Thus he proceeds step by step; and as he approaches his own
times, his digressions become richer, more ample
in detail, and more trustworthy. In his account of
Amalric, he dwells at greater length on the condition of Egypt; he gives whole treatises on the
position and age of the Egyptian Babylon, on the
origin of the Fatimite caliphate, on the number of
the mouths of the Nile, the increase of the Delta,
and the Indian traffic across the Isthmus of Suez.[27]
His researches go far back into antiquity; and
wherever he finds differences of opinion, he does
not rest until he has solved them. He invariably
gains his object, which is to obtain a sure foundation for the facts he relates; and, with the same
view, he never omits to mention the death and
succession of popes and of the Roman and
Greek emperors; giving in most cases a short
review of their reigns, and a description of their
most remarkable qualities. He was not likely
to pass over such subjects. He had seen how

[27] xix. 14, 19, 22, 26.

T 2

the Patriarchs of Jerusalem had maintained their rights, or had suffered injustice in Rome; the quarrel between Frederic I. and Alexander III. had been felt even in Christian Syria; he himself had negotiated important treaties with the Emperor Manuel, and had attempted to benefit his native country. These circumstances had not only facilitated his task at the commencement, but were of great assistance to him in working out the plan of his history. He had got far beyond the ideas of the first Crusaders; above all things he looked for logical connection and historical coherence.

Arrived at this point, we shall proceed to institute a comparison between William of Tyre and the earlier authorities, and shall then examine the method he has pursued in making use of his materials. It is not difficult from this point to trace, in all directions, the contrast hitherto only indicated in particular instances, of his personal character and his intellectual activity.

As we have before observed, we possess many narratives of the Crusades, some written by the actors themselves during the progress of the events, while others derive their origin and their widespread notoriety from the wonder of contemporaries. A large army, enthusiastic beyond example, without unity, almost without leaders, and only actuated by one common impulse, had recovered the Holy Sepulchre. They were in a foreign land; the war was over, and yet everything resembling civil, social, or indeed any sort of government, was totally wanting. They ruled only the ground upon which they stood. The population was hostile; he who chose to stay, had to trust solely to his own right-arm and his good sword. Under such circumstances, with feelings of entire sympathy, and hearts full of that enthusiasm which had armed Europe, were the first narratives of the Crusades composed. The West seized upon these manifold and vague traditions; the ideas which these deeds called up were not less lively in the breasts of the auditors; each one selected only those descriptions which touched his own imagination, and if he found none such he invented them. The original sources told little that was logically connected; at any rate, we can discover but little, and there is much to disbelieve in individual cases. The tradition of the legend has an original unity and a wide significance, but not of a kind to be of use to the historian of daily events, and of the laws deducible from those events.

We will now return to William of Tyre. He was devoted to his country, which then represented a political whole, if any country did. It is true that, chiefly owing to William of Tyre's representations, a conviction has gained ground that the condition of the Christian possessions in Syria was hopelessly deteriorating; that religious and patriotic sentiments had vanished; and that even the old warlike spirit was no longer to be found. We always hear of the wickedness and weakness of those times, and are astonished that, considering the power of Noureddin and Saladin, the destruction of the Christians was so long delayed. I confess that I do not discover so much in William of Tyre's expressions, (the Arabic authorities give a very different story,) nor can I quite agree in what is to be found in his work corroborating their views. In the first place, they were far superior in material power, as William of Tyre often states, to the former generation. Under Baldwin IV. they were able to raise a force of more than twenty thousand men. William of Tyre says: "We had an army more powerful than that which any kingdom has ever raised within the memory of man."[28] As to the moral condition of the armies, avarice and immorality were on the increase; many places may have been more frequently sold or betrayed, but I cannot quote any case from which a falling off of martial valour can be inferred.

[28] xxii. 27.

Frequent as were the defeats, they were nearly always caused by the imprudence of the leaders and want of discipline of the soldiers, never by cowardice or sheer inactivity on either side. It is true that the influence of the first kings had ceased; they had, year by year, sent out their roving parties to pillage the country. But the real reason was, that they now formed a state among other states; they no longer stood face to face with a reckless enemy with whom no law was to be kept. They had come to a tacit understanding with those who, although implacable enemies, were still regarded as men possessing equal rights with themselves. At any moment an armistice or a truce was possible; and the war, when it commenced, was carried on in regular form. In the internal policy of the kingdom, the corporations exhibit the same political life: they were numerous and regularly organized. It is true that frequently the interests of the public were sacrificed to those of the corporation. For example, the two great Orders of the Knights Templars and Hospitallers did great mischief by their pride and obstinacy. But in general, facts speak louder than the denial of historians, as to the existence of unity of purpose. It was at this period of decay that circumstances resulted, in the formation of that body of laws called the Assizes of Jerusalem. The aristocracy had various representatives whose abilities no one contested. The wealth and importance of the cities is abundantly proved by the taxation ordered in 1182 ;[29] and examples of any, excepting those who belonged to the Orders, neglecting to comply with the requisitions of the State, are rare. From Guido's time they cease to be so. On a general review of this state of things, we shall find many defects, but we shall reverse the usual judgment, that at this juncture the noblest attempts of individuals failed to act upon the depraved condition of the masses. That which was really wanting to the State during its whole existence was an able ruler, capable of giving a strong impulse to the desire for progress,— a prince such as Bohemund during the First Crusade. But even such a one, under the conditions in which he was placed, would scarcely have offered a lasting resistance to the attacks of Saladin.

If this is acknowledged, and if it be further conceded that William of Tyre was thoroughly imbued with the views above indicated, we cannot fail to be struck with the contrast which he offers to his authorities for the First Crusade. William of Tyre was by nature calm and dignified, not susceptible of those emotions which tend to excitement

[29] xxii. 23.

or fanaticism. His excellence does not display itself in brilliant actions or in striking words, but he wins our esteem by his quiet virtues. He exhibits self-possession rather than force; he awakens our confidence, if not our admiration. As an historian he is conscious of the discordance of his authorities, without being able to conquer the difficulties they present; and as a statesman he fails to master public affairs, but he discerns and judges them in a manner which few of his contemporaries would have been capable of doing. He consistently lamented Amalric's covetous policy towards Egypt;[30] and he showed lively gratitude to the Emperor Manuel, his most powerful protector. But he never exercised any practical influence on politics, and never, in spite of all his efforts, succeeded in promoting the Greek interests.[31] We may remark that he never forgets, in the author, his position as Chancellor. He passes rapidly over the events of 1148, and is obviously reticent on later domestic affairs. He complains bitterly how difficult it is to tell the truth without giving offence, and promoting fresh dissensions in the kingdom. But his caution has this merit: it produces an extreme

[30] Lib. xx. c. 11.
[31] See, for example, the negotiations he began with Philip of Flanders.

anxiety to injure no man. He constantly accompanies his statements with the assertion that common report stated so and so, but that he had not discovered anything certain on the point. Occasionally his disclaimer is almost comical: "It is said that the King, as is reported, may have known such and such a thing;" and the like, frequently concerning the most unimportant matters. If we concede, what indeed is obvious, that this way of thinking is directly at variance with the sentiments of the First Crusade, what are we to say of the influence that general literature exercised upon him? He quotes the Roman poets as frequently as the Bible; he confirms his description of the miseries of those times by referring to Livy; and he is deeply imbued with classical philosophy. It is important here to remark that he scarcely perceives the distance that exists between himself and his authorities; between the times of Godfrey of Bouillon and of Amalric. In his own, as well as in former times, he sees the ordinary course of human affairs,— happiness and misery, heroism and weakness, rise and fall. In drawing comparisons, he does not hesitate, as we have before mentioned, to declare the reign of the first king of Jerusalem to be the happiest period, and one never likely to return.[32]

[32] Compare xxi. 7. In the ninth book he recognizes the dan-

This tendency, which has only been indicated in general, will become more evident when we trace its influence in the manner in which the materials are treated in detail. The feelings of most men are naturally expressed in the most marked manner when the object to be described has attained its culminating point. For instance, in the First Crusade, which was the product of religious and martial enthusiasm, the mind was fixed, on the one side, on the contemplation of heavenly things, and, when possible, on miraculous manifestations; on the other side, on the various displays of heroism, or (so prevalent in those times) those of the spirit of adventure. It is well known that towards the close of the eleventh century Europe was teeming with visions, dreams, and miracles. That there was an immediate intercourse with Heaven was the conviction of every one. This feeling coloured the whole mental existence of the pilgrims, whose character and modes of thinking were formed in a manner totally independent of the hierarchical power of the Church. I have already mentioned to what an extent the contemporary authorities were pervaded by this feeling, and have pointed out the traces of various other

gerous position of Godfrey of Bouillon very clearly. But the personal picture that he draws of this prince, spite of all the author's zeal for inquiry, keeps alive the old feeling of former times for that prince.

tendencies in William of Tyre. But apart from his secular knowledge and habits of thought, we can recognize even in his religious opinions a totally different origin. He is full of the spirit which animated the Christian Powers in the East toward the close of the twelfth century; the interests of Christianity are still prominently put forward, but the mystical enthusiasm has vanished; and, in lieu of the zealous asceticism which characterized that period, we perceive hierarchical tendencies. It is no longer the pilgrim or the mere ecclesiastic who writes, caring only for ecstatic visions or penitential practices: we recognize the bishop, whose life has been passed in the bosom of a well-organized Church, and in the transaction of temporal affairs of the most important nature. Albert says of Peter the Hermit, after he had fallen asleep, "In visu ei majestas Domini Jesu oblata est." William of Tyre says, "Visus est ei Jesus Christus quasi coram positus exstitisse."[33] The difference in expression sounds trifling, but in it we see the contrast between a miraculous reality, and a pious but natural dream. In Albert's account, Peter goes to the Pope, the Pope goes to Clermont, and on the 8th of March, with wonderful rapidity, Walter the Penniless was with his thousands on the frontiers

[33] Albert, i. 2. William of Tyre, i. 11.

of Hungary. We perceive that Albert here recognizes a miracle,—the immediate interference of Heaven. But even here William of Tyre finds a natural solution, in which however a religious enthusiasm, somewhat modified and conformed to reason, is still traceable. He relates how Peter the Hermit visits all countries, stirring up men's minds, and actively promulgating the allocution of the Pope. In Albert's narrative the matter ends there; after Peter has fulfilled his mission, there is no need of any further mention of the issue. But William feels it necessary to have a more satisfactory conclusion, and states afterwards how the Surians, after the taking of Jerusalem, gave him, their deliverer, their warmest thanks.[34] As before mentioned, William of Tyre, in his account of the finding of the Holy Lance, follows Raymond of Agiles, who in this passage tells of infinite signs and wonders from heaven. The greater portion of these are wholly omitted by William of Tyre, whose account is, from quite different reasons, almost as short as Albert's.[35] He again follows Raymond in the narrative of the election of Godfrey as king. The account of an event of such importance may have appeared to him too short; at any rate, he determined to amplify it by additional details. There is no question that on

[34] viii. 23.   [35] Raimond, p. 179.—William of Tyre, ix. 2.

this point he had the richest choice of materials.
There was scarcely another occurrence which had
been so much amplified by enthusiastic tradition.
Visions, miracles, all the glory of heaven and earth,
had been here brought together by Albert and
others.   But all this touched him little; an insignificant anecdote, the chief point of which was the
complaint of the servants at having to eat cold meat,
was inserted with some satisfaction in lieu of these
splendid wonders.   It was sufficient for him that
Godfrey's religious fervour was excited by fine altar-
pieces; he willingly omits all supernatural ornaments. He comes later to Godfrey's earlier history,
and even here again he discards nearly all that is
miraculous.

The further he proceeds in his narrative, the more
rare are the opportunities for displaying this dislike.
With scarcely any exception he remains on the
firm ground of ordinary matters of fact.   I only
remember one passage where there is express mention of a miracle; but even here he brings forward the arguments against a solution by natural
causes, in so circumstantial a manner as to induce
us to suppose that he was not convinced himself.
He does not exactly deny it, but he shows no enthusiasm.   He inserts the story because he had
heard it, but he would have held the same view of

Divine Providence, had nothing of the sort come to his knowledge.[36] Occasionally expressions such as these occur: an individual misfortune, or the general deterioration of their position, was caused by the wrath of God at their sins.[37] Meanwhile it requires no great investigation to see how great is the contrast between such opinions and the belief in miracles entertained by his predecessors. In one place he examines into the causes of the decay of the state;[38] he gives three reasons: the first of which is, the anger of the Lord; but he puts in the same class the weakness of the existing race of men, and the union of the formerly disunited Turkish kingdom. Naturally, and as befitted an orthodox Christian of those days, he is far from denying the general providence of God; but that God interferes in any other way except by the operation of natural causes, is, to him, rather a matter of history than of actual experience. In one

[36] The Holy Cross puts out the fire of the steppes through which the army was marching. A white knight then leads the Christians through pathless mountains. It was distinctly observed that on their camping he had vanished, and was never seen more (xvi. 11, 12). It was the unlucky expedition of Baldwin III. against Bosra. It was said that the Franks had never suffered such misery in Syria, and stood so much in need of Divine assistance. Under these circumstances prodigies arose, as they did on a former occasion during the siege of Antioch by Kerboga.

[37] xx. 19.   [38] xxi. 7.

word, the ground of his religious views is, that he recognizes only one mystical fact; namely, the existence and the sensible action of the Church, in the hierarchical form it had then assumed. He dwells upon this development with the greatest enthusiasm; first, so far as it concerned his own immediate sphere, but also with a view to the more important unity of Roman Christianity. On this point he had made the most accurate and original researches, in which he displays all the advantages of his historical skill. I have in a previous passage attempted to show, that from him alone true information is to be obtained of the fate of Dagobert, the first Patriarch. We have no doubt the same may be said of later doubtful events. I will only mention one example,—his account of the Patriarch Radulph of Antioch.[39] The amount of detail, the perspicuity and ease of his narrative, show clearly how much his mind was occupied with these topics. We are the more thankful to him, as without his account the important change in the state of men's minds in Syria would have been almost unknown to us.

When we turn to the temporal side of these events, we see a similar coincidence. Instead of adventures, we meet with campaigns; instead of

[39] xv. 12–17.

chivalrous single combats, we read of regularly constituted armies and kingdoms. The change runs through the whole book; I will quote one instance, more with the object of bringing this change prominently to view, than for the sake of proof. The contest for Antioch was the culminating-point of the knightly exploits of the Crusaders of that day, and William of Tyre took, as the authority for his narrative, that very writer who had the greatest love for such subjects. Albert of Aix details the adventures with the utmost fullness. The knights surpass themselves; the princes are covered with glory; the feeble and unlucky succumb; the strong attain to honour and wealth: and so it goes on in endless detail, without however the idea of any plan. It was the chief object of William of Tyre to arrange his work upon some system. In the first place he shows how little feeling he had for romantic heroism, as he omits a number of the anecdotes of Albert of Aix, with the remark that, considering the brevity which he aimed at, it was impossible for him otherwise to get through the endless materials. He connects together the thread of the narrative, which, with his knowledge of the other authorities, could not be difficult, and thus produces a whole, which, if we did not know its origin, might be considered well arranged and rational enough. But

with this order the whole freshness of the chivalrous spirit evaporated; it died out with that freedom from plan from which it drew its life and sus-
tenance. It is still a question whether the Archbishop's rational history can maintain its ground
against a picture drawn from the original sources;
how far also these authorities represent a plan of
proceedings, and whether they represent the plan
which William of Tyre describes.

The following remark seems not to be out of
place here. William of Tyre gives several accounts
of the number of fighting-men in the contending
armies, differing from the authorities that have come
down to us, and which he therefore obtained from
other quarters.[40] In the 'Gesta Francorum,' in
Raymond and Albert, we likewise find other statements on the same subject. They sometimes agree
with, sometimes vary from, those given by William
of Tyre. Where they vary, it is from a difference
of motive worth attention. In the original authorities the fact itself is treated as a matter of indifference, and the statements are mostly very loose.
The interest to them arose from a far different consideration; namely, the power of the Lord, who

---

[40] On the whole of the first crusading army consult i. ii., extr.
i. iv. 12, and also concerning the number of troops at Jerusalem
and Ascalon.

gave the victory to the few over the many. As the power of the Lord was everything, it necessarily followed that the real number of fighting-men was quite unimportant.[41] William of Tyre, however, did not take this view of the matter: he desired, very naturally, to obtain a surer foundation for his facts. It is to be regretted that he has not given us more frequent and better-arranged statements. Some later passages raise doubts as to the correctness of the numbers in the first parts of his works. In the later portion he talks of a Turkish army of twenty thousand, or at most forty thousand, men; and adds with emphasis,—"Dicebatur a senioribus regni principibus, quod a primo Latinorum in Syriam introitu nunquam tantas vidissent hostium copias."[42] These accounts are evidently more reasonable than the enormous numbers given in the earlier books.

There is no question that the turn of William of Tyre's mind has contributed materially to our knowledge, not only of ecclesiastical, but of temporal matters. The constitution of the kingdom, the subject to which we now allude, is not in-

[41] Fulcher, in the later portions of his work, gives this matter another turn, and complains of the smallness of their number, and how willingly they would have had larger armies.

[42] William of Tyre, xxii. 16: here it is 20,000. xx. 21, where the same matter is mentioned, he gives 40,000 men.

deed treated with the same interest and detail as
the history of the Church. On the contrary, in a
few passages only is anything directly relating to
it mentioned. But the whole book, springing from
a soil politically prepared for it, bears traces of
its origin. It would be wrong to imagine that we
could treat of the Assizes of Jerusalem in a comprehensive manner without reference to William of
Tyre. He does not often deviate from the original
authorities, but he clothes their dry and meagre
outlines with great variety of incident and interesting personal details. This however more properly
applies to the history of the First Crusade.

Narrative of the First Crusade.

We have praised the talent displayed in the style
of William of Tyre, in which there is a union of
good taste, vigour, and lively perspicuity. We
readily recognize these same merits in the original
works giving descriptions of the First Crusade.
But the comparison with his authorities renders
a closer examination necessary. It is clear that
he completely remoulds the form, if not the
contents, of his originals. This deserves praise;
for much coarseness, and many discrepancies and
contradictions, vanish under a process which, out
of such discordant materials, produces a complete

whole. On the other hand, we must confess that, together with what is objectionable, he destroys much that is significant, and frequently substitutes for what was a vivid picture a commonplace narrative. He writes history with a skill and liveliness that carry his readers away; but his predecessors, with greater coarseness and less skill, have the art, although in another manner, of writing both vividly and dramatically. Albert of Aix thus relates the march of the priest Gottschalk through Hungary:—"Dum per aliquot dies moram illuc [near Messburg] facerent et vagari cœpissent; Bavari vero et Suevi, gens animosa, et cæteri fatui, modum potandi excederunt, pacem indictam violarunt, Ungaris vinum, hordeum, et cætera necessaria paulatim auferentes, ad ultimum oves et boves per agrum rapientes occiderunt, resistentes quoque et excutere volentes peremerunt, cæteraque plurima flagitia, quæ omnia referre nequivimus, perpetrarunt, sicut gens rusticano more infulsa, indisciplinata et indomita. Juvenem quendam Ungarum pro vilissima contentione palo per secreta naturæ transfixerunt in foro plateæ." William of Tyre gives the following version of this passage: —"Alimentorum abutentes opulentia et ebrietati vacantes, ad inferendas enormes indigenis se contulerunt injurias: ita ut prædas exercerent,

venalia foris illata publicis violenter diriperent
et stragem in populo committerent, neglectis le-
gibus hospitalitatis. Commiserunt gravia in locis
quam plurimis, turpiaque nimis et relatione in-
digna." It is clear that the attempt to condense
his predecessor's narrative was not the sole aim
of William of Tyre. In Albert's account one
image follows another, and one fact explains the
other. William of Tyre, on the contrary, limits
himself to a bare recital of the events, which
he might have represented in equal detail. While
Albert, after his fashion, boasts of the purple
banners and the golden insignia, William of Tyre
merely says, the army marched in great pomp from
one place to another. At Dorylæum, says Fulcher,
was Bishop Adhemar with four other bishops, beside many priests in white garments, who hum-
bly besought God for victory. Many went to them
for confession, and princes were in the heat of
the fight. William of Tyre describes it thus:—
"Dominus vero Podiensis cum multis ejusdem of-
ficii comministris populos admonent, hortantur prin-
cipes, ne manus remittant, sed certi de victoria di-
vinitus conferenda, interemtorum sanguinem ulcis-
cantur, et de fidelium strage fidei hostes et nominis
Christiani non patiantur diutius gloriari."

Here there is no abridgment; on the contrary,

William of Tyre is more detailed than Fulcher, but rhetorical amplification takes the place of simple reality. We may remark incidentally that the fact differs materially from that mentioned by Fulcher, and exactly as we should have expected from our previous observations. While Fulcher gives us a picture of the battle, in which confusion reigned,—the priests in anguish and terror on their knees, people coming to them in the midst of the turmoil for absolution, and the like,—William represents the clergy solemnly assembled, as it were, in order of battle, headed by their chief; and in a becoming state of enthusiasm urging on the warriors to do battle for the Lord.

A comparison with any of his authorities gives similar results. Raymond of Agiles, who troubles himself little with artistic composition, at the close of his introduction begins his narrative thus : —"So the Count of Toulouse and Bishop Adhemar marched through Slavonia and had many difficulties to encounter in the way, especially from the winter season. Slavonia is a wild, pathless, and mountainous country. For the space of three weeks we saw neither bird nor beast." He then observes how the wild inhabitants molested them, killing many stragglers, and easily evading pursuit by flying into the mountains. He adds,

" I will not omit one glorious act of the Count;" and relates with some detail the success of an ambush for the natives devised by Raymond. "Above all," says he, " it is impossible to narrate the deeds then performed by the Count. We were forty days in Slavonia, when the fog was so dense that we could actually grasp and handle it. All this time the Count was not idle one moment; he was the first to advance and the last to retreat, and remained armed day and night, until he had led the army through, without any serious loss." Here we at once recognize the eye-witness, who conveys to us the impressions he himself felt. Rough as are his forms of speech, he transports us at once into his own position and his own feelings. We grope our way with him through the mist and over the mountain-passes, and exult over a general by whose skill and vigour the army was saved.

Whilst this author presents the event itself, William of Tyre gives a history of it. He first relates the departure of the Count, and gives an account of his forces; then passing to Slavonia, he collects all the topographical notices scattered through the work of Raymond of Agiles, into the framework, as it were, of a quiet description. The army reaches its destination after great difficulties, throughout which it was admirably protected by thc Count. William of Tyre ends without having omitted a single fact or description; but likewise without having succeeded in one instance in giving the impression of his original. It must be admitted that he exhibits the lively sympathy with his sub-ject in general which is produced by a warm patriotism; but in the single statements of these early events he shows more interest in the compo-sition of his history than in the history itself.

This continues into the middle of the book. The account of the defeat of Raymond of An-tioch, in the year 1119, given by the Chancellor Gauthier and followed by William of Tyre, ex-hibits the same striving after historical skill, and the same want of simplicity of apprehension. There is no question that, with a feeling for method and clearness, William of Tyre omits much that is foreign to the matter; the arrangement and con-nection of the whole are much more distinct than in Gauthier. But in spite of these advantages his narrative has not the character of the original. His picture is correctly drawn, but its colouring is dull and differs from the original. His ruling passion is unity of design. He reduces all the inequalities of the originals to one uniform measure. By these means a broad and harmonious whole is indeed obtained, but all appearance of real life is destroyed, and an analysis of his materials is rendered impossible.

We recognize the same method of proceeding on another subject. William of Tyre, in the first books of his history, quotes a number of letters, docu-ments, speeches, and treatises, copied, it would appear and has been frequently believed, from authentic sources.[43] I believe them indeed to be all a pure invention of the Archbishop, unsupported by any earlier tradition. Such are, for instance, at the very beginning, the negotiations of Peter the Hermit with the Patriarch of Jerusalem. We do not find them in this form in any of the original authorities known to us. We can indeed trace their origin to Albert of Aix, although his narrative differs materially. I must maintain the same with regard to a thing which has been more generally accepted, the speech of Urban II. at Clermont.[44] Frequently as this has been quoted as a genuine document, I neither see external evidence of its au-thenticity, nor do the contents appear consonant to the spirit of those times. In this elaborate docu-ment, full of elegance and learning, there is no

[43] On the strength of his assertions, the Hist. Litt. de la France, viii. 600, considers Godfrey as the author of particular letters to the French historians. Examples of such a use in this sense are to be frequently found.

[44] Lib. i. c. 15.

in trace of the feeling dominant at that time, namely, boundless and extravagant fanaticism. In no way does it differ, either in thought or expression, from the treatment in the rest of William of Tyre's book. This may be said of other matters, to which we shall have to allude.

I pass over the speeches and letters inter-changed between Duke Godfrey and King Kalma-ni, briefly to consider the more important nego-tiations with the Emperor Alexius. There is merely a reference to the mission to Godfrey, given word for word from Albert's narrative; on the other hand, the requisition of Bohemund to make war upon Alexius, and Godfrey's refusal, is told *in extenso*, and in William of Tyre's most elaborate style.[45] But the conviction is forced upon us that we have before us an amplification of the let-ters given by Albert of Aix, exactly as we have in cap. xi. of the curt speeches of the Emperor to Godfrey.[46] The connection may appear more doubt-ful in the narrative of the embassy of the Emperor to Bohemond, as well as in that to the Count of Toulouse, which are not to be found in his autho-rities for those times, Baldrich[47] and Raymond of Toulouse.[48] I have no doubt that this also was a

[45] Lib. ii. c. 6, 10.—Albert, ii. 7, 14.
[46] Albert, c. 16.   [47] Baldr. p. 93.
[48] Raymond, p. 140.—William of Tyre, ii. c. 13-16, 18.

pure invention of William of Tyre. The contents of
the two letters are of the most general kind; their
form is precisely that used by the Archbishop, and
not at all like the Greek, as we may see in various
passages of Anna Comnena. Radulf proceeds in
a similar manner: he likewise introduces in a direct
speech the embassy to Bohemund, but does not attempt to conceal his own invention.

A further example, still more characteristic of
William of Tyre, is to be found in the negotiations about Nicæa. I must here premise, as well
known, that Alexius with great skill forced the
garrison of the town to a compromise, without any
reference to the Crusaders, and took possession of
the place, without allowing them to have any part
in the capture. In William of Tyre's narrative,
Tatikios took possession of the town, which, it is
said, the princes did not resent, as they would
not otherwise have been able to remain. He
lets this opinion escape in a letter addressed to
Alexius, wherein the princes request the Emperor
to send them a sufficient garrison, foreseeing that
they would soon be forced to break up their quarters.[49] We now know for certain that they were
exceedingly embittered by the loss of such a
booty; that they refused to hold intercourse with

[49] Lib. iii. c. 11.

the Emperor, and were only induced by urgent entreaty to open fresh negotiations. We know further that the Greek troops in Nicæa were quite numerous enough to defend the place, strong as it was, even against the Crusaders themselves. There could be no meaning therefore in the request for reinforcements. William of Tyre's intention seems to me clear enough; he neither wished to mix himself up with the passionate and vague questions of that period, nor did he believe (at all events he had no wish to relate) the intrigues of the Emperor, the lust for plunder of the princes, nor to touch on the various negotiations that passed. He had in his mind the picture of two great and admirably constituted Powers, and he represents their negotiations in the manner which seemed to him fitting. In a passage that follows immediately afterwards, it is stated, " In pactorum serie quæ inter eos inita fuerant, hæc formula dicebatur interserta; quod si aliquam de urbibus," etc.[50] This is in fact simply a new version of Albert's statement, that the princes had promised to restore the towns, lands, and villages;[51] the decision as to the plunder is of course added. A similar

[50] Lib. iii. c. 12.

[51] "Promiserunt enim juramento, nihil de regno imperatoris, non castra non civitates nisi de ejus voluntate seu dono retinere." —Albert, ii. 28.

proceeding is obvious (lib. vi. c. 15) in the account of the embassy of Peter and Herluin to Kerboga. He adopts Fulcher's account of the message with which the emissaries were entrusted, and Baldric's for the negotiations with the heathen emir. In both cases everything rough and uncourtly is excluded; they are made to discourse in the most diplomatic manner, and not with the wild zeal of lawless warriors fighting for religion's sake.[52] And so it is in all cases. I consider none of these statements as really original, or indeed as having any claim to be reckoned so. The first that I find trustworthy is the letter of Dagobert to Bohemund, in which instance there is no reason to doubt the express statement of William of Tyre.[53]

I have purposely dwelt somewhat at length upon this point, partly on account of the general acceptance which these representations have obtained, partly of the importance of the matter in forming a judgment on William of Tyre. Were the facts authentic, we must accept the Archbishop as an original authority, and a very important one. But now they serve admirably to define the position which he holds in relation to the original authorities.

[52] Fulcher, p. 393. Baldrich's paraphrase is still stronger (p. 119). The identity is too manifest to make any quotation necessary. William of Tyre, vi. 15.

[53] William of Tyre, x. 4.

We see how the general state of affairs, William's own position and modes of thought, and the manner in which he acquired and dealt with his materials, are dependent on each other. Another point remains, the decision of which must determine the literary position of his history. Without an examination of his critical method, our inquiry into the purpose and practical application of his history would be useless.

We have already suggested, that William of Tyre abstained from incorporating Arabic narratives into his work, as resting on such totally different grounds from those of Christian writers. The discrepancy between his Christian authorities apparently did not strike him; it is true he corrects occasional errors, but he never rises to a view of the whole. There are indeed traces of such an attempt, but it soon becomes evident that it is the result of an external influence. The second book contains the march of the separate bodies of troops through the Greek Empire. He first lays Albert of Aix under contribution, for the narrative of the march of the Lorrainers; he refers for Bohemund's advance to the 'Gesta Francorum' or to Baldrich; for that of Raymond of Toulouse to Raymond of Agiles; and lastly, he takes from Fulcher of Chartres his account of the march of the Northern French.

He thus always goes to the best authority—a countryman or a personal companion—for his account of each Prince. It ought not to affect our judgment, that he also inserts from other quarters much that is erroneous, and for which there is no authority.[54] This is unavoidable from the nature of such traditions. But this circumstance is conclusive, that he differs widely from the unhistorical Albert of Aix, and that he aims at preserving the historical value of his narrative, by divesting it of all legendary forms.

If we remember his personal character, and how foreign to his sober and well-regulated mind were all miracles and adventures, all poetry, whether religious or secular, it will appear more surprising that he should place any reliance on Albert of Aix, than that he should alter his narrative. On the other hand, if his scepticism was so strong as to lead him to reject it, he could easily throw out its poetical elements, and give to the dry residuum an historical character. But after he had stripped the political and military parts of all adventure, and substituted hierarchical forms for mystical excite-

[54] Such are to be found at pp. 705, 708, 710; how Bohemund has some spies roasted; Baji-Sijan suspects Firuz; Tancred and Robert of Flanders storm Antioch; how Raymond of Toulouse, even before the capture of the city, protests against Bohemund's assumption of its government.

ment, there still remained traces of the legendary origin of his history, in the contradictions, internal and external, which it contains, and the fables which are at variance with reason and experience. If William of Tyre were freed from these objections, his work would be complete and his task fulfilled. But on comparing it with some of the passages quoted in our criticism of Albert of Aix, we perceive how little he kept this object in view.

Albert places the peace between Godfrey and Alexius in January, 1097, and shortly afterwards mentions it as having been signed about Christmas, 1096. William of Tyre dismisses the last statement altogether, and confirms the first from other sources. In other respects he follows Albert word for word.[55] The latter describes the battle of Dorylæum, with a great display of poetical but useless detail. The distrust inspired by such a mode of writing is confirmed by a comparison of the statement with the original authorities. William of Tyre uses them all indiscriminately. He omits all Albert's poetical forms, and comments on the discrepancies of his statements, without expressing any scepticism concerning the narrative as a whole. He omits whatever bears clear evidence of a fabulous origin,—whatever is in obvious contradiction

[55] William of Tyre, ii. 10–13.

to the original authorities,—and places side by side two reports of the same occurrence, as if they related to different events.[56] What remains after this process he adds to the narrative of the original authorities, not perceiving that he has only saved a dead and worthless mass.

Albert first leads Prince Sweyn of Denmark to Nicæa, then back again to Constantinople, and thence to his defeat by Solyman. William of Tyre at once copies the whole story, only altering one point,—the absurd journey back to Constantinople.[57]

Duke Godfrey, according to Albert, is wounded in a fight with a bear near Antiochetta, and is in consequence confined to his bed for many months. But immediately after, we find him engaged in fierce battles, leading the army, and, clad in armour and with flying banners, breaking the ranks of the heathen host. William of Tyre unhesitatingly copies the one occurrence from Albert, but he omits the other. Here, as in other places, the want of sense in the passage made him hesitate to admit it. But he had no doubt as to the general narrative, the whole of which was open to suspicion.

He proceeds in this manner throughout the book. All that Albert tells, without rhyme or reason, of

[56] William of Tyre, iii. 13, 15.
[57] Id., v. 20.

the Turkish affairs, William of Tyre weeds out, yet he cannot emancipate himself from the influence of these reports on other facts. We have before quoted similar proofs of his manner of dealing with the legend of Peter the Hermit; how in the account of the embassy to Kerboga he mixes fable and history, and endeavours to give to Albert's narrative of the siege of Antioch an air of historical truth. His criticism is in the main conservative, but without any valid reason: out of two discrepant accounts he endeavours to make one true one, by taking away here and adding there, until the angles are smoothed down and a flat but insipid polish is attained. William of Tyre was quite conscious of this in his later books, but only when Albert's deviations touched him on the tenderest point. He makes use of Albert in the manner I have described, until the foundation of the kingdom of Jerusalem. He then leaves him, and never refers to him again. He does not allude to the cause of this sudden mistrust, but I believe it is attributable to Albert's account of the Patriarch Dagobert and Arnulf. We have shown the strongly-marked contradiction that appears between these two authors, and the passion with which William of Tyre devoted himself to that portion of his narrative. We cannot therefore wonder that he subsequently wholly re-

x 2

jected an authority which threatened to undermine his historical faith.

It is to be regretted that he did not apply the conviction thus forced upon him to his treatment of the earlier part of his history. We hesitate not to assert, that it is solely owing to his work that the prestige of legends in this portion of history has endured for so many centuries. The distrust which must have arisen, had the original forms of the legends been preserved, vanished before the historical air he imparted to them. The idea of the leadership of Godfrey of Bouillon, miraculous in its origin and in all its results, and terminated by a marvellous death, would not have satisfied men's minds long. William of Tyre deals with the whole cycle of the traditions as he does with individual cases. He passes over in silence the divine interposition, and the events in which it was manifested; but he accepts all the glory ascribed to Godfrey of Bouillon, and creates the idea of his character which has remained in force even to this day. According to this idea, Godfrey was the leader of the Crusades neither by the express choice of man, nor by the miraculous dispensation of God; but his wisdom, strength, righteousness, and his other virtues, gradually raised him to the highest place,—a view which a sceptical age readily accepted. William of

Tyre was regarded as an original authority, and no one thought of disputing his claim to that character. His representation was taken to be the true one. The original legend, scattered far and wide, and with no great name to guarantee its truth, fell into oblivion, or its splendours and its marvels only served to embellish and magnify the events that actually occurred. Men spoke of the strong enthusiasm, of the passion for miracles of that age, in which embellishments to truth were natural enough. But no one imagined that these very embellishments were the real originals, and that what was supposed to be the truth was only a diluted reproduction of them.

Unless I greatly err, the positive nature of William of Tyre's book, concerning the First Crusade, is characterized in the foregoing description. William of Tyre represents a phase which, in the literature of every nation, immediately succeeds the development of legendary tales: the distinction between historical and poetical creations disappears; the writer attempts to unite the former with the latter. He does not perceive that the truth of the one and the poetry of the other are thus lost; he proceeds with his work with talent and vigour, and it bears the impress of his character. It is true that this view lowers his repu-

tation for trustworthiness: we divide his work into
two equal portions, one of which is admirable; the
other, as concerns its contents, is totally valueless
as an original authority. It was the more necessary to prove the unity of these two portions, from
the personal character of the author. The position
he has chosen as mediator between legend and
history is the natural consequence of that character. How much he sacrificed to such a mode of
treating his materials is evident enough, and every
reader will doubtless resort, if he can, to the original sources.

CHAPTER IV.

EPOCHS OF A LATER LITERATURE.

Whether we investigate each single work, or take a general survey of the literature subsequent to William of Tyre, two points have to be considered : first, those originals which at that period exercised a predominant influence ; and next, the position of the writers with regard to the events which they were about to describe. It will suffice here to recognize and to attest the character and the turning-point of the different epochs. Our space will not allow us to enter into the subject with the fullness required by biographical or critical examination. In fulfilling these requirements, the object appears to be attained, of assigning the just position, according to the materials, to later additions and emendations. The selection of the materials that have come down to us has been made with this view. Provided the results of the examples I have adduced are not weakened by some authority which I have overlooked, I am content not to have passed over any of the more important, or omitted any of the most striking points of the narratives. The great mass of monographs, which might have explained many peculiarities, have been left unnoticed. The same applies to all the histories of a purely national or patriotic tendency, such as almost every nation of Europe possesses on the subject of the Crusades. Such an inquiry would require a special work, and would afford little available for our purpose.

We shall perceive a similarity of proceeding in this province of history when treated as a whole, as when we examined the views of contemporary authors. Among the latter I include the original authorities, the Legends, and William of Tyre. Even in the literature of a later period, the views contained in these three sources of information seemed for a time different; without question, at the beginning, the influence of the original authorities preponderated; which they owed to their greater circulation, if not to the talent of the writers. The Legends, by blending poetry with history, combine the attractions of both. William of Tyre was read, but it was only after the lapse of a long period that his account of these events became extensively known. Although, under these circumstances, the views taken of persons and of events varied, still, on the whole, the judgment as to the general importance and the particular details of the Crusades remained fixed. The ecclesiastical point of view predominated, and only on trifling points assumed a more chivalrous or mystical colouring. But in a second period, this state of opinion completely changed: William of Tyre becomes the exclusive authority. In process of time, the original sources are more consulted, though but few notices from them are incorporated into the groundwork of the Archbishop's narrative. The glory of Peter the Hermit and Godfrey of Bouillon, ascribed to them by William of Tyre, is celebrated in proportion as the ecclesiastical, poetical, or patriotic interest prevails. Even the negative philosophy of the eighteenth century leaves the facts untouched, however much it busied itself with the motives and the consequences of the Crusades. Lastly, the tendency of modern literature has been to restore them on all points to their old position.

I will here mention—chiefly for the sake of the place where it was written—a short history of the Crusades, compiled in 1218 by a certain Scholasticus Oliver.[1] In the camp before Damietta, on the very spot where but a few years before William of Tyre wrote and acted, Oliver merely employed himself in condensing Fulcher of Chartres, taking probably such extracts as suited his purpose from the 'Gesta Francorum.' I have not met with any later mention of this essay.

But the work of Vincent, Bishop of Beauvais, has attracted great attention, and had a wide circulation, although his 'Mirror of History' gives no detailed narrative of the First Crusade.[2] It is a mere compilation, deficient in critical and descriptive power. The beginning—up to the words "Secundum bellum fuit Nicææ"—is copied from Siegbert of Gembloux, and the commencement of Baldrich is repeated. Baldrich remains his leading authority, occasional extracts from Siegbert and William of Malmesbury being added. Insignificant as the work is, the great reputation in which Vincent of Beauvais was held in the Middle Ages

[1] Oliv. Schol. Historia Regum Terræ Sanctæ, quam in obsidione Damiatæ apud Ægyptum compilavit, in Eccard. Corpus Hist. M. Æ. t. ii.

[2] Vinc. Bellov. Spec. Hist. xxv. 96. For the account of the several editions see Ebert, Bibl. Lexicon, s. v. Michaud, Bibl. iii. 323, gives a detailed notice of the history of the Crusades. Vincent died in 1264.

caused it to be much used, partly as sole authority, partly mixed with others. The translator of Bernhard, of whom we shall treat in another place, quotes him among his authorities. Archbishop Antoninus somewhat later quotes him also, together with some passages from William of Tyre. Hermann Corner has scarcely any other authority for his knowledge of the First Crusade: he includes in his work the narrative of the 'Mirror of History,' with all its quotations.[3] The great Belgian Chronicle does exactly the same, only that it contains the history of Gulfer and his lion,[4] first mentioned, I believe, by Godfrey Vos. He derives also from Raymond (whom he calls Martin Agiles) an account of the Holy Lance, and of the transmission of letters by pigeons captured near Cæsarea.[5]

In Germany the narrative of Eckhardt, which we have described as being current in the twelfth century, is occasionally met with in the thirteenth. The Luneburg Chronicle, which ends with the year 1285, gives it at length. The chronicle of the priest Andreas Kraft, of Ratisbon,[6] gives a second copy of it, equally diffuse. Robert, Baldrich, and Siegbert are the authorities of Alberich's

[3] Herm. Com. in Eccard. Corpus, t. ii. p. 630.
[4] In Labbé, Nova Bibl. t. ii. p. 292.
[5] Pistorius, Script. vi. 129.
[6] Both are in the first volume of Eccard. Corpus Hist. M. Ævi.

narrative, to which some passages from William of Tyre and the lost work of Guy of Châlons have been added.[7]

In the beginning of the fourteenth century we meet in England with a compilation from Siegbert and the monk Robert, in the 'Flores Historiarum,' by Matthew of Westminster, who continuéd this work down to the year 1307. The narrative is remarkably short, but the eulogy of the Duke of Normandy by Robert is not omitted (p. 40, *apud* Bongars).[8]

Again it is Siegbert, with some additional particulars from the 'Gesta' or the copyers of that work, who has furnished John of Ypres with materials for his narrative of the Crusades.[9] John of Ypres died in 1383, and his Chronicle reaches from the year 590 to 1294. William of Tyre is his authority for some of the dates, and for the incident of the refusal of Godfrey to wear the golden crown at Jerusalem.

Gobelin Persona, who continued his Cosmodromium to the year 1418, gives only a summary account of the Crusades, and does not refer spe-

---

[7] Alberici Chron. ad a. 1096. The article in Michaud's Bibliothèque gives a more detailed account.

[8] The whole is copied word for word in Walsingham's 'Hypodigma Neustriæ,' which ended in 1417. (Camden, p. 441.)

[9] Chron. S. Bertini, in Martene, Thesaurus, t. iii. p. 593.

cially to any original authority. The communication by means of pigeons, already mentioned, from Cæsarea, is copied word for word from Raymond of Agiles (P. 173, *apud* Bongars).[10]

Blondus, in the third and fourth book of his second Decade, takes a wider circuit; his object is not only to mention, but to describe the Crusade. He had access to Andreas Dandolo, to William of Tyre, and, apparently, to the French text of Bernhard; nevertheless he invariably follows Robert the Monk, to whom he frequently alludes.[11] He copies from him the good and bad indiscriminately, and by his confused way of writing spoils much that was valuable in the work of Robert the Monk.[12] Moreover his style is without colour, and his narrative without life. The whole composition, like all that this author has left, is of inferior value.

Platina, who has interpolated into the Lives of Urban II. and Paschal II. a narrative of the First Crusade, does not rank much higher.[13] Robert the Monk serves also as the groundwork

[10] Meibom, Script. t. i. p. 62.

[11] L. iv. "In Venetorum monumentis invenio (Andr. Dand. in Muratori Script. xii. p. 256). Fatetur ingenue Robertus S. Remigii monachus, quo hæc certiora sumuntur, fatetur Guilielmus et ipse scriptor Gallicus," etc.

[12] Compare the occurrences in Constantinople and what is said of Baldwin's rule in Tarsus.

[13] In the ' Vitæ Pontificum.'

to Platina, as is evident from a cursory comparison.[14] The account of Godfrey's humility at the Holy Sepulchre is the only passage taken from William of Tyre. But, beside copying the blunders of others, Platina has many of his own.[15] His style is somewhat more polished than that of Blondus, and the whole book less pretentious and shorter. Nevertheless the general tendency is the same; the religious character and influence of the Crusades is the central idea; but there is no special mention either of Peter the Hermit and his visions, nor of the mystic or human superiority of Duke Godfrey.

On a general view of these writers, we find some departure from the original authorities, but they are still current until the end of the fifteenth century. Eckhardt and Siegbert are most frequently quoted. Their statements from the ' Gesta ' come down to us chiefly in the forms given to them by Baldrich or Robert; in the latter, mixed with some portions of oral tradition. Fragments from William of Tyre are here and there intro-

[14] There can be no doubt that the ' Gesta,' and not Albert, is the latest authority. We may recognize Robert in the manner in which Hugo and Godfrey are glorified at Dorylæum, and in which Pyrrhus admires Bohemund's great qualities.

[15] The statement that Godfrey and his brother Baldwin were the first to enter Jerusalem.

duced, but he exercises no influence in enlarging the view of the subject as a whole ; this indeed is entirely lost sight of. The annals are short, and display great poverty of expression. Almost the only idea of any importance is, the recognition of the Pope as the originator and active leader of the general religious movement.

At the same time a mode of treating these events, entirely at variance with that which we have been considering, found remarkable sympathy and furtherance. I have already alluded to the Legends of the Crusades, at first fostered unconsciously by the national spirit of the people, and falling by degrees into the hands of the poets, who worked them up into artistic forms. Had a complete separation of literature from actual life been then effected, we might have omitted all allusion to this branch of the history of literature. But the poets of the romances to which we refer had no idea of being mere inventors, or of quitting the interest which attaches to the incidents of actual life, for a wider and more arduous range. " We could not understand the existence of these romances," says Fauriel, speaking of the poems of the Carlovingian period[16], " if we sup-

[16] Revue des Deux Mondes, vii. 539, 554.

posed that they were invented exactly as they now are, and, as a connected whole, three hundred years after the events they celebrate. We can only comprehend them regarded as the expression of a lively and unbroken tradition." The same may be said of the romances of the Crusades; they also invite the barons to listen to captivating stories and truthful songs; they also relate actual events, *"vieille histoire, haute histoire."* The powerful effect produced by this union of poetry with tradition merits our attention.

I must, however, confine myself to little more than titles of books and brief notices of their contents. None of the romances to which I now refer have ever been printed in a complete form; they come down to us in extracts. The historical narratives founded upon them are contained in obsolete editions. In most cases the mere mention of the title will suffice to justify the place we assign to it in the collection.

In characterizing the contemporaneous legends, we traced the numerous forms under which they brought individual facts before our eyes; at the same time we noticed one ruling idea which pervades them; namely, the poetical glorification of Duke Godfrey as the leader chosen by God for this enterprise; and we mentioned the poems of Gandor of Douay and others, in which this subject assumed an artistic form. We now see that the preference visible in the literature of the thirteenth, fourteenth and fifteenth centuries for epic tales of chivalry, extended to the subject of the Crusades. The north of France was especially the land of poetry on the Crusades; though traces of the same are also found in Germany, Holland, England, and Italy. The mode of development followed the usual course. In the thirteenth century the poetical feeling was stronger, and the epos found expression in metrical forms. After the fourteenth century, measure and rhythm gave way to a diffuse romantic prose; belief in the truth of the narrative increased; while the poetic fictions were so mingled with the most varied historical statements, that cultivated readers were unable to distinguish poetry from history.

The oldest poetical reproduction of the subject known to me, after the poem of Gandor, is by a German of great celebrity. The Imperial library at Vienna possesses an epic by Wolfram of Eschenbach, on the expedition to the Holy Land, under Godfrey of Bouillon; to which is appended a narrative of the Syrian campaign until 1227.[17]

Gandor's 'Knight of the Swan' was translated into prose in the fourteenth century, and many ex-

[17] Lambecii Commentar. de Bibl. Cæsar. ii. 911: ed. Kollar.

tracts from it have been published.[18]   It is manifest that, in the process of transmission, numerous
alterations and additions were made; religious excitement, which was not remarkable even in Gandor, has altogether vanished, and is replaced by a
hurried series of adventures. I pass over the mythical account of the grandfather of Godfrey of Bouillon, from whom the poem takes its name, and will
select a few passages from the history of the Crusades itself.

The scene is laid at Mecca, where the tomb of
the god Mahound floats in the air: the heathen
are assembled, the Sultan of Persia, the great Emir
Corbara, and many other kings around them. The
mother of Corbara, Calabre the learned, arrives,
and prophesies the fall of Jerusalem by the instru-
mentality of Godfrey and his brothers. This story
had already been current among those who took a
part in the Crusades. The 'Gesta Francorum'
treats of it at some length. On this announcement
Cornumarant goes to Europe in disguise, in order
to kill the three brothers. He is recognized, and
states his readiness to do homage to the Duke,
whose high destiny fills him with reverence. The
Duke, in order completely to dazzle the Turk, summons all the bishops to his reception. To enhance

---

[18] Mélanges tirés d'une grande Bibliothèque, vi. 4.

his dignity, the princes of Artois, Flanders, the Palatinate, and of Hainault, represent themselves as the officers of his Court. Godfrey of Bouillon here announces his intention of fulfilling the prophecy, and the princes determine to place themselves under his guidance. What had begun merely as a show became a reality : the Pope, the Emperor, and King Philip of France, gave in their adhesion; but before they started on the expedition, the Duke was obliged, in single combat, to make good his claim to Lorraine, and put his rival, here called Arnulf, to death. At length Peter of Amiens arrives from Rome to preach the Crusade, and from that point we find ourselves on the well-known ground of Albert of Aix or of William of Tyre. In the end Godfrey of Bouillon, as lord of Jerusalem, marries the beautiful Florie, sister of Corbara, and daughter of the learned Calabre of Holofernia.

I think these extracts will confirm the judgment I have pronounced; but in those times the world was satisfied with such absurd fables, which were reproduced in great numbers until the middle of the fifteenth century. An old catalogue of Parisian manuscripts gives no less than fifteen of these chronicles extant.[19] 'Godeffroy de Billon de la Con-

---

[19] In the Hist. de l'Académie Royale, i. 314 : among these fifteen, however, the Chevalier du Cygne might have been in-

queste d'Oultremer,' or with some such title; two
of them are "*rymé*," but are also extant in a prose
version; the rest appear to be all in prose. That
the contents do not differ in any important points
from the narrative I have described, appears to be
beyond a doubt, both from the pre-eminence given
to Godfrey, and from the positive assertions of the
best-informed writers.[20]

These histories soon attained to a wide-spread
popularity.[21] 'Les Faits et les Gestes du preux Godeffroy de Bouillon' were known in all countries.
In France, a work of N. Chrestien on this subject
was printed in 1499. Le Noir translated the Latin
work of 'Desrey de Troyes' in 1511; and in 1580
that work went through a second edition. In Italy,
the young Ariosto translated one of these romances,
under the title of 'Goffredo Bajone;'[22] and in 1481
William Caxton gave an English version of this
or some similar work. A Dutch version appeared

cluded. The statements in the Mélanges, vi. 1, are not at any
rate correct.

[20] Mélanges, i. c.

[21] The following notices are taken from Ebert's Bibliogr.
Lexicon, article "Godefroy de Bouillon." Görres' introduction
to the 'Lohengrin,' p. 76, mentions a Godfrey of Prabant, quoted
by Pütrich, p. 18, and an Icelandic Godfreysaga; nevertheless
the other quotations of the passages (concerning Desrey and
Ariosto) are too incorrect for me to rely on his statement.

[22] Fernow, Life of Ariosto, p. 57.

at Haarlem about 1486; and a German one was printed at Augsburg in 1502.

This suffices to show the tenacity of the belief that Godfrey was the real leader of the Crusade,—a belief that existed long after William of Tyre had become the chief authority among the learned. Even to this day, the idea of Godfrey's superiority to the other Crusaders is only driven out of men's minds by the weight of authority, and then only for the moment.

The service rendered by William of Tyre and his followers to historical truth appears very great, in comparison with the writers we have mentioned. Until the time arrived for subjecting the original authorities to the test of a searching criticism, William of Tyre and his followers gave currency to statements which had at any rate an air of probability and of historical research. The first labourers in this field, though superior in some respects to many of their successors, yet furnish little to a knowledge of the First Crusade, and form no epoch; I shall therefore notice them briefly.

Jacob de Vitry, afterwards Cardinal and Bishop of Tusculum, wrote before the year 1240 a connected history of the kingdom of Jerusalem, taken entirely from William of Tyre.[23] His work justly

---

[23] Historia Hierosolymitana, in Bongars, i. 1047. He makes use of William of Tyre from i. 15.

enjoys a high reputation, not on account of the historical narrative, which has no original value, but from the numerous topographical and statistical statements which form the larger portion of his compilation. Towards the close of the same century the Venetian Marino Sanuto, borrowed from him the historical information required for his remarkable book the ' Secreta Fidelium Crucis.'[24]

Shortly after Jacob de Vitry had published his compilation, William of Tyre again appears as the chief authority of a long and popular narrative of the Crusades. Matthew Paris, in his ' Historia Angliæ Major,' copied almost entirely from William of Tyre, adding various notices from William of Malmesbury, or from the ' Gesta.'[25] At the same time his notions of critical examination or skilful compilation are but faint. In many cases he confuses time and place, simply from being unable to arrange well-authenticated facts in a connected narrative.[26]

I may also here call attention to a passage in Petrarch's treatise on the ' Vita Solitaria' (book ii. sec. 4, c. 1, 2). The earnestness with which, even in his poetical works, Petrarch endeavoured

---

[24] In Bongars, ii. 130. [25] Historia, p. 22.
[26] Compare the events in Constantinople and the occurrences in Cilicia and Cappadocia.

to excite men's minds to a new Crusade, is well known.[27] The passage to which I allude, in praise of Peter the Hermit, has the same object, and we instantly recognize the influence of William of Tyre, whose tenth and twelfth chapters are borrowed nearly word for word. Petrarch then proceeds:— " I need not write further on this subject, as the matter is made public in two goodly volumes, written in the vulgar tongue (*sermone vulgari*), and in a tolerable style. I see on this point the minds of their authors moved in different directions," etc. It would have been curious to examine this difference of their opinions, but I have failed even to discover to what Italian work Petrarch alludes.

In the second half of the thirteenth century ✓ the Treasurer Bernhard—an author of whom we know nothing beyond his name—translated the whole work of William of Tyre into French, and brought down the narrative to the departure of the Emperor Frederick II. The book had been lost until a few years ago, when Michaud discovered a manuscript copy in Paris, and published ample extracts in his ' Bibliothèque des Croisades,'[28] from which however nothing is to be learned beyond the

[27] Canzone 5, Sonetto 107.
[28] Bibliothèque des Croisades, ii. 555.

identity of these narratives, as far as concerns the first half, which is taken from William of Tyre. About the year 1320, a Dominican of the name of Pepin of Bologna made a Latin version of Bernhard's work,[29] in which the author allowed himself much latitude, and made alterations and additions from Vincent of Beauvais.[30] Singularly enough, the vision of Peter the Hermit was passed over in complete silence.

From the same materials, but with a much warmer sentiment, the Archbishop Antonine of Florence compiled, about the year 1450, that portion of his ' Summa Historialis ' which treats of the history of the First Crusade.[31] With the exception of some statements taken from Vincent of Beauvais, William of Tyre is his chief authority. In the words of the introduction we may trace the influence of the legends. Jerusalem was delivered under the leadership of Godfrey of Bouillon, who, together with his brothers Baldwin and Eustace, fought against the Turks with marvellous fortitude. William of Tyre, with some exaggerations as to re-

---

[29] In Muratori Script. vii. p. 663.

[30] He makes a free compilation from letters and speeches. Cap. 10, 11, 13; c. 22: the Greek emperor is called Romanus Diogenes. Cap. 25 : Baldwin of Tarsus is not mentioned. Cap. 26: a free narrative of the events at Edessa, etc. Some passages are taken from Vincent of Beauvais, c. 8, 9, 78, 80.

[31] Pars ii., p. 665.

ligious sentiment, is the main foundation of the
work. Although there is a total want of critical
investigation and narrative power, the book has
been largely used and quoted by later authors.

Without comparison, a work of much greater
interest is that of Benedictus Accolti, 'De Bello
à Christianis contra Barbaros gesto,' libri iv. Accolti, born at Arezzo, and afterwards Secretary to
the Republic of Florence, where he died in 1465,
followed the legal profession, which, together with
the general tendency of the times, led him to
a deep study of the ancients. His book betrays
the influence of the Latin writers, and a conscious striving after historical art. He cares less
for matter than for form, and he writes with
more of a social than an ascetic spirit. His
diction is rich and elegant, but occasionally over-
loaded with ornament. He neglects the critical
for the narrative portion; he praises nothing and
condemns nothing, and puts speeches in praise of
the Crusades in the mouths of Urban, Bohemund,
and others. The contents are chiefly taken from
the narrative of William of Tyre. It is the most
elegant version of that author with which I am
acquainted, singular as the subject appears dressed
in an antique garb. The book, which ends with
the death of Godfrey, had a great reputation, and

went through many editions; the last was printed in 1731. Dempster added to it a commentary, written without spirit or much learning.[32] I leave others to decide whether Warton is right in saying that Accolti's work gave the first idea of his poem to Tasso;[33] but it may be confidently asserted that the style and manner which he first applied to this subject long prevailed among historians. The influence of antiquity, then dominant in the widest provinces of literature, thoroughly pervaded this particular field. I will only mention two examples, written in the beginning of the sixteenth century, and used and imitated by most of the modern writers. George Nauclerus, in his 'Historia Chronica,'[34] did not devote much time to inquiry: he seems to have exclusively consulted William of Tyre, and him often in a very cursory manner. The polish of the style is not so obvious as in Accolti's work, and the result is not nearly so good. The sentiments are more worldly, especially in the history of Godfrey's government. The conquests and the well-regulated administration of affairs are praised at great length, whilst personal or religious ex-

[32] His chief authorities are Platina and Antoninus. It is true that he quotes contemporaries in many places. His critical review of the latter is wholly useless.

[33] Mill's History of the Crusades, i. 150.

[34] Tom. ii., gener. 37.

cellence is dismissed in a few sentences.[35]   Paulus
Emilius of Verona surpasses him in careful research.
In the fourth book of his 'Res Gestæ Francorum' he gives a detailed history of the Crusades.
His chief guide is William of Tyre, but he also
makes use of Guibert and Albert of Aix.[36]   The
language is good and concise, though he affects to
clothe the eulogy of the French, which is the main
object of his history, in words or turns of sentences
founded on classical models.

The. character of these works is completely in
keeping with the general tendencies of the period.
The tasteless forms were in the highest degree popular; at the same time there arose a certain taste
for learning.   Compared with the manner in which
Blondus used his authorities, these compilations
from William of Tyre show a considerable progress,
not to mention the 'Gestes du preux Godefroi,'
which are nearly forgotten.   The calm frame of
mind in which these narratives are written is agreeable: we recognize the artist who takes a pleasure
in his work. without the bias of personal interest.
The period we have next to survey is not remarkable for impartiality.

[35] Page 164.
[36] Page 108: there were supplicating Syrian Christians at
Clermont. Page 109: the decrees of the Council were made
known to the whole world in one day.

Thomas Fuller compiled the 'Historie of the Holy Warre'[37] chiefly from Paulus Emilius and other later authors.   He also looked into William of Tyre and some other original authorities, and never rises beyond the facts thus obtained.   But at the very beginning he discloses the totally differ- ent point from which he starts, by asserting that the Pope encouraged the Crusades for his own special advantage, and sent Peter the Hermit to Jerusalem in order that he might return from thence as an apostle sent from God.   This is not a rationalist opinion on his part, but the expression of the hosti- lity of an Englishman to the Papacy, as is clearly seen in the following phrase, which is also a good example of his style :—" England, the Pope's pack- horse in that age, which seldom rested in the stable when there was any work to be done," etc.   Fuller is, as far as I can remember, the first to discuss the often mooted question of the righteousness of the Crusades.

The History of the Crusades by Father Maimbourg is more celebrated, and stands on a very different footing ; it is at the same time affected by outward influences.[38]   The work is dedicated to Louis XIV.,

---

[37] The third edition, printed at Cambridge, 1647.

[38] Histoire des Croisades pour la Délivrance de la Terre Sainte.   Third edition.   Paris, 1685.

whose favour the writer enjoyed ; and the influence of the Court pervades it in every part. The author has a good opinion of himself, a fund of religious zeal, tempered by a genuine dash of modern good sense ;[39] but above all things he knows he is writing for great people and the best company.[40] Such are the circumstances which have chiefly affected Maimbourg's opinions. There is little depth or soundness of research, though he makes a great parade of authorities and quotations. At that time Bongars' Collection was about to be published. He nowhere critically examines the original authorities, but relies implicitly upon William of Tyre. Moreover the quotations are jumbled together in the most careless and confused manner. Maimbourg has no mean talent for clearness and vivacity of expression, but evidently thought more of the fate than of the contents of his work.

The prevalent state of opinion did not long maintain its ground. Maimbourg halted between religious excitement and scepticism ; but the spirit of

[39] Page 13 : Peter in the temple at Jerusalem. "L'hermite s'étant éveillé sentit ou du moins crut qu'il sentait dans son âme les effets d'une impression," etc.

[40] For example, he says he would mention the princes of the Crusades, according to his authorities, " si les personnes de qualité qui prétendent que quelques-uns de leurs ancêtres aient eu part à ces guerres saintes, me font la grâce de m'envoyer de bonnes mémoires," etc.

the eighteenth century was decidedly opposed to implicit faith, and restlessly active in remodelling science and art. A series of works were written, in greater or less detail, which threw light upon the Crusades, and which, taking different views of the facts, subjected the products of the eleventh century to a searching criticism. Voltaire is the foremost of these writers; the part in his 'Essai sur les Mœurs'[41] touching on the Crusades is very weak in point of research, for he does not even name any other authorities than William of Tyre, Anna Comnena and Elmacin, and those he scarcely used. At the same time it exhibits a remarkable contrast with the later narrative of the Crusades, by the clear decision of judgment and charms of style which distinguish his writings. De Guignes, in his History of the Huns, is more bitter and more learned, but he is dry and tasteless compared with Voltaire. He says in the very beginning :[42]—" Parmi les Francs une multitude de gens sans aveu, et de libertins, sortirent de l'Europe et ne passèrent en Asie que pour s'enrichir, se lever de plus en plus à leurs vices et y trouver l'impunité; les crimes de ceux-ci, le fanatisme de quelques autres, et le mélange bizarre de religion et de chevalerie, ont fait désap-

---

[41] Cap. 54, vol. xxiv. of the Zweibrück edition.
[42] Histoire des Huns, t. ii. p. 13.

prouver dans un siècle plus éclairé ces sortes de guerres." His criticism of the authorities is not such as to make this section the best part of De Guignes's celebrated work. Whatever names may appear on the margin, he takes nearly all his materials from William of Tyre, and makes many blunders whenever he quotes Eastern authorities.[43] I cannot speak more favourably of that section of this author's work devoted to the trade of the French with the Levant.[44]

Mailly's often-quoted work, 'Sur l'Esprit des Croisades,' is far better on all points. It is in four volumes, and reaches to the end of the First Crusade. The authorities are better investigated than by De Guignes, although the author depends more upon the judgment of the 'Histoire Littéraire de la France' than upon his own criticisms. For all accounts of particular events, William of Tyre is Mailly's principal authority. He is very lavish of

[43] At p. 85, the year 1097 is given for the taking of Jerusalem by the Egyptians, and Zonaras and Jacob de Vitry are the authorities quoted. At p. 196, it was mentioned, on the authority of William of Tyre, that Kilidje Arslan had been with Kerboga's army.

[44] He argues that the Crusades were chiefly brought about by the impediments thrown in the way of the trade of the Franks, and that this was the best excuse for them. The accounts of the trade of the Merovingians are good, but the Essay is very incomplete and faulty in many parts.

his philosophical reflections; but he takes as he finds them the order of events, the characteristics of the chief personages, their actions and their influence. Maier, who takes his materials chiefly from De Guignes, and Heller, who is largely indebted to Mailly, compiled works for German readers which are too worthless to require serious mention.[45]

"Urban and Peter!" exclaims Heller, "the corpses of two millions of men lie heavy on your graves, and will fearfully summon you on the day of judgment."[46]   There was a strong reaction against this violent condemnation; but the sentiment which prompted it was by no means extinct; and even to the present day it has occasionally found expression in various languages. Haken's History of the Crusades[47] is written in this spirit: the barbarism of the Middle Ages, the fatal fanaticism, the mad impulse to action, meet with continual reprobation; and he studies the authorities more diligently than any earlier writer holding these views, and engrafts a tolerably complete series of other statements, likewise authentic, on the narrative

[45] Maier, 'Versuch einer Geschichte der Kreuzzüge in ihren Folgen.' Berlin, 1780. Heller, 'Geschichte der Kreuzzüge nach dem heiligen Lande.' 3 vols. Frankenthal, 1784.

[46] Page 16.

[47] 'Gemälde der Kreuzzüge.' 4 parts. Frankfurt, 1808.

of William of Tyre. The author, tried by modern standards, is open to the charge of want of taste and turgidity of style, and of a pathos frequently out of place.[48]

Mills' History of the Crusades,[49] as far as outward form goes, is far preferable to Haken's, and little inferior in the diligence bestowed upon the collection of materials; but the absence of methodical criticism is seen in the patriotic leaning to William of Malmesbury, and still more clearly in the appendix characterizing the original authorities. Here and there a slight doubt is expressed concerning Albert of Aix and William of Tyre, but always with regard to some particular fact, never from general views of the grounds on which their narratives rest. By far the safest authority in the whole work appears to be De Guignes, according to whom the interest of commerce, next to the pilgrimages, exercised the most powerful influence on the origin of the Crusades.[50]

But the spirit of the eighteenth century is still more clearly shown in the passages on the Crusades

[48] The Essay of the same author, in Ersch and Gruber's Encyclopædia, article "Bouillon," closely follows Wilken.

[49] Charles Mills' History of the Crusades, 2 vols. 2nd edition. London, 1821.

[50] Peter's oration is mentioned at page 38, but not his dream.

in Lebeau's ' Histoire du Bas-Empire :'[51] "Ces ex-
péditions nommées saintes," he says in one place,
"qui l'auraient été en effet si l'esprit de la religion
chrétienne était un esprit de guerres et de con-
quêtes,—if it was really intended to free the East,
and had Constantinople joined the Crusaders,—but
although the Holy Places deserve our veneration,
this will scarcely justify the murder of those who
desecrated them," etc. We see that neither the
sources nor the forms of the religious enthusiasm
of the eleventh century were understood by this
writer. I should scarcely have mentioned the work,
which belongs rather to general literature than
to history, had not St. Martin's name led me to
expect special information from Oriental sources.
But this is not the case. Albert of Aix, William of
Tyre, and even Marino Sanuto are the chief authorities; and, with few exceptions, the work is mainly
founded on Michaud's History of the Crusades.

Lastly, St. Maurice's ' Résumé de l'Histoire des
Croisades'[52] is wholly unimportant. It is written,
after the modern French historical fashion, in a
glowing romantic style, and only repeats the matter
found in the best-known authors concerning the
First Crusade. The Crusades, he says, were not

[51] Edited by MM. St. Martin and Brosset, T. xv. p. 301.
[52] Paris, 1826.

the product of a general religious excitement ; they were the work of the Popes, whose tottering (*sic*) hierarchy could only have been saved by such means. Tasso's poem and brilliant fictions kept the world in a state of illusion until the eighteenth century ; "mais les lois de la vérité sont imprescriptibles," etc.[53]

That this opinion is not universally accepted at the present day, is to be attributed as a lasting merit to Wilken. Generally speaking, when Wilken began his History,[54] the exclusive conceit that prevailed in the previous century had somewhat abated, and the feeling (of the Germans at any rate) had reverted with affectionate enthusiasm towards the Middle Ages. Wilken, with great and sound learning, endowed with a remarkable power of narrating, undertook to turn this feeling to account, and to represent to our age the Crusades as they appeared to contemporary actors and writers. His work gave him, and with justice, the first place in this province of history. No one doubts its merit, and I have no intention of lessening it by attempting to indicate in what respect some later history may be a further progress in the right di-

---

[53] P. 324. He uses Condorcet's motto: "Les Croisades, entreprises pour la superstition, servirent à la détruire."

[54] The first volume appeared in 1807.

rection. The chief point is, that even with Wilken's knowledge and freedom of mind, he has not attained to a complete mastery over his materials. The 'Gesta' and its copyists contradict each other in the same breath, according to circumstances: Albert of Aix and William of Tyre, William of Tyre and the original authorities, are annealed together; and, in a much higher style but with precisely the same objects, the method of the Archbishop of Tyre reappears. It is scarcely necessary to quote individual passages, or to illustrate the consequences of this mode of dealing with the subject. The case is not much altered by the fact that on particular points the statements of William of Tyre or Albert of Aix are amended or contradicted by some extracts from the original authorities. The radical distinction between historical and legendary tradition is nowhere clearly defined; and in no case, even in the original authorities, is the individual evidence tested by the general character of the report. The sentiment that prompts this proceeding is higher than any we recognize in William of Tyre; we see the same veneration for the records of those times, and this constitutes the great charm and merit of the work. It is, in effect, a similar, but somewhat more developed form of William of Tyre. The representation of Peter as the original cause

of the war, of Godfrey as its Agamemnon,[55]—the
numerous legends forged by Albert of Aix and his
imitators,—are reproduced in the same form which
the Archbishop has impressed upon them, as it
would seem, for all ages to come. In particular instances, the ascetic colouring of most of the original
authorities, and the chivalrous tendency of most of
the legends, have suggested many a picturesque
passage to Wilken. Hence his work has a livelier
and more religious character than that of William
of Tyre, but it is conceived in the same spirit.

It seems strange to find a deeper religious
feeling in Wilken than in a writer of the twelfth
century, and a few words on this circumstance
will not be out of place here, as they will serve
to mark another characteristic of this work. The
expression of this religious fervour arises less from
the author's actual opinions, than from the conscious attempt on his part to narrate the history
of those times in a spirit in accordance with their
own. We readily admit that this mode of writing
history is an advance compared with that of the
preceding century, and that the author's enthusiasm
communicates itself to the reader. But it is also
necessary that the enthusiasm felt should naturally

[55] After Tasso, I have only met with this expression in Heeren,
in his well-known prize essay of 1808.

spring from the subject, and that not only the author, but the events which he records, should compel us to adopt his views. The narrative should make us forget that these views are originally foreign to our mind; if this effect be produced, no one will doubt the sincerity of the narrator, whatever be the art of his style. This task will naturally be much easier to a contemporary writer, himself taking part in the events he narrates; yet it is scarcely attainable even by him. The success of a more modern author will exactly depend upon the skill with which he conceals this assumption of a foreign dress and mode of thought. For example, when Raymond Agiles speaks of the knights errant of Christ, who began the holy war by the command of God, and who mowed down the godless crew with pious joy, we witness with a feeling of sympathy the deep passion displayed. We see side by side the rudeness and the blind prejudice, as well as the exuberant force and energy, of that generation. But it is only because this union of qualities is so vividly portrayed, that a natural interest and a clear perception of it are developed in us. An historian, on the contrary, in the real sense of the word, who, as a matter of course, considers his readers on the same level as himself, must endeavour to write in the language of his own time: and in this age we cannot regard the Crusades as a holy war, or the pilgrims as the people or champions of God; we can only describe a council as "an assembly of venerable fathers." When this is the case, unless the immeasurable difference between the actors and the hearers has been previously explained, the picture must be confused and out of keeping. This is the effect produced in Wilken's work, by the prominence given to the ascetic element of the original authorities over the spirit of William of Tyre.

Although this defect does not, like some we have before pointed out, concern only particular portions of the work, but runs through the whole, still the importance of the history, in many respects, cannot be denied. Wilken has the great merit of having been the first to use Oriental authorities with good results. The narrative is lucid and full of life; it has epic breadth, without being tiresome; and is cast, as it were, in one mould, without being monotonous. We might wish for greater distinctness in grouping his subjects, but the richness and vividness of the details must satisfy the most critical reader. Wilken unquestionably far surpasses all his predecessors; nor can any subsequent writer, for the amount of service rendered, claim to be ranked on the same high level.

From the first appearance of Wilken's work to the present day, it has had a success such as few works have enjoyed. In Germany the book still holds undisputed pre-eminence, so far as we can judge from later histories of the Crusades. Funke's sketches are not without a certain freedom of judgment; but from first to last he renounces all pretension to that learned mastery of the subject, which alone would entitle him to be regarded as independent of the assistance he derives from Wilken. The sketches, however, will always be read with interest; every page displays the most generous opinions, a just appreciation of facts, and remarkable talent for arrangement. The portions of Von Raumer's 'Hohenstauffen' relating to this subject, as well as Van Kampen's 'History of the Crusades,'[56] owe still more to Wilken. Von Raumer has, at any rate, a profound and extensive knowledge of the original authorities, and forms his judgment on his own grounds; whereas Van Kampen generally possesses only an average knowledge of his materials, and takes his views for the greater part from Heeren's 'Essay on the Crusades.'[57] It would be an endless

[56] Von Raumer's 'Hohenstauffen,' books i. and iii.; the first edition. Van Kampen, 'Proeve eener Geschiedenis der Kruistogten,' 4 parts. Haarlem, 1824.

[57] He also owes much to Regenbogen, who competed for the prize of the Paris Academy, with Choiseul-Daillecourt and with

undertaking to enumerate the various criticisms and views on the Crusades which are to be found in other historical works; and the only effect of it would generally be to confirm the uncontradicted fact of Wilken's influence. I will, however, mention that Schlosser's narrative, in the third part of his ' History of the Middle Ages,'[58] is on many points in striking opposition to William of Tyre: his objections are chiefly founded on the original authorities. Matthias Eretz of Edessa, and the 'Gesta,' are treated as the best sources of information. Schlosser has not been able wholly to discard the Legends, and the statements in the text are frequently at variance with those in the notes; for instance, on the subject of Peter the Hermit and the Assizes of Jerusalem.

Meanwhile historical science has taken a similar turn in France; after Wilken and Schlosser, we may mention Michaud and Capefigue. Michaud's ' History of the Crusades ' holds a similar position in France to that of Wilken's in Germany: at any rate, it is introduced to his readers with the same pretensions. There is no lack of large promises in prefaces and expositions; several fellow-labourers

Heeren; but whose manuscript was lost in its transit through the post-office, and was only published in 1819.

[58] The first part of the third volume, p. 129.

contribute original, and often most valuable papers, and Michaud himself has devoted four large volumes to a criticism of the original authors, which Wilken has omitted to do.[59]   Moreover his talent for narration is unquestionable, and the style, although somewhat inflated, is rounded, and full of vigour and life.   His judgment differs materially from the negative tendencies of the preceding century ; and he shows a correct and distinct appreciation of the conditions of a former age, and of opinions which he does not affect to share.   But these many merits are thrown into the shade by two defects. First, valuable as is the material contained in the ' Bibliothèque,' the critical and methodical research is very inferior to that displayed by Wilken.[60]   Not to mention his remissness in not distinguishing between original and secondhand authorities, we are at a loss how to designate Michaud's arbitrary selection from among his materials.   He makes continuous use of Albert of Aix and William of Tyre, all through the first and second volumes of

[59] First in the ' Bibliographie :' then in the ' Bibliothèque des Croisades.'

[60] I can here only speak of the events in the ' Histoire des Croisades.'   With reference to the ' Bibliothèque des Croisades,' the matter may be looked at from other sides ; but the results would be the same.   The article " Godefroy de Bouillon," in the ' Biographie Universelle,' also by Michaud, is defective in criticism to a greater degree than any part of his history.

his history ; and the discrepant statements of his authorities are often cited without comment. This Wilken, although he does not go deep or far enough, never omits. The preface announces that it was not difficult to discriminate between the true and the fabulous in the original authorities. And this may be true, if, with Michaud, we consider as fabulous only the stories of prodigies and their acceptance. But it is stated further on, that the contradictions between the authors of the various nations—Franks, Greeks, and Saracens—are almost impossible to solve. This is repeated in the text, and in the notes we frequently read that in such a place the narrative of Albert of Aix and that of Anna Comnena may serve to correct each other. In most cases the author is content to add particular statements taken from one original, to those of another, without caring whether the latter were in direct contradiction to the fragments thus interpolated. Our wonder that the manufactured speeches in Robert the Monk are used as originals,[61]—that mention is made of Baldrich and of Guibert a hundred times,—that Tudebod is seldom quoted, and the ' Gesta ' never,—ceases when we find the description of the Council taken from Aubert's ' Histoire de la Conquête de Jérusalem,' as if

[61] Vol. i. p. 209.

it were a contemporary chronicle; and the ritual of
the consecration given from the 'Pontificale Roma-
num' as a formula belonging to the year 1095.[62]
Concerning Raymond of Toulouse, we find the incident, first related, we believe, by Mariana, that he,
as a reward for his brave deeds, received the hand
of Doña Elvira from King Alfonso; a fact which had
been doubted, but completely proved by the 'Histoire de Languedoc.' Michaud has not taken the
trouble to examine the sources; nor has he even observed that Dom Vaissette alludes to the want of
contemporary reports, and only rests his statements
(incorrectly as it happens) on Roderick of Toledo.[63]
From a list of similar cases I will only mention one
example, as it illustrates the manner in which this
author deals with a question between Legend and
History; and this is more important than a few
individual errors. The visit of Bohemund and Baldwin to Godfrey of Bouillon, at Jerusalem, is correctly
described, as given by Albert of Aix and Fulcher of
Chartres; it is there said that Godfrey accompanied
the princes on their journey home, as far as Jericho,
but then returned to Jerusalem, where he appeared

---

[62] Vol. i. pp. 99, 126.

[63] Roderick, in the passage cited, mentions only the marriage,
not the victories which were supposed to have recommended the
Count as a son-in-law.

as a lawgiver before the assembled barons, citizens, and Syrians. In fact, the whole is taken from the Assizes; although it is expressly stated in a part of the appendix, that all this appears to be a collection of legends, and that it is impossible to tell how much concerning the Assizes related to Godfrey, or to a later time. Yet in spite of this admission, the time and place, the cause and manner, of the law-making are given in the text with the utmost composure.[64]

This leads me to the second point; namely, the manner in which a number of stories taken for good or for bad from original authorities are interpolated into the groundwork. The events they tell of may possibly have occurred, but they are valuable only as poetical creations or historical romances. They are totally devoid of authenticity, and the historian might have left them to his reader's fancy or to the pencil of the artist without any injury to his reputation. On the council of Piacenza, putting aside its European decrees, we possess but one short notice of Bernold, that Greek ambassadors had there besought help against the Saracens. Michaud states[65] that the attention of all was fixed on the Ambassadors of Alexius; after they had addressed the assembly, Urban supported them with

[64] Vol. ii. pp. 14, 537.   [65] Vol. i. p. 97.

all the arguments which the interests of religion and of Christendom could suggest ; nevertheless the Council came to no conclusion on the subject. The story of the Council of Clermont is still more dressed up.[66]   The author makes Peter the Hermit depict to the assembly the misery of the Eastern world; he adds, " En racontant les malheurs et la honte des Chrétiens, Pierre avait le visage abattu et consterné, sa voix était étouffé par des sanglots, sa vive émotion pénétra tous les cœurs." I will not take upon myself to assert that Peter the Hermit could not have been at Clermont, but it is certain that there is no mention anywhere of his speech or of the effect of his eloquence.[67]   Peter the Hermit is a second time introduced, to give the author an opportunity to display his powers of description, in the account of the embassy to Kerboga, which is embellished and amplified in the same manner.

We will quote one more case, where William of Tyre's account has been dressed up falsely. William of Tyre relates, simply enough, from Albert

[66] Vol. i. p. 103.

[67] William of Tyre, i. 14: the only place in which his name is mentioned, " promulgatis canonibus, qui pacem, suggerente Petro Heremita, quæ de rebus perierat, reformarent, qui verbo sibi injuncto debitam gerebat sollicitudinem, novissime ad hanc exhortationem se convertit, dicens;" then follows Urban's speech. The text is obviously corrupt.

of Aix, that Baldwin had rejoined the main army at Meraasch, and that it was only respect for Godfrey of Bouillon that saved him from Bohemund's wrath for his conduct at Tarsus. By the advice of an Armenian called Pancratius, he had determined, in spite of the small number of his immediate followers, to advance into Mesopotamia. The diminution of his force was caused by the general disapproval of his conduct to Tancred. Michaud first gives a lively description of Baldwin's ambition, and then goes on to say, that as the devil took Christ, so Pancratius took the Prince, to the top of a mountain, and showed him all the country round; a long speech is then inserted, in which Pancratius enlarges upon the fruitfulness of the land and the ease with which it can be conquered. Baldwin was filled with worldly desires and ambitions. His wife died; but while the requiem for the dead sounded, he thought only of the glories of this world. He appealed to the princes, but found no response. With some trouble he collected a small body of men, but the princes determined forcibly to restrain him from his unholy scheme. He then hurried on his preparations, and separated himself silently and in secret from the rest of the Crusaders.[68] The only comment we have

[68] Michaud, i. p. 250.

to make is, that none of these interesting particulars are to be found in the original authorities.

In all essentials, therefore, the relation to William of Tyre is the same ; for even Michaud's supplementary matter is mostly embroidered on the groundwork borrowed from the Archbishop. These premises being granted, the work deserves all praise. It shows great diligence and plastic fancy, activity of thought and power of expression. But it fails in one great essential: there is a lack of careful investigation, and, above all, of the sense of conscientious research in small matters. Had it not been for this, an active inquiring spirit like Michaud's would scarcely have rested content to be merely a continuator of William of Tyre's method of writing history. Where he does go beyond William of Tyre, it is more in the manner of Torquato Tasso, whom he frequently cites ; among other passages, that in which Baldwin's character is given, as if its authenticity could be strengthened by such means. Judging from his own poetical attempts, (the best name for these inventions,) we can comprehend his admiration for the ' Gerusalemme Liberata;' though, after much examination, he gives the preference to the ' Gerusalemme Conquistata' for its greater historical truth.[69] As

[69] In a special appendix to the first volume.

William of Tyre interwove the historical matte: of the original authorities with the legends of Albert of Aix, so has Michaud combined the poetical master-piece of the Italian poet with the historical work of the Archbishop.

If we turn to Capefigue, who promises an en-tirely new view of the Crusades, in his work on the French Kings,[70] we find in every line unmis-takable evidence of the position and manner of the author. A few short extracts will suffice to give an idea of the whole, and for this purpose I will give the characters of Godfrey and of Tan-cred, both taken from the third volume, relating to Hugues Capet. First of all, we learn from his polemic how important Tasso has become to the Frenchman of the present generation. Twice in a short space the poet is called, "le grand corrupteur de l'histoire." The author warns his readers, as St. Maurice did before him, against Tasso's influence, and allows no part of his narrative to pass uncontra-dicted. But what Capefigue gives us instead is by no means better. We meet with clever phrases in particular instances, and with foregone conclusions on all subjects, occasionally verging upon the truth, but seldom attained by searching investigation. He says of Tancred, at page 120, "Il montait un puis-

[70] Hugues Capet et les Rois de la troisième race, t. ii. and iii.

2 A

sant coursier, se couvrait de rudes armures et bri-
sait des lances ; son caractère était sombre, méfiant,
irritable au dernier point, et aucunement sociable ; il
portait avec lui le type agreste et indomptable des
montagnards." Apart from the utterly romance-like
colouring of this portrait, which must either delight
the reader, or cause him to lay the book down at
once, it would be difficult for the author to support
the whole of his theory by any authority, though it
might be possible to defend some part of it. But
now we come to Godfrey. He says of him, at page
72, " Godefroy, élevé par de vieux serviteurs dans
la sauvagerie de la chasse et de la guerre, le barbare
Godefroy des Ardennes et de Souabe, proclama l'an-
tipape Anaclet. Mais—là finit la vie grossière et
sensuelle ; comme l'empereur Henri IV, il éprouva
à l'aspect de Rome un profond repentir ; l'homme
de chair et de sang s'agenouilla devant les pompes
de l'Église catholique." Under the influence of these
penitent and contrite feelings, Godfrey takes the
Cross and enters upon the government of Jerusalem
and of Palestine,—a joyless desert country, deprived of all temporal splendour. This view is not
without some foundation of truth. No one will
deny the influence of religious asceticism on the
progress of the Crusades, which indeed it is part
of the object of the whole book to show ; as

we find it expressed on occasion of the quarrel
between Henry and Gregory.[71] "Au moyen-âge
le Catholicisme est la pensée sociale, le mobile de
la civilisation; la féodalité est la matière forte qui
résiste au mouvement des idées." I will also grant
that this thesis contains a certain amount of truth,
although the reverse might be maintained with equal
plausibility; but there can be no doubt as to the
judgment on Capefigue's way of relating particular
facts. Out of a general idea he creates a numerous series of deeds, persons, and opinions; for
one that is correct, he produces a hundred that are
false, and he allows himself the greatest poetical
licence. We can easily conceive how, in spite of
the entire variance of their views, Albert of Aix
should be treated by Capefigue in particulars as
an original authority. In fact, Capefigue's mode of
writing trenches as much on the province of legend as anything that Albert of Aix has left; for
what else is it but legend, to clothe a precon-
ceived idea in free and graceful forms, which can
only by courtesy be called history? If we take
this measure of the whole, we can feel but small
interest in the examination of the separate parts
of the work. There are admirable remarks upon
certain facts, and there is a fullness and freshness of

[71] Tom. ii. p. 185, and *passim*.

narrative which deserve no small praise, if we can get over the origin of his materials. But it is evident that no real advance in historical knowledge can be made by such labours as these.

THE END.

Lightning Source UK Ltd.
Milton Keynes UK
UKHW012145170119
335727UK00009B/558/P

9 780282 077198